INDIAN INDUSTRY
Energy Management

INDIAN INDUSTRY

Energy Management

Editor

RATNAKAR GEDAM

Akashdeep Publishing House

Akashdeep Publishing House
4374/4B, Ansari Road,
Darya Ganj, New Delhi-110002.

INDIAN INDUSTRY: *Energy Management*
First edition, 1991
ISBN 81-7158-226-5

PRINTED IN INDIA

Published by Akashdeep Publishing House, New Delhi, and Printed at Sangita Printers, Delhi-53.

Preface

Indian Industry has to encounter numerous problems on account of scarce resources, inadequate infrastructure and other inputs. The efficiency of inanimated source of energy depends upon organizational structure and energy management. The efficiency of enterprise as whole is a function of commulative total efficiency of all operations, activities, output etc. The human energy coupled with electrical, heat, and chemical energy calls for greater role for energy management. The uninterrupted source of energy is prerequisite for greater volume of output but for given duration of available source of energy, the maximum output per unit of energy consumed is always aimed at by energy management. Maximizing the output per unit of energy consumed is good index of conservation of energy as well as success of energy management. To raise the engineering efficiency of any process or plant call for greater role for energy management.

In this book, the selected topics have been included to present overview of the industrial activities.

Editor

Contents

1

An Approach for Conservation of Electrical Energy—A Case Study in A Heavy Assembly Industry

N. Venkataramiah, I. S. S. S. Ganesh***

Introduction

Electrical Energy constitutes one of the key inputs to any industrial activity. In view of the various restrictions imposed by Electricity Boards, from time to time, it is necessary to evolve a plan of action for optimum utilisation of this key input. This paper narrates various approaches adopted by Hindustan Shipyard during power crisis for conserving electrical energy. These approaches helped the organisation to tide over the crisis and also helped the Shipyard to formulate a long term proposal for conserving electrical energy.

Hindustan Shipyard is one of the pioneer ship-building yards in India. There are as many as 17 production sub-departments in the above organisation. Shipbuilding is a heavy assembling industry involving multitude of organisations

* Manager, Plant Engg., Hindustan Shipyard Ltd., Visakhapatnam.
** Sr. Indl. Engr., H.S. Ltd., Visakhapatnam.

and skills. This industry is extensively labour-oriented and any set back to production activity should be interrupted for maintaining delivery dates stipulated in the contacts. In this industry, electrical power is required for providing services like compressed air, running heavy duty cranes, catering to the requirements of welding, running ventilation system in closed spaces and for general lighting purposes. In addition, electrical power is also required to operate various machines in shops.

In the year 1979-80, the shipyard experienced a severe power crisis. Every quota had been drastically reduced from 31,166 units a day to 21,833 units a day. Peak load restrictions are also imposed stipulating a maximum permissible demand of 1,733 KVA. In spite of these restrictions, it was decided to maintain he same tempo of production for keeping up the contractual delivery dates. This was necessary because any slackness in production tempo might affect the manufacturing schedules and ultimately result in delayed deliveries, thereby the shipyard would be facing stiff competitive market. Under these circumstances, various alternative methods were adopted for conservation of electrical energy with an objective of maintaining the stipulated quotas and at the same time ensuring a smooth flow of production activity.

Observations and Analysis

In order to deal with the above situation, data was obtained from past records and analysed. The analysis of the data yielded the following information.

(i) Shop-wise energy consumptions were established from the past data.

(ii) Demand was recorded for every half-an-hour and demand curves were plotted for locating the peakload occurrences. From the demand pattern, it was observed that, peakloads occur during 6.30 a.m. to 8.00 a.m., 9.15 a.m. to 11.15 a.m., 12.15 p.m. to 2.15 p.m. and between 5.30 p.m. & 7.15 p.m.

An analysis of loads revealed that major contribution comes from welding sets, running of air compressed and provision of lighting facilities inside the ships' structure under construction.

An analysis had been made and the consumption of electrical energy by various groups and the consumption of each group as percentage of total energy consumption was observed to be as follows :

Equipment/Area	*% Consumption*
Machinery	15.04
Compressors	26.60
Welding	28.18
Cranes	13.10
Lighting	17.08

Alternative Plans Adopted

Staggered Holiday System

An analysis of different services in Production Departments revealed that the following services constitute vital services to production activity. They are—

Services	*Connected Load in KW*
Heavy Duty Cranes	1000
Air Compressors	930
Lighting	400
Ventilation Systems (Inside ships)	150
Welding System	2000 (Staggering & diversity will not effect.)

It was observed that the diversity factor of the above load was very high. Therefore, it was necessary to minimise the diversity factor for the above loads for achieving the peakload restrictions. As these services were catering to requirement of all Production Departments, the load on the services could be reduced only, if the services get a relief by cutting down loads of some production departments. As it was not desirable to cut-down the production departments loads during normal working, this proposal was introduced. Under this plan, the entire production group was divided into seven categories and for each category, a different day was given as a weekly holiday. It was observed that by introducing this scheme, only 2000 cft. compressor could meet the requirements instead of running 3,000 cft. and 1000 cft. compressors. It was also observed that the maximum demand for the production division, would also be reduced in addition to the reduction in the maximum demand of the above services. By introducing this Scheme, it was noticed that the peakload was scaled down to 1825 KVA. In addition to reduction in maximum demand there was also saving in electrical energy, because of the reduction in loads on the above services. The electrical energy requirements were brought down to 19,241 units a day, resulting in a savings of 18% over normal requirement.

Eventhough, this scheme was operating successfully and yielding the desired results, problems were experienced as regards wage payments because of staggered holidays. In addition, the Management was forced to introduce certain restriction on peakloads during night times, due to restrictions imposed by the State Electricity Board. Therefore, the 2nd alternative proposal was introduced.

Revised Shift Timings

From the demand pattern of various departments, it was observed that there would be peakload occurrences, if all the departments were to work simultaneously. It was also observed from the working pattern that there was a general down trend in pattern in the afternoon and at the end of the shift during E-1 shift. Similarly, it was observed there was downward trend at the end of E-2 shift. It was also deserved that Welders constitute maximum load from production shop and a scheme should be worked out by properly facing the working hours of welders. Keeping these observations in view, revised shift timings were worked out assuming that by adopting different shift timings for different groups, peakload for one group would occur when there was a slackness of working pattern in the other group. By this proposal, the peakload occurrences were evened out. They new shift timings are as follows :

E-1 Shift 6.30 a.m. to 3.00 p.m.—All outfit Departments and welders in shops and ships at Jetty.

E-2 Shift 2.30 p.m. to 11.00 p.m.—All outfit Departments and welders at Jetty.

New Shift 9.00 a.m. to 5.30 p.m.—All steel Departments in shops and berths and welders in Steel Departments.

From the above shift timings, the welders load at Jetty was spread over both in E-1 and E-2 shifts. The welders load at berths was shifted to a new shift. By introducing this scheme, the maximum demand was maintained around 1700 KVA. As most of the people were brought under day shift, there was a substantial saving in lighting load consumption. As a result of this scheme, the energy requirements were brought down to 16,227 units a day. The demand pattern reveals that peakloads were restricted after 6.00 p.m.

In spite of the successful operation of the above scheme, there were certain grievances from work force, because of new shift timings. The union requested that lunch and tea break were not suitable to the workmen in new shift. In order to avoid hardships to work force, the scheme was revised as follows.

Shift System on Zonal Basis

In this scheme, the entire production group was divided into two major zones viz., all steel departments in zone 1, and all outfit departments in zone 2.

The revised shift timings were introduced with a view to evenout the peakload occurrences by minimising the demand on services. The scheme also aimed at savings in energy consumption on lighting by bringing all work force during day time. The revised shift timings were as follows :

E-1 Shift 6.30 a.m. to 3.00 p.m.—Zone 1
E-2 Shift 10.00 a.m. to 6.30 p.m.—Zone 2

By introducing this scheme, only 2000 cft. compressor was put to use. In addition, cranes at births were operated in E-1 shift and cranes at jetty were operated in E-2 shift. By this method, the peakload of different groups were phased out resulting in a reduction in peakload. By this proposal, management was able to maintain the peakload around 1700 KVA, and the energy requirements were also worked to be around 18,000 units a day.

Conclusions

By adopting the above schemes, frequent trippings of power supply, were completely avoided. These approaches helped to derive the benefit of continuity of production tempo apart from substantial savings in electrical energy from 31,166 units a day to 18,000 units a day. Certain drastic measures such as layoffs, retrenchments, contemplated earlier during power crisis were completely avoided by methodically tackling the above problem.

The data obtained from the above schemes provided insights into the areas of wastage of electrical energy. This helped the management to formulate long-term proposals for eliminating such wastages. Some of the permanent proposals introduced are :

(i) Priority sequence for various equipments along with their energy consumption was established for each shop.
(ii) The lighting systems have been relocated so as to reduce unnecessary lighting points.
(iii) Usage of air compressors was selectively regulated.
(iv) Suitable systems were evolved for a better utilisation of cranes and reduction of idle trips.

2

Wealth from Waste

*F. L. Lobo**

Introduction

Not so very long ago, waste could just be discharged into the environment—the air, the sea, rivers, barren land—it was not of much concern to management. Newly constituted industrial areas would boast about their location advantage of proximity to the sea or a river for discharge of effluent. But today, the management of waste forms an integral part of the production-consumption cycle. It is developing into a well defined system with related procedures and technology.

In mass production, waste can take on astronomical proportions. For example, in an iron and steel works, about 1.1 tonnes of solid waste is generated for every tonne of steel produced. One can well imagine the problems of materials handling and disposal when the production runs into millions of tonnes.

While high operating costs may be a cause for closer attention to waste management, it is now being realised that

* Francis Lobo & Associates, Consultants in Management, Pune.

there is money in waste. In the U.S.A., the "throw away society" is coming to a slow but certain end and in its place is emerging an $ 18 million tonnes of waste generated annually by individuals, government and industry.

The subject is discussed under the following heads (i) Management principles to be supplied, (ii) Measurement and assessment of performance, (iii) Techniques used, and (iv) Management Action.

Management Principles

The application of the following principles will facilitate the success of a waste management programme.

Principles of Numbers

Economics of scale apply to the collection and utilisation of waste. An individual item of waste may have little value, but when available in large numbers, uses can be found. For example, it has been estimated that the aluminium foils on the milk bottles which are thrown away in a city like Calcutta, would amount to Rs. 3,000/day.

Principle of Identity

All resources are inert, have no value and are unproductive until a human being identifies a use for them. We are discovering today new value in terms like the water hyacinth and gobar.

Principle of Emphasis

Results, as in all other areas, are in proportion to the emphasis given. The idea of preparing compost from vegetable waste was given to two schools in Calcutta. In one school the idea ended up where most ideas on wealth from waste end up—in the waste paper basket. In the other, the Don Bosco High School, the idea was tried out and proved to be successful winning for the school public appreciation and for the students, knowledge and experience.

Measurement and Assessment

What is Waste ?

Waste is anything that has (a) No valve, (b) Lost a significant portion of its value and (c) Negative value, i.e., costs are to be incurred for its transportation, disposal and containment, e.g., nuclear waste.

Value Lost in Waste

This can be expressed by the following equation :

Per Unit of Waste

Costs incurred (in Value lost Original Retained in waste = value — value — production of the waste + in collection, transportation, segregation, disposal and containment.

For example, if we consider steel scrap, the figures may look something like this

Per Kg. of Waste

Value lost in waste	Original = value — say	Retained value say	Costs incurred (in — production + handling) say
	Rs. 3.50	Rs. 1.80	Rs. 0.25
	= Rs. 1.45		

(The retained value will be reduced to the extent that all waste is not recovered and some of it is lost by contamination with other materials, discharged as affluent, pilfered, etc.)

Some of the characteristics of retained value are :

(i) It could fluctuate, e.g in 1981 heavy melting No. 1 scrap varied between Rs. 1850/ tonne and Rs. 2150/ tonne, stainless steel sheet cutting (non-magnetic scrap from Rs. 9,600 to Rs. 14,000.

(ii) Prices of the scrap may be even higher than that of the original raw material; e.g., scraped components.

(iii) The retained value may be very substantial, depending on the condition, e.g., while the price for M.S. and alloy steel turnings and borings scrap could be in the range of Rs. 1500/tonne, the price of M.S. light scrap could be as high as Rs. 2,600/tonne.

$$\text{Waste Index} = \frac{\text{Value lost in waste}}{\text{original value}} \quad \text{e.g.} \ \frac{\text{Rs. } 1.45}{\text{Rs. } 3.50} \times 100$$

say 40%

Waste Audit

An audit of the operations should be conducted to assess the total value lost in waste. The total picture can be obtained by the following :

For Raw Materials

A material balance. This will identify the losses occuring at each stage of manufacture on the composition and characteristics of each type of waste.

Determination of the loss of value in the waste.

For Capital Investment

Determination of the loss of value in unutilised assets (based on the returns obtained by the company or others where the assets are utilised) such as land, buildings, machinery and personnel.

This should also include costs involved in maintaining idle assets.

Determination of the loss of value in items which are scrapped e.g. spares and capital goods

The above data will give a picture of the company's potential for improvement and, if comparative data of comparable firms is available, its competitive position.

Techniques

In the war on waste, the strategies that can be adopted are as follows

Reducing the units of waste

Increasing the retained value

Reducing the costs of collection, etc.

Reducing the Units of Waste

By application of appropriate technology; e.g., Continuous casting

It is estimated that use of this technique for manufacture of copper rods would save to the extent of 5% in consumption.

Electrolytic deposition of paints and metals to reduce wastage of materials.

By using recycleable reuseable containers and packagings, e.g.

Packing cases received with incoming materials being used for despatching outgoing material,

cones for ice cream which are consumed along with the ice cream.

By preventing damage and spoilage in storage and use, e.g.

in certain areas of the country it is estimated that 25% of the grain is destroyed by rodents ;

proper oiling and greasing of moving parts.

By using the correct specification of material will prevent wastage of high value material when lower value material can be used, e.g.,

A switch over from copper cadmium catenary wire to alluminium alloy.

Spheroidal graphite in place of bronze bearings.

Increasing the Retained Value

By effective Extraction and Separation. Extraction and separation can be manual, mechanical, electrical, magnetic, biological or chemical. Examples of application of this are:

recovery of chemicals from effluents;

platinum and palladium from catalytic converters;

Carbon black, oil and steel from tyres;

extraction of silver from used films and hypo solution;

zinc ingots from zinc dross/ash from galvanising pots;

tin from tin dross

using hitherto unused lean or complex ores and raw materials;

recovery of lead from storage batteries.

Upgrading scrap by sorting out commodity-wise, e.g.,

Today in the U.S.A. there are 15,000 firms that make a business of recovering and re-selling used parts from the 10 million autos, trucks and buses that are taken off the road each year. In spares there may be parts that can be re-used, e.g. switches and precious metal.

Finding alternative uses, e.g.

In India it is estimated that we throw away as much food as would feed 60 million people;

waste office stationary, e.g. one side used cyclostyled paper can be used for scribbling pads;

waste water after treatment can be used for irrigation;

straw used for packing, as cattle feed.

Recycling of material, e.g.

making metals like aluminium and steel from scrap;

recovery of used oil;

making paper from scrap paper. More than 500 of the 700 paper mills in the U.S.A. depend exclusively on waste paper;

making glass from scrap. In the U.S.A.; 600,000 tonnes of glass are crushed and re-cycled each year;

polyethlene and similar scrap can be re-cycled.

process water cnn be treated, cooled and re-cycled

Consolidating waste, e.g.,

quilt making; small unusable pieces when joined together can make a large usable and decorative covering;

small pieces of soap can be pressed together to make a usable cake of soap;

pelletisation of fine material;

use of fly ash for making bricks.

By conversion, e.g.,

chemical applications—gobar gas plants, oils and gases from forest waste, power from the water hyacinth;

artistic applications—handicrafts, hand made paper;

mechanical and electrical applications—energy from tidas waves, the sun;

utility applications—paper and cloth bags from used material.

By re-building, e.g.

It is estimated that around the world billions of dollars are wasted every year by scrapping machine parts and tools which could have been saved by re-conditioning.

Re soling of tyres.

Re-conditioning of conveyor belts.

Re-conditioning of furniture and building

By mixing, e.g.

granulated slag of steel mills used in cement production;

in steel mills, mill scales along with the dust and fines generated at basic refractory materials making section, find their way into the sinter plants.

chopped up pieces of old tyres are being mixed with asphalt as a paving material.

By collection, e.g.,

antiques, stamps,

Reducing the Cost of Collection and Storage

The cost of collection, storage, transportation, containment, can be controlled by proper segregation at the point of scrap generation by

preventing contamination and collecting waste at regular intervals;

pre-determining alternative uses for excess production, e.g., divert production in excess of export orders to the domestic market;

managing obsolescene. Obsolescene is normally a gradual process and the environment changes gradually over the long term. Symptoms of changes are evident long before the change itself actually occurs. Hence, if one is alive to the environment, one can reduce the impact of slow moving and obsolete materials;

inclusion of appropriate clauses on removal of waste and excess materials in construction and installation contracts.

Management Action

To ensure that effective feasures are taken, management should take the following action

Set specific objectives for each manager for conserving and re-cycling materials.

Set norms for economic usage of materials.

Develop appropriate technologies for using waste.

Maintain a data bank on possible uses of waste—off grade products, by-products, residues, surplus equipment, surplus material, waste scrap.

Set up a system for exchange of surplus items within the company and with other companies.

Maintain an inventory of problems for which solutions are to be found.

The key factor for success in waste management is "information. What are the items of waste ? How can they be used ? Where/whom is the know-how available for converting the waste into items of value ? Problem solving today is not merely a matter of logic and reasoning; it depends largely on a bank of knowledge and information. Management must, however, be aware that information collected but not uses is, itself, a waste.

Conclusion

Summing up the deliberations of the conference of experts on waste re-cycling for development, the U.N. official observed : "Waste utilization, in short, should be part of the closed loop system of production-consumption cycle. The world is about to enter a new age of the post Industrial Society and, with it, probably, there will be enormous global-waste generation unless mankind turns the tide by converting waste into wealth".

3

Role of Industrial Engineer in Survey and Assessment of Fire Losses and Measures for Loss Prevention

A. M. Gawarikar

Introduction

The primary purpose of such a survey is to establish the cause and to fairly assess the extent of loss or damage. To a large extent the achievement of this objective depends upon the experience and efficiency of the person undertaking the work of surveying. In the case of damage it requires that the Industrial Engineer should have an understanding of the special characteristics or properties of the goods, machines, plants and systems which are involved. Moreover, he needs to be familiar with such treatment as may be recommended to minimise the loss.

The increasing complexities of modern techniques, in industry and trade, requires the assessor to keep abreast of the rapid strides being taken in the field of science and technology. An Industrial Engineer, due to his knowledge of inter-disciplinary systems involving engineering, costing, economics, plant layouts and various systems used in plants, can assess the loss and damage accurately and suggest improvements in process, operating methods, layouts of plant, building and equipment and its safety measures by which total losses can be minimised in the interest of the insured and the underwriters.

Industrial Engineering can be used to advantage in this field. The basic objective of the survey of major fire or breakdown is to establish cause, extent of damage, cost of damages and method for minimising these losses. It is only an Industrial Engineer who can help in minimising losses by suggesting proper methods of work, material handling, maintenance, inspection and plant designs. It is a well known fact that functions covered by industrial engineering are complex and involve almost every activity connected with industry.

Aim

In this paper, I have dealt with the basic procedures that should be followed in assessment of fire losses including calculations of loss of profit after careful examinations of terms and conditions of policy.

Cause of Fire

There are many possible causes of ignition of a fire in industry. Ignition can be caused by heat or by electric spark. Short circuition can arise any time by accident or from damage. Often added to these are the inadvertant lapses on the part of workmen.

Assessing the Total Loss

The loss are damage can be partial or total. For assessing the cost of damage to building, machinery and other assets, it is necessary to find out the value of the items at the time of loss. The depreciated value of fixed assets is an important consideration. Hence, while estimating the value of the items at the time of loss Industrial Engineer must consider the following : (a) Effect of time, (b) Wear and tear due to use, (c) Previous accidents (reason). (d) Capacity of owner to carry out maintenance, (e) Obsolessence, (f) Fall in market value,

(g) Appreciation in market value, and (h) Inventions of new machines.

Quantitative evaluation of assests used is important while determining the value of the assests. Often factories work overtime and in different shifts and some times plant may be lying idle. Following table gives rough idea about the rate of depreciation in different shifts :

Types of Assets

	Ist	*IInd*	*IIIrd*
Factory tools and equipments	10%	12½%	15%
Machinery	7½%	10 %	12%
Electrical equipments	12½%	15 %	18%
Furniture & Fittings	10 %	12½%	15%

Actual rate however depends upon the type, nature of assests and on the extent of fatigue or strain which can be evaluated by inspection on site.

Loss of Profit

Once the extent of damage is established, Industrial Engineer has to study loss of profit to the Company due to damage/stoppage of the work. The Industrial Engineer with the help of various financial statements can find out the status of the Company. For ascertaining the financial position of the company, reference should be made to the director's report and Chairman's speech.

It is thus imperative for the Industrial Engineer to take the following steps : (a) Study all data connected in financial statements or otherwise given to the chartered accountant with a view to understanding their significance, (b) Obtain information about the raw material, work in process and finished goods inventory level and inventory control methods adopted by the Company, (c) Tabulate all relevant information in a logical manner. For the purpose of interpretation for profit, a number of statements can be prepared. The more important of such statements are as under : (i) Comparative Balance Sheet, (ii) Comparative statements of manufacturing cost. (iii) Comparative statements of working capital, and (iv) Comparative statement of working capital.

A. Comparative Balance Sheet

	Years	*Increase*	*Decrease*
Liabilities			
Capital Liabilities			
Capital			
Equity			
Preference			
Reserve and Surplus			
Capital reserves			
Revenue reserves			
Secured Loans			
Debentures			
Bank Loans			
Deferred payment liability			
Unsecured Loans			
Subsidies from Banks			
Current Liability and Provisions			
Sundry creditors (including bills payable)			

Tax provisions

Proposed dividends

Assets

Fixed Assets

Land

Building

Machinery and equipments

Investments

Current Assets

Debtors and bills receivable

Stocks (1) Finished goods

(2) Goods in process

(3) Materials

Unexpired amounts

Loans and advances

Cash

B. Miscellaneous Expenditure

	Years	*Increases*	*Decreases*
Materials used			
Productive labour			
Factory expenses			
Total manufacturing cost			
Total net increase/Decrease			

Comparative Statements of Earnings and Expenses

	Years	*Increases*	*Decreases*
Earnings			
Net sales			
Loss : cost of goods sold			
Profit			
Net increase/decrease			
Expenses			
Selling			
Advertising			
Administrative			
Financial			
Depreciation			
Taxes			
Total expenses			
Net increase/decrease			
Summary			
Net increase in earnings			
Net decrease in expenses			
Increase/decrease in Net Profit.			
Current Assests			
Cash			
Debtors and bills receivable			
Finished goods			

Goods in process

Materials

Unexpired amounts

Total corrent assets

With the help of these statements the Industrial Engineer can ascertain the loss of profit due to damage sustained to the machinery/equipments/plants.

The Industrial Engineer can now clearly project a picture of total loss/damage due to fire and loss of profit to the Company. He should suggest methods for loss prevention after careful study of the followings : (a) Industry type and the process of production, (b) Volume of production, and (c) Type of product/machinery.

It will thus be clear that the Industrial Engineer can make recommendations first towards preventing the occurrence of a fire, i.e. elimination of possible sources and causes of ignition and secondly towards providing the most efficient installations and equipment to fight a fire if it does occur.

There are many possible causes of ignition of a fire in a industry. Ignition can be caused by the overheating or can be due to electric spark or short circuiting. The possibilities of ignition by such causes can be reduced by proper protection of electric circuits, flame proof equipment where necessary, generous ventilation at places where inflammable vapours may collect, and adequate best insulation of the boundaries of heat sources.

The second recommendation has to be fire protection of efficient fire fighting installations and equipment which must constantly undergo review and investigation. Space will not permit a detailed or complete description of all the types of installation and appliances used but the more important are as follows : (a) Water spraying system (automatically controlled by electronic fire alarm system), (b) Steam drenching (if possible), (c) Methyl bromide system (toxic), (d) Carbon dioxide installations, (e) Foam system, and (f) Fire main system having various hydrants.

Conclusion

The present discussion is a pointer to an important fact of an Industrial Engineer's duties. It would not be incorrect to surmise that with his knowledge of engineering and non-engineering disciplines, he is best suited to assess the loss/damage due to fire, loss of profit and evaluate the needs of introducing fire fighting techniques and equipments. Indeed that in itself can assist in minimising the losses to the national assests.

4

Industrial Energy Analysis Part-I (Fuel Conversion Chain Model)

*Siddhartha Bhatt M.**

Abstract

This paper describes two techniques for industrial energy analysis : Specific Energy Consumption Model and Fuel Conversion Chain Model. It also gives the necessary energy conversion data for evaluating energy consumption in industries involving the use of thermal and mechanical energy. As an example, the model is applied to the case of HMT Foundries.

Part-II gives a Gross Energy Conversion Chain Model, Part-III is devouted to Energy Economic Flow Model and Part-IV deals with Energy Economic Flow Model.

Introduction

The Indian Industry, in general, has neglected energy analysis because :

(i) Energy costs constitute a minor portion of the total production cost.

* Scientist, Central Power Research Institute, Bangalore-560012'

(ii) Energy costs can be easily transferred onto the customers. The industries maintain their profit margin and add the energy costs to the product cost. Thus, increase in energy costs does not affect profits.

(iii) Many industries have no idea of how much can be saved through energy conservation schemes. They feel that savings are too small and it is not worthwhile to spend time on such "unproductive ventures".

(iv) Most industries do not have persons conversant with or having spare time for energy analysis. Employing a professional organisation or trained hands would be too costly for small industries.

(v) Even if there are agencies or organisations interested in conducting energy analysis as a project programme, small industries tend to be secretive and would not like to reveal details about their energy consumption.

(vi) In regions where electricity and fuel are scarce, the industries would like to buy energy through clandestine deals or by bypassing electrical connections or by destroying the energy meters, rather than study their process for energy saving, optimisation and substitution. Such industries find it very convenient to solve their energy problems by bringing corrupt officials.

(vii) The general small and medium scale industries are concerned over factors affecting day-to-day profits rather than long term goals.

Despite these trends, it is well known that energy is the most important factor affecting industrial productivity. Several techniques of energy analysis have been evolved. The two models described in this paper are the Specific Energy Consumption Model and the Fuel Energy Conversion Chain Model.

These will be useful in all types of industries involving mechanical power and thermal energy.

Specific Energy Consumption Model

The energy cosumption is evaluated in natural units. The magnitudes of the n energy inputs (Ei : i=1 to n) are separately recorded along with the raw materials and products. For example in the manufacture of V tools and Parting tools from high speed steel, electricity, coal, kerosene and human power are used. The quantity per day and per unit product are determined. Charts are made for daily monitor. In the remarks column, details of disruption of power breakdown of machinery, repair work, work hold-up due to non-availability of energy etc., are recorded.

In some cases, the process comprises of several stages, each situated in different buildings. For such systems, multi-stage energy flow diagrams are drawn. The output of a previous stage will form one of the inputs of the next stage. For example, in the manufacture of a certain automobile part, foundry, machine shop, heat treatment shop, etc., can be considered as separate stages and specific energy consumption can be evaluated for each stage.

The time interval for each stage must be 1 day or at most 3 days. Higher times will average out small variations and sometimes hide important observations. A study of the daily charts over a period of a few months reveals a lot of details such as :

(i) The average product energy consumption.

(ii) The effect of machine breakdown on energy consumption.

(iii) The energetic performance of kilns, furnaces, prime movers, etc., with time.

(iv) The variation of energy consumption for different grades of raw materials and fuels.

Table 1

Specific Energy Consumption Table

Sl. No.	*Particular*	*Unit*	*Qnt.*	*Qnt./day*	*Qnt./day*	*Remarks*
1	Main input (r.m.)			—	—	
2	Main output			—	—	
3	Electricity	kWh	—			
4	Coal	kg	—			
5	Diesel	1	—			
6	Kerosene	1	—			
7	Human labour	man-hr	—			
8	Animal power	a-hr	—			

(v) Comparison of data with similar manufacturers abroad may give an idea of the energetic efficiency.

Fuel Energy Conversion Chain Model

To get a quick overall picture of operation and usefulness of this model, consider two foundries producing ferrous castings :

(i) Foundry – A : Uses an induction furnace (thermal efficiency=90%) powered by electrical energy and consumes 750 kWh/tonne of casting of on a 'per year' basis.

(ii) Foundry—B : Uses a cupola (thermal efficiency= 25%) fueled by hard coke and consumes 250 kg coke/ tonne of casting on a 'per year' basis.

If one considers the energy consumption at the Usable energy end, i.e. at the foundry inlet. Foundry A consumes 2.70 GJ/tonne and Foundry B consumes 8 GJ/tonne. The energy inputs measured at the foundry inlet point are based on different datum levels. Alternatively, one can measure the energy consumption on a common datum level—coal mine. At the mine point Foundry A consumes 32.54 GJ/tonne and Foundry E consumes 29.76 GJ.

The energy consumption can also be measured at another point—the task end or the useful heat end, Foundry A consumes 2.43 GJ/tonne and Foundry B consumes 2 GJ/tonne.

Thus, the point in the energy conversion chain, where the two systems are compared, also important. Theoretically the useful energy (heat) must be the same for both systems, but Foundry shows a higher consumption probably because of electric failures in firing period. Even though Foundry A consumed less energy at the Useable energy end, at the resource end, this consumes more energy. As far as national resources are concerned, Foundry B is more efficient. Also, at the task end, the Foundry A is being operated at below optimum efficiency.

Without tracing the individual energy conversion chains of each fuel, it is impossible to come to these conclusions. Application of Conversion Chain Analysis to industrial energy systems will lead to much broader understanding of the problem.

Energy Comparison and Addition on a Common Scale

Fuel and non-fuel energies undergo long conversion chains in the process of their production, transportation and use. The energy chain starts from the point of resource availability and terminates with the performance of useful tasks. National energy consumption is estimated at the resource end—coal mine, oil well, etc. The actual usage is at the task end—factory, vehicle, house, etc.

The movement of an energy form along a conversion chain involves two changes : a chage in physical or chemical form and a change in position. The example of a conversion chain is that of electrical energy—coal at mine, coal at thermal plant, electrical energy at the thermal plant, electrical energy at the load point and finally useful energy output of the last conversion device, i.e. induction furnace in the above example. Diesel has a conversion chain as follows : crude oil at mine, crude oil at mine surface, diesel at refinery, diesel at distribution point, diesel at inlet of engine, SHP of engine, useful mechanical power.

Conversion chain analysis helps in the following :

(i) Find the relationships between the energy and the useful energy.

(ii) Analyse the multiple-source energy systems and facilitate :

(a) the addition of different forms of energy (independent of each other), at corresponding points in the conversion chain.

(b) standardisation of key points in the conversion chain where addition of energy is valid.

Operational Definitions in Conversion Chain Analysis

Clear specification of the starting point and end point of the chain are needed to make the energy conversion operative for actual calculation.

Resource end energy (*R*) is the starting point in the energy conversion chain, e.g. coal at mine, oil in oil well, gas in gas well, rice husk at mill, water in dam, firewood in forest, etc.

Usable energy (*S*) is the energy in the useful form just prior to its utilisation for end use, ag., diesel at pumpsite, electricity at load point, coke at furnace site, oil stored for use in kiln, etc.

Task end energy (*T*) is the salvation point in the energy conversion chain. It is the ultimate useful energy output of the last energy conversion device, e.g. shaft power, heat or light.

Conversion chain is the transition from R to T through S.

During the transition from R to S, certain external energy inputs are added to the conversion chain, e.g., diesel for train in transporting coal from the mine to the factory. Such external energy inputs have their own resource and energy, usable energy and task end energy and form a mini-energy conversion chain. Such a chain is called a *Sub-Conversion Chain.*

The Sub-Conversion Chain in turn has external energy inputs, e.g., diesel used in a train which transports coal may need electricity. Here coal forms the main conversion chain, diesel forms the sub-conversion chain and electricity forms the sub-sub-conversion chain. Thus, a main conversion chain may have 'm' external energy inputs and each of these may have 'm_1' external energy inputs and so on. It is observed that the magnitudes of the contribution from sub-conversion chain is only about 5% that of the main conversion chain and the magnitude of the contribution form sub-sub-conversien chains may be about 0.05%. Thus, the external energy input at the

Useable energy end of the Ist sub-conversion chain set only is considered. All the secondary contributions are neglected.

The *Conversion Chain Efficiency* is the ratio of the task end energy to the resource end energy needed for its production

$$\eta_{cc} = T/R \qquad \ldots(1)$$

The *External Energy Efficiency* is defined as the ratio of the Resource end energy needed for a particular task to the sum of the Resource end energy and the total resource end energy components of all the external energy inputs of the sub-conversion chain. Though this efficiency is for the whole conversion chain, in practice it is only for the R to S portion.

$$\eta_{EE} = R/(R + REEI) \qquad \ldots(2)$$

where, $$R_{EE} = \sum_{j=1}^{n} R_j$$

Suppose there are 'n' external energy inputs associated with the main conversion chain, each of these forms its own sub-conversion chain. The resource end energy of such a sub-conversion chain 'j' is Rj.

Useable Conversion Chain Efficiency is defined as the ratio of the useable energy to the resource end energy for a particular conversion chain. This is *independent of the task performed.*

$$\eta_{ucc} = S/R \qquad \ldots(3)$$

End Point Device Efficiency is the ratio of the end energy to the useable end energy needed to perform this task. This is the usual value quoted as overall device efficiency. It is the overall efficiency of the last device in the conversion chain and is independent of the conversion in the Pre-useable energy portion of the conversion chain.

$$\eta_d = T/S \qquad \ldots(4)$$

The Integrated Conversion Chain Efficiency is so, called because it integrates the decrease is available energy of main source and the external energy inputs into one expression. It is the ratio of the task end energy to the sum of the resource end energy and the total resource end energy component of all the external energy inputs of the sub-conversion chain.

$$\eta_{ICC} = T/(R + REEI) \qquad \ldots(5)$$

$$\eta_{ICC} = \eta_{CC}\, \eta_{EE} = \eta_{d}\, \eta_{UCC}\, \eta_{EE} \qquad \ldots(6)$$

Energy Conversion Data

For actual calculations dealing with industrial energy all the three efficiencies, ηd, ηUCC, ηEE must be determined for a particular situation. Of these ηId depends on the device being used in the factory, ηUCC is general in nature and ηEE depends on the transportation distance.

Useable Conversion Chain Efficiency Relationships

(i) 1.1 tonne of rice husk at the mill = 1 tonne of rice husk at the utilisation point (90.2%).

(ii) 1.42 tonnes of dry firewood or 1.73 t of wet firewood on the tree of the plantation = 1 t of dry firewood at the end point of usage (70.4%).

(iii) 1.05 t of saw dust at mill = 1 t of was saw dust at the utilisation point (95%).

(iv) 3.5 t of coking coal in mine = 1 t of coke at the utilisation point (33.7%).

(v) 2.23 t of coal in coal mine = 1 tonne of coal at the utilisation point (44.9%).

(vi) 11.44 t of dry firewood on trees in the forest = 1 t of charcoal at the utilisation point (14.1%).

(vii) 2.04 t of crude oil in oil well = 1 t of diesel at the utilisation point (48.5%).

(viii) 2.30 t of crude oil in oil well = 1 t of kerosene at the utilisation point (43.5%).

(ix) 2.02 t of crude oil in oil well = 1 t of petrol or LPG at the utilisation point (49.5%).

(x) [(1.26)η^{-1} trans] t of coal in mine = 1000 kWh of electricity at the point of utilisation (11.4 ηtr). It can be taken as 1.4 t for some cities to 2.1 t for very remote villages.

(xi) [1277.14 η^{-1}trans] kWh of potential energy of water in the dam = 1000 kWh of electricity at the point of utilisation (78.3η tr).

Detailed calculations have been worked out by the author in Bhatt, 1982[1].

General Relationships for Calculating the External Energy Inputs per Unit Useable Energy

All External Energy Inputs (EEI) are either living energy (human energy and draft animal power) or fossil fuels (diesel, petrol or coal). The relationships between the resource end and useable energies are :

$$R_{EEI} = S_{EEI} \text{ (for living energy)}$$

$$= 2\, S_{EEI} \text{ (for fossil fuels)} \qquad \ldots(7)$$

The relationships based on 1 tonne of fuel (or 1000 kWh elect.) at the useable energy end are as follows :

(*i*) *Charcoal and firewood for rural areas*

$$S_{EEI} = K\,(A + 12.40 y_1)\ 4.18 \text{ MJ} \qquad \ldots(8)$$

where K = 1.12 A = 440 ...charcoal

K = 1.42 A = 64.4 ...firewood

and y_1 = no. of hours of operation of the animal cart.

(*ii*) *Charcoal and firewood for urban areas*

$$S_{EEI} \text{ (firewood)} = 5.94\,(64.40 + x_1\, 1.60 + x_2\, 0.14 + x_3\, 1.55) \text{ MJ} \qquad \ldots(9)$$

$$\text{SEEI (charcoal)} = 4.68\ (440 + x_1\ 1.68 + x_2\ 0.18 + x_3\ 1.62)\ \text{MJ} \qquad \ldots(10)$$

where 'x' is the distance in km :

x_1=truck (forest to railway station)

x_2=train (main journey)

x_3=truck (to end use point)

(*iii*) *Coal and Coke*

$$\text{SEEI (coal)} = 9.32(25.5 + 0.69\ x_1 + 1.45\ x_2)\ \text{MJ} \qquad \ldots(11)$$

$$\text{SEEI (coke)} = 5.31\ (49.3 + 1.41\ x_1 + 1.66\ x_2)\ \text{MJ} \qquad \ldots(12)$$

where x_1=train (main journey)

x_2=truck (railway station to end use point)

(*iv*) *Diesel, Kerosene, Petrol and LPG*

$$\text{SEEI} = k(A + 0.075\ x_1 + 0.11\ x_2 + 1.92 x_3 + c_4 x_4 + e_5)\ 4.18\ \text{MJ} \qquad \ldots(13)$$

where k=1.14 A=117.3 for retail kerosene purchase
k=0 A=0 for others

c_4=1.68...kerosene, petrol and diesel for urban areas

1.47 ...kerosene, petrol and diesel for rural areas

2.57 ...LPG for urban areas

1.51 ...LPG for rural areas

c_5=20.60...LPG for urban areas (tempo transport)

=0 ...for others.

'x' is the transportation distance in km,

x_1 ...pipeline (oil well to port)

x_2 ...ship (port to refinery)

x_3 ...train (refinery to town)

x_4 ...truck (to end use point)

(*v*) *Thermal electricity from coal*

SEEI (electricity) = 5.27 (25.5 + x_1 0.69) (η trans)$^{-1}$ MJ ...(14)

x_1 = train (mine to power plant) (km)

Calorific Values of Fuels

Table 2

Calorific Values of Industrial Fuels

Sl. No.	*Fuel*	*Unit*	*HCV*
1	Electricity	MJ/kWh	0.2778
2	Coal	MJ/kg	26
3	Soft Coke	MJ/kg	27
4	Charcoal	MJ/kg	29
5	Metallurgical coke	MJ/kg	32
6	Furnace Oil	MJ/l	38
7	Kerosene	MJ/l	40
8	Diesel	MJ/l	46
9	Butane	MJ/kg	46

Note : These are approximate values and actual values must be determined experimentally.

Table 3

Energy Consumption Pattern in HMT Foundry[2] for 1982

Sl. No.	*Energy*	*R*	*S*	*T*	*NEEI* (%)
1	Electrical power	8.610	5.430	4.887	100
2	Furnace oil	0.074	0.036	0.022	93
3	Kerosene	0.069	0.003	0.002	93
4	Hard coke	0.757	0.340	0.085	84
	Total	9.510	5.809	4.996	—

Note : R : resources end energy, S : useable end energy and T : task end energy. All the energy values are in GJ/tonne.

Results

The Fuel Energy Conversion Chain model is applied to the case of HMT Foundries. The fuel consumption data is obtained from Bilagi, *et al*, 1982[2] HMT I & II Foundry, Bangalore produces heavy duty inoculated Grey Iron Castings for its Machine Tools. The fuels used are electrical energy LDO/furnace oil kreosene and hard coke. The energy consumption has been evaluated at the resource end, useable energy end and task end.

Discussions and Conclusions

The paper describes two methods of evaluating energy consumption in industries which utilise mechanical power and thermal energy. In the specific energy consumption model, the energy consumption per unit product is evaluated on a daily basis. If it is a multiple stage energy system, the enery is evaluated for each stage. Study of the results accumulated over few months or a year will provide valuable data which may lead to decisions regarding conservation. The total cast iron melted in HMT Foundries 1982 was 7008 tonnes. Of this 6196 was melted electrically and 812 t by coke. The resource end energy for casting alone was 6/460 GJ/tonne (coke+electricity). In addition, auxiliary electricity (2.907 GJ/tonne), furnace oil (0.074 GJ/tonne) and kerosene (0.069 GJ/tonne) were consumed at the resource end. The miscellaneous energy was 3.050 GJ/tonne. The total energy was 9.51 GJ/tonne as indicated in the table.

The resource end energy for casting alone in HMT Foundries (1982) for various alternatives is :

(i) Total hydro electricity (7008 tonnes of casting) = 4.27 GJ/tonne

(ii) Thermal electricity (7008 tonnes =29.24 GJ/tonne

(iii) Coke (7008 tonnes) =23.20 GJ/tonne

(iv) Thermal electricity (6196 t) +coke (815 t) =28.54 GJ/tonne

(v) Hydro electricity (6196 t)
+coke (815 t) =6.46 GJ/tonne

If the calculations are made at the source end, i.e. in terms of electrical units and kgs of coke, the energy consumption for thermal and hydro electricity will not be any different. Whether the electricity is transmitted from a distance of 100 km. or 1000 km. the energy will be the same at the source end. But if one evaluates the conversion chain efficiency, the difference will be obvious. The same is true for transportation of coke. The technique desribed in this paper can be used to determine the ηCC, ηEE, ηn and ηICE for any industry located anywhere in India. By very simple calculations a variety of optimisations, efficiency maximisations and energy consumption minimisations can be achieved.

5

Investment Decisions of Heavy Earth Moving Equipments

*M. Mandal**

Introduction

The company 'C' has been engaged in producing Iron Ore from early of this century along with two parallel companies in the region and has expanded rapidly into both marine construction equipment and for shipment of iron ore to the different countries.

Most of the company's capital investment is used on plant and Equipment in the different projects. For this, management policy recently stated that all future investment on project should be linked to the projected production programme based on the export marked availability. Thus, long-term strategic planning plays a vital role in decision-making and, of course, include intuition after clear cut demarcation based on quantitative aspects of decision-making. This revealed to ensure the utilisation of resources equipments (e.g. Dozers, Excavators, Dumpers, Drilling equipments, etc.) in best possible manner to have the return on investment with great accuracy on projected pace.

* Industrial Engineer, Tata Exports Limited.

The author was involved in this model building exercise. After discussions with policy makers of the company, it was aimed to develop a decision model for building the potential production capability of the company in its different iron ore projects based on the probability of obtaining new contracts for shipment of Iron ore to the foreign countries.

Problem Identification

It reveals from the international market survey of Iron Ore and the potential evaluation of this particular company that there is enough demand of its Iron Ore. The exercise was concerned in developing a model which would give a clear cut guideline regarding the equipment programming for the new and or existing iron ore projects for expansion. The questions to be answered were :

(a) What is the optimum designed capacity of the equipments ?

(b) What is the optimum achievable capacity of the equipments ?

The designed capacity may be defined as the level of output attainable from an equipment when it is assumed that there are no operational or lost time delays, i.e. all the equipment available time is used for machine running at standard speed and the ancillary activities (Unproductive Time) necessary to maintain this. The achievable capacity may be defined as the level of the output attainable from an equipment when it is operating under normal conditions with specified methods and organisation for face operation and all the associated manual operations are carried out at standard performance along with the random delays which will be termed as 'Lost time delays'. Therefore, achievable capacity of any equipment is obtained by short time effort with all system manned at standard for which the operating management could be held accountable. Reasons which can account for production below this level may be : (a) Unforeseen Geological Trouble, (b) Labour Disputes, (c) Mechanical and lectrical Failures, (d) Undermanning occuring during festival days etc.

In respect of these factors, it is important to incorporate the effect of each of these and should carefully be quantified. Following the analytical techniques as stated above, the designed and achievable capacities for individual equipment operation groups are computed after detailed Indusrtial Engineering studies.

Principles for Optimising the Mining and Excavation System

In surface mine operations, the excavation system is dependent on the total quantity of material to be handled, the physico mechanical properties of the iron-ore and the over burden material, the phasing of production, the weather conditions of the locality and the geo-mining conditions of the area under working. Once established, the normal rate of excavation can be ascertained to remain virtually a constraint, unless major changes occur in the market or the capital structure of the organisation. The overall size of the mining excavation plan is dependent on the iron content in the orefi the strike length of the deposit available for benching, the required benchwidth, the height of working faces and the number of operating benches. Slopes should be steep enough to give economical recovery of iron ore and flat enough to ensure safety. Here also optimisation plays a vital role in designing the stability of the working slopes and it is beyond the scope of this paper for establishing technical parameters.

Problem Definition

Examination of the company's requirements showed that for any new combination of the iron ore project or group of projects, the following steps were necessary :

(a) Examine ordering documents of the HEM Equipments for the proposed Iron Ore project(s) and check the clients estimation of the designed capacity.

(b) Based on technical data from the manufacturer's

manual, draw up a total balance of equipment fleet composition to fulfill proposed production programming.

(c) Simulate the earth moving operation by using computer. Results of the equipment utilisation, delay in each of the sub-system of operation, queue lengths studied for further equipment fleet compositions.

(d) Using the data from 3 as guideline, further computer runs with different excavators, loarders, dozers, drills, dumpers etc. were made until the individual equipment is matched in the system concept to produce optimum efficiency and output.

(e) Based on information from 1, project sequencing is made over a period of time, say 300 working days for 2 shifts operation a day.

(f) Transportation of Iron Ore and overburden material from the work side to the proposed destination by various capacity of dumpers is estimated based on results from the computer simulation exercise of 4 and the finding of 5.

(g) Labour, material and fuel costs together with equipment operating costs are evaluated.

(h) Assumptions are made and constraints identified for the purpose of investment analysis.

(i) Linear programming model (LP) is designed to find the meximum present value of contribution using input results from the final simulation runs.

(j) Investment decisions taken based on finding of 9.

Mining Cycle of Earth Moving Operation

The cycle of operation in any surface mining may be summarised under the following heads :

—Preparation of the working site (i.e. Drilling etc.)

—Blasting of the Material for the ease of digging and loading.

Loading by the excavators on to a transporting equipment.

—Transporting the material from loading site to the unloading point.

Activity of Earth Moving Operation

Empty dumpers arrived at the loading site area and queued up to wait for their turn to be filled up with excavated iron ore/over burden material by the excavators. After being filled up, the dumpers moved away from the loading site to travel a distance 'a' before reaching the check point located at the boundary of the Iron ore project where records were being maintained. The dumpers then travelled a distance 'b' to the site where the iron ore or over burden materials were discharged. It may be mentioned here that for overburden removal it needs no checking and weighing, but records are maintained based on the volume that individual dumpers carried. The empty dumpers then returned by travelling a distance 'c' and arrived at the loading point to complete its cycle of operation.

Assumptions

Assumption which were made for the purpose of the study are outlined as follows :

(a) All dumpers took on a full load before leaving the loading point.

(b) No overtaking was allowed in any travelling activity.

(c) All entities in the queues were to be on first-in-first-out basis.

(d) The discipline for service at the loader was on first-come-first-served basis. The same was followed at the unloading point.

Simulation of Mining Cycle Time Components

To complete a cycle of operation, the time required was the sum of all the component times. The cycle for the earth moving operation included the elements of loading, hauling and unloading. Time studies were made for the evaluation of each of these sampling from each of the frequency distributions of elemental time in the cycle would lead to the establishment of total time for a cycle. Further cycle times were provided by subsequent random sampling.

In order to simulate reality in a model, it is essential to incorporate the variable factors which would affect performance in the real-life situation omitting the unpredictable or uncontrollable factors.

The model divided the cycle into eight elements represented by the following activities :

(a) Dumpers being loaded by the excavators at loading station near the face.

(b) Loaded dumpers travelling a distance 'a' of the haul road.

(c) Loaded dumpers stopping at the check point and being recorded.

(d) Loaded dumpers travelling a distance 'b' of the haul road.

(e) Loaded dumpers discharging at the proposed discharged point.

(f) Empty dumpers travelling a distance 'c' and returning to the loading point.

(g) Empty dumpers arriving at the loading point near the face.

(h) Queue for loading by the excavators.

The time required to complete a single element of a cycle

was treated as an independent random variable with known distribution either as a function or as a histogram. The parameters of the distributions were obtained from estimates of real world situation based on previous experience and records and using a knowledge of anticipated job conditions and equipment performance statistics.

In the simulation model, two sizes of dumpers were assumed. This was essential because, a carrying out actual earth moving operation, a certain proportion of the trucks were being hired from outside on material handling basis.

Sensitivity Analysis

Independent computer runs were made to simulate the actual conditions using different combinations of two sizes of dumpers. The outputs of each run of the simulation model recorded the number of times, each activity was started, of two sizes of dumpers. The outputs of each run of the simulation model recorded the number of times each activity was started, the length of queues and the time duration each operation was delayed in the queue.

From the number of times, each activity was started and completed, the utilisation of the entities and thus the productivity of the system were established. The number of loads carried by each of the large and small size dumpers were then calculated. With all these information, it was possible to carry out an analysis of viable computer runs and select a short list of six potential alternatives (i.e. step 4). These alternatives provided the answers to the questions raised earlier.

As mentioned earlier, financial analysis of these alternatives was then undertaken (steps 5-10). This involved the application of accounting techniques (e.g. discounted cash-flow) to a linear programming (LP) model (step 9) along with intution before the final decision was taken.

6

Storage Cost Parameter for An Inventory Mode

*S. Acharya**

Introduction

Shortage phenomenon is rife in inventory systems of most business enterprises. But, the extent of shortage depends on the inventory policy adopted by the enterprise. To extirpate shortage will beget a need to maintain a large (theoretically infinite) quantity of stock to meet with a fortuitously high demand. To carry such an unforeseen high demand would mean a pyrchic victory in so far as the cost or carrying a large inventory over a long period, might outweigh the likely benefit. Thus, it is expedient to minimise the total financial implications engendered by shortage on one hand and procurement and carrying of inventory on the other. Minimising of total relevant inventory costs is effectuated normally through a wee bit of shortage embedded in the resulting policy. Ergo, it is undersirable to shriek, over an occasional shortage that might have ensued in the wake of implementation of an optimal policy.

* Executive Indl. Engineer, Salgaocar Bros. Pvt. Ltd., Goa,

Two situations may encompass the shortage phenomena : (i) actual shortage of stocks (this shortage entails a loss of production in a production inventory system and rids the good will of customers by depriving him of his demanded finished goods in a sales inventory system), (ii) apparent shortage during which expediting efforts are additionally made for timely building up the stock that depleted below the danger mark so that production does not suffer. These two situations of apparent and actual shortage occurs in varying combinations. The resultant etched out of these two situations the shortage cost parameter.

Shortage cost parameter may be distinctly ascribable to each unit of stock that goes short when demanded. Or, it may be expressed as a fixed sum when an item runs out of stock irrespective of how many units of it. These parameters are often expressed over the year or the procurement cycle. Determination of such a parameter is essential in formulating a total relevant cost equation for an inventory system with a view to optimising it. Policies otherwise elicited will be non-optimal and impute an additional cost (2).

In this paper, an approach has been evolved to formulate a model for computing the fixed shortage cost parameter per procurement cycle. Such cases of fixed shortage costs are common in production processes where shortage of a particular raw material begets a fixed amount of loss irrespective of what number or quantity. As an example in a blending process, if one item is short, it does not matter by what quantity, blending perhaps cannot start bringing about a fixed loss in production. Similarly in an assembly operation where the sole unit that the enterprise may be assembling cannot be assembled because of nonavailabiliy of a particular component (may be several units of this component are employed in the assembly, but the final assembly gets delayed by almost the same period of time if this component be short irrespective of by how many number of units of it).

Mathematical Formulation

Shortage cost parameter employed in the total equation of an inventory model embodies two elements : (i) actual shortage cost parameter, and (ii) apparent shortage cost parameter. Based on the percentages of time (a) production actually was impeded due to shortage in the preceding planning horizon, and (b) an impending shortage was overcome due to expediting efforts; these two parameters are computed for a particular raw material as follows.

Determination of Actual Shortage Cost Parameter

Actual shortage cost is the cost of impairing the production process through either direct loss or the necessity and hence an alteration of the schedule. For a production inventory system, the methodology to assess this cost parameter is enumerated in the following four steps.

Probability of Actual Shortage under Past Inventory Policy : Under the actual shortage situation, production had to be discontinued when a particular raw material was not available. The number of hours of occlusion of production owing to shortage of a particular raw material (for which the shortage cost parameter is to be established) reflected the inventory policy of the preceding planning horizon.

The general expression for probability of shortage for any inventory policy, given by order quantity, x, and buffer stock, r, can be denoted by the function $P_s(x, r)$. But, in the preceding planning horizon, the value of this probability of shortage for the corresponding inventory policy could be T_1/T, where T_1 was the hours of stoppage of production due to shortage of the raw material and T was the normal production hours during the planning horizon. Hence,

$$P_s(x, r) = T_1/T \qquad ...(1)$$

Production Volume Lost due to Shortage.

If for any machine, i, of output rate, O_i, of the firm

employing m machines, the number of hours production stopped was lij due to the shortage of the raw material, then the total volume of production foregone during month j could be given by.

$$L_j = l_{1j} O_1 + l_{2j} O_2 + \ldots\ldots + l_{mj} O_m \qquad \ldots(2)$$

For the entire planning horizon of n months, production volume foregone could be

$$L = \sum_{j=1}^{n} L_j \qquad \ldots(3)$$

Money Value Surrendered Due to Shortage :

During the hours of shortage, while production was impaired, neither the raw material was utilised nor other operating expenses (excluding direct labour) were incurred as the direct labour and overhead costs remained unaltered. Direct labour and overhead costs attributed to each unit of output increased as the output volume decreased (with in a range as practically it does while shortage occurs). Para-phrasically, had there not been shortage, the output volume would have gone up at the cost of only direct material and other operating expenses (excluding direct labour). The monetary opportunity foregone due to shortage is worked out as follows.

For a particular product, production of which got impaired due to shortage of the raw material, i.e. :

V be the direct material and other operating (exclusive of direct labour) costs per unit of output,

P_1 be the level of output that could have been achieved without shortage,

P_2 be the level of output that was actually achieved with the shortage,

p be the selling price per unit of the product assumed

to be constant over the range P 2 to P 1 levels of output,

f_1 be the fixed (overhead plus drect labour) cost that could have been accounted per unit of the product had the output level been P1,

f_2 be the fixed (overhead plus direct labour) cost actually accounted per unit of the product as the production levelled P2.

Then, $P_1 > P_2$, and $P_1 - P_2 = L$ of relation 3, is the volume of output foregone due to shortage of the raw material. The corresponding sales revenue surrendered is $(P_1 - P_2)p$.

If the production were not hindered, net profit realised would be

$$P_1 p - P_1(f_1 + v) \qquad \ldots(4)$$

But, actual net profit realisable with the hindrance of production was

$$P_2 p - P_2(f_2 + v) \qquad \ldots(5)$$

The net profit relinquished owing to shortage of the raw material from relation 4 to 5 was :

$$P_1 p - P_1(f_1 + v) - P_2 p + P_2(f_2 + v) \qquad \ldots(6)$$

Since total overhead plus direct labour cost in both the circumstances is the same, $P_1 f_1 = P_2 f_2$. Hence expression 6 can be reduced to

$$(P_1 - P_2)\ (p - v) \qquad \ldots(7)$$

Even if the additional sales volume of $P_1 - P_2$ units was expected to be sold only at the production cost of $(f_1 + v)$, the net profit surrendered because of shortage would be (substituting $v + f_1$ for p in relation 7)

$$(P_1 - P_2)\ f_1 \qquad \ldots(8)$$

Evaluation of Actual Shortage Cost Parameter :

If F be the actual shortage cost parameter, then the expression for shortage cost for any inventory policy (x, v) will be

$$F.P_s(x, r) \quad ...(9)$$

For the yester planning horizon's inventory policy, the probability of shortage $P_s(x, r)$ of expression 9 assumed a value T_1/T.

And, since money value surrendered due to the occurrence of shortage of the raw material is nothing but the cost of shortage,

$$F(T_1/T)+(P_1-P_2)\ (p-v)$$

$$\text{Or, } F=(T/T_1)\ (P_1-P_2)\ (p-v) \quad ...(10)$$

Determination of Apparent Shortage Cost Parameter

The situation of apparent shortage comes into being when the item likely to be short is replenished through additional expediting efforts, e.g. sending messenger, telephoning, etc. For the yester planning horizon, these expediting efforts could be quantified with a bit of subjective arbitration.

Let F be the apparent shortage cost parameter during any planning horizon; and c_1 be the cost of sending messengers, c_2 be the cost of telephoning and so on for the yester planning horizon, then the total cost of expediting could be

$$c_1+c_2+........ \quad ...(11)$$

With the probability of apparent shortage expressed as $1-P_s(x, r)$ the apparent shortage cost expression becomes

$$1-P_s(x, r)\ F' \quad ...(12($$

Substituting the value of $(1-T_1/T)$ of probability of apparent shortage for the yester planning horizon in expression 12 and equating the result with the apparent shortage cost in expression 11,

$$(1-T_1/T)\ F'=c_1+c_2+......$$

Or $F=\dfrac{c_1+c_2+\ldots\ldots}{1-T_1/T}$ ...(13)

Shortage Cost Parameter

The total fixed shortage cost parameter, K, is sum of the actual shortage cost parameter, F and apparent shortage cost parameter, F' and is given by

$K=F+F'$ ...(14)

Combining the relations 10, 13 and 14

$K=(T/T_1)(P_1-P_2)(p-v)+$

$(c_1+c_2+\ldots\ldots)/(1-T_2/T)$ ...(15)

changed to railing structure system.

Case Study

In a consumer product blending and packaging firm, 1775 units of output could not be produced during 1012 operable hours in the preceding year of total 116545 operable hours because of shortage of a particular raw material. The overhead and direct labour costs per unit of output was Rs. 0.40. The firm could overcome the situation of impending shortage of the raw material by expediting through telephone calls and sending messengers. The cost to telephone calls was Rs. 1000 and that of sending messengers was Rs. 500 during the entire year for this material. The profit margin (after recouping the total cost) was Rs. 0.40 per unit of the product.

Thus, $T=116545$ hours, $T_1=1012$ hours, $P_1-P_2=1775$ units of output, $f_1=$ Rs. 0.40, $c_1=$ Rs. 1000 and $c_2=$ Rs. 500

$p-(v+f_1=$ Rs. 0.40 $\quad\therefore p-v=$ Rs. 0.40
$+$Rs. 0.40 $=$ Rs. 0.80

Substituting the above values in the relation 15, the shortage cost parameter to be considered for future modelling becomes,

$$K=\frac{116545}{1012}\times 1772\times 0.80+\frac{1000+500}{1-1012/116545}$$

$$=163532+1513=\text{Rs. }165045$$

Conclusion

It is important to figure out the shortage cost parameter for evolving optimal inventory control policy by minimising the total relevant cost equation for the inventory system. But precaution has to be taken to ensure authenticity of records of the costs of expediting and hours of production stoppage due to the particular raw material under study. In a multiproduct firm, it may be assiduous to prorate the overhead costs for each product. In cases of raw materials common to all products the differences arising out of overhead allocation is more likely to be diffused and hence the above formulation can be employed. Also, for other critical and high value raw materials, it might be ingenious to develop the shortage cost parameter as outlined above.

7

Economic Analysis of Energy Proposals

W. C. Turner, K. E. Case**

Abstract

Economic analysis of energy related projects is becoming more and more of a problem. Various governmental tax incentives and regulations along with the perplexing problems of multiple rates of inflation often make such analysis difficult and complex. Multiple rates of inflation occur when one cash flow (e.g. energy) inflates at a different rate than other cash flows.

This paper examines the problem, and presents a technically correct way of analyzing cash flows with multiple rates of inflation. Some surprising results are presented showing that great care must be taken in choosing inflation and interest rates. Finally, a survey is made of various tax incentives for energy projects.

* School of Industrial Engineering and Management, Oklahoma State University, Stillwater, Oklahoma. Reprinted with permission from Proceedings 1979 Fall, I.E. Conference, AIIE.

Introduction

Analysis of energy proposals presents some interesting and potentially perplexing problems to the energy manager. While many sectors of the economy are experiencing inflation, the energy manager faces a particularly high rate of inflation for energy costs. Treating inflation properly in energy related economic analyses has become a matter of great interest and considerable misinformation.

In addition, state and local governments have passed tax incentives including substantial tax credits, in an attempt to speed the adoption of favourable energy management projects. While these incentives are not difficult to use, the energy manager may be unaware of the potential opportunities available as well as their net positive effects. For example, a simple 10% investment tax credit on first cost often swings an undesirable investment to one which is cost effective.

This paper attacks both of these areas. First it discusses correct and incorrect ways of handling single and multiple rates of inflation. Then, the paper surveys the various Federal and State tax incentives and shows how to incorporate them into the analysis. The paper does not work on the problem of forecasting energy cost, but rather leaves that to the analyst.

The energy manager should remember that the future of energy cost is *almost* unpredictable with any certainty. Therefore, the technique used must take this into account through sensitivity analysis or some other technique.

Inflation and Before-Tax Analyses

Inflation has been a problem in economic analysis for some time now and much has been said about it. White, Agee, and Case (2) briefly discuss the subject and imply that there are two typical ways to handle inflation. They are :

Method 1 : Express cash flows as "then current" dollars. These may or may not be increasing at a constant rate k

Combine the interest rate i and general inflation rate j using i'=i+j+ij to discount the cash flows to present worth.

Method 2 : Express all cash flows as "constant dollars". If K=j, these cash flows are simply expressed in today's dollars. If K≠j, "constant worth" dollars are found by inflating at the rate k and deflating at the rate j. All cash flows are then discounted to present worth using interest rate i.

Single Inflation Rate

The correct use of these methods is illustrated in the following example. Also, a common incorrect method is shown.

Example 1 : A $10,000 investment is under consideration. If in place today, it would save $2,000/year. Such savings, however, are expected to follow the general inflationary rate of j=k=8% over the seven year life of the investment. At the end of this period, the investment has negligible salvage value. Interest is i=10%.

Method 1 :

	2160	2333	2519	2721	2939	3174	3428	
θ	↑	↑	↑	↑	↑	↑	↑	
	1	2	3	4	5	6	7	End of Year
10,000								

Modified interest rate = i' = i+j+ij =
.10+.08+.10(.08)=.188

End of Year	*"Then Current" Cash Flow*	*Present Worth Factor at i'=.188*	*Present Worth Cash Flow*
1	*2*	*3*	*4*
0	−10,000	1.0000	−10,000

(*Contd.*)

1	2	3	4
1	2,160.00	.8418	1,818.18
2	2,332.80	.7085	1,652.89
3	2,519.42	.5964	1,502.63
4	2,720.98	.5020	1,366.03
5	2,938.66	.4226	1,241.84
6	3,173.75	.3557	1,128.95
7	3,427.65	.2994	1,026.32
			−263.16

Due to the negative net present worth, the investment is not cost effective.

Method 2 :

2,000 2,000 2,000 2,000 2,000 2,000 2,000

θ ↑ ↑ ↑ ↑ ↑ ↑ ↑

10,000

End of Year	*"Constant Worth" Cash Flow*	*Present Worth Factor at i' = .10*	*Present Worth Cash Flow*
0	—10,000	1.0000	−10,000
1	2,000	.9091	1,818.18
2	2,000	.8264	1,652.89
3	2,000	.7513	1,502.63
4	2,000	.6830	1,366.03
5	2,000	.6209	1,241.84
6	2,000	.5645	1,128.95
7	2,000	.5132	1,026.32
			−263.16

Note that Method 2 results in the same negative present worth as does Method 1. Again, the investment is not cost effective.

Incorrect Method

Probably the most common error committed in inflationary analysis is illustrated here. The savings or positive cash flows are allowed to increase at the inflation rate k, yet the cash flows are discounted at only the interest rate.

End of Year	*"Then Current" Cash Flow*	*Present Worth Factor at i'=.10*	*Present Worth Cash Flow*
0	−10,000	1.0000	−10,000
1	2,160.00	.9091	1,963.64
2	2,332.80	.8264	1,927.93
3	2,519,42	.7513	1,892.88
4	2,720.98	.6830	1,858.46
5	2,938.66	.6209	1,824.67
6	3,173.75	.5645	1,791.50
7	3,427.6 ;	.5132	1,758.93
			3,018.01

The incorrent method illustrated above indicates that the investment is clearly cost effective.

It should be obvious from the above results that it is *incorrect to inflate annual cost and not increase the discount rate* by the general inflation rate and the product of the original discount rate and the general inflation rate (i.e., i'=i+j+ij). Also it appears safe to state that *Method 2 (express cash flows as "constant worth" and use interest i as the discount rate) is easier to use when j=k.*

Multiple Inflation Rates

Inflation rates need not always follow the general inflation rate. Some economic components, for example energy costs, may inflate at a high rate, while other components may be closer to the general inflation rate. Multiple rates of inflation are demonstrated in the example to follow.

Example 2 : A \$10,000 investment is required to install a recuperator on a boiler. If in place today, \$2,000/ year in energy costs would be saved. Due to the steep rate of increased energy costs, the savings will increase at $k1=20\%$ during each year of the seven year life of the recuperator. There is also labour intensive maintenance that would cost \$1,000/ year if in place today, and increase by $k2=8\%$ each subsequent year. The general inflationary rate of $j=8\%$ is expected to continue throughout the life of the project. The recuperator will have a negligible salvage value and interest is $i=10\%$.

In Method, 2, the modified interest rate $i'=i+j+ij=.10+.08+.10\,(.08)=.188$ is used to discount the "then current" net cash flows. A negative present worth results, indicating that the investment is not worth while.

In this method the general inflationary rate of $j=8\%$ is first removed, resulting in a constant worth cost flow which is then discounted to present worth using interest of $i=10\%$. Note that the negative present worth of -291.19 matchs the present worth of Method 1.

Incorrect Method

All too often, vendors will develop programmes that lead a Customer to believe he should use an inflation rate k on energy and not modify the discount rate i. This can lead to dramatic over energy consciousness. This is illustrated in the following analysis where energy savings are inflated at $k1=20\%$, but maintenance is held at "constant worth" and discounting is done at only the interest rate $i=10\%$.

Obviously, using "then current" savings, "constant worth" maintenance and discounting at the interest rate makes

Method 1

End of Year	*Investment*	*Then Current Savings at k1=.20*	*Then Current Maintenance at K2=.08*	*Then Current Net Cash Flow*	*Present Worth at i'=.188 i=i+j+ij*
0	—10,000			—10,000	—10,000
1	—	2,400	—1,080	1,320	1,111.11
2	—	2,880	—1,166.40	1,713.60	1,214.16
3	—	3,456	—1,259.71	2,196.29	1,309.91
4	—	4,147.20	—1,360.49	2,786.71	1,399.03
5	—	4,976.64	—1,469.33	3,507.31	1,482.15
6	—	5,971.97	—1,586.87	4,385.10	1,559.84
7	—	7,166.36	—1,713.82	5,452.54	1,632.61
					—291.91

Method 2

End of Year	*Investment*	*Then Current Savings at k1=.20*	*Then Current Maintenance at k2=.08*	*Then Current Net Cash Flow*	*Constant Worth Cash Flow at j=.08*	*Present Worth Cash Flow at i=.10*
0	—10,000			—10,000	—10,000	—10,000
1	—	2,400	—1,080	1,320	1,222.22	1,111.11
2	—	2,880	—1,166.40	1,713.60	1,469.14	1,214.16
3	—	3,456	—1,259.71	2,196.29	1,743.49	1,309.91
4	—	4,147.20	—1,360.49	2,786.71	2,048.32	1,399.03
5	—	4,976.64	—1,469.33	3,507.31	2,387.02	1,482.15
6	—	5,971.97	—1,586.87	4,385.10	2,763.36	1,559.84
7	—	7,166.36	—1,713.82	5,452.54	3,181.50	1,632.61
						—291.91

End of Year	Investment	Then Current Savings at $k1 = .20$	Constant Worth Maintenance	Present Worth Cash Flow at $i = .10$
0	—10,000			—10,000
1	—	2,400	—1,000	1,272.73
2	—	2,880	—1,000	1,553.72
3	—	3,456	—1,000	1,815.23
4	—	4,147.20	—1,000	2,149.58
5	—	4,976.64	—1,000	2,496.18
6	—	5,971.97	—1,000	2,806.55
7	—	7,166.36	—1,000	3,164.32
				5,261.31

this investment appear highly desirable when it is not. Many programmes will enable the analyst to inflate maintenance cost but it is always done at the general rate j. Even if this were done in the above example, the answer would still be highly positive, leading to an incorrect decision.

In the multiple inflation rate case, Methods 1 and 2 are about equally easy to apply, the answer being the same either way, Method 1 or Method 2 are mathematically consistent, and one may be selected over the other at the discretion of the analyst.

Modified Energy Inflation Rate

Method 2 can be modified and simplified by inflating those economic components for which $j \neq k$ by a single factor k'. This would be in lieu of inflating the cash flows at a rate k and deflating them at rate j.

The modified inflation rate is given by

$$k' = \frac{1+k}{1+j} - 1^*$$

where, as before :

k' = modified component inflation rate

k = specific component inflation rate

j = general inflation rate

For example 2, the modified inflation rate for the energy savings component is

$$k' = \frac{1.20}{1.08} - 1 = .111111$$

In Modified Method 2, those components increasing at the general inflation rate (maintenance) are expressed in "constant worth" dollars. Those components increasing at a rate

* See Appendix for Derivation.

Modified Nethod 2

End of Year	*Investment*	*Modified Savings at j'=.111111*	*Constant Worth Maintenance*	*Net Cash Flow*	*Present Worth at i=.10*
0	—10,000			—10,000	—10,000
1	—	2,222.22	—1,000	1,222.22	1,111.11
2	—	2,469.14	—1,000	1,469.14	1,214.16
3	—	2,743.48	—1,000	1,743.48	1,309.91
4	—	3,048.32	—1,000	2,048.32	1,399.03
5	—	3,387.02	—1,000	2,387.02	1,482.15
6	—	3,763.36	—1,000	2,763.36	1,559.84
7	—	4,181.50	—1,000	3,181.50	7,632.61
					—291.91

Table
Present Worth

Correct : $\left(\frac{(1+k)}{(1+j)(1+i)}\right)^n$

	j/k	4	8	12	16	20
	6	.4491	.5849	.7545	.9645	1.2229
n=7	8	.3940	.5132	.6619	.8462	1.0729
	10	.3465	.4513	.5821	.7442	.9436
	j/k	*4*	*8*	*12*	*16*	*20*
	6	.3187	.4648	.6686	.9497	1.3330
n=10	8	.2643	.3855	.5546	.7878	1.1057
	10	.2200	.3209	.4617	.6557	9204
	j/k	*4*	*8*	*12*	*16*	*20*
	6	.1799	.3169	.5468	.9255	1.5390
n=15	8	.1359	.2394	.4131	.6992	1.1627
	10	.1032	,1818	.3137	.5310	.8830

Table
Present Worth

Correct : $\left(\frac{(1+k)}{(1+j)(1+i)}\right)^n$

	j/k	4	8	12	16	20
	6	.3615	.6367	1.0986	1.8597	3.0924
n=15	8	.3731	.4810	.8300	1.4050	2.3363
	10	.2074	.3653	.6303	1.0669	1.7741

1
Multipliers at i=.10

Approximate : $\left(\frac{1+k-j}{1+i}\right)^n$

j/k	4	8	12	16	20
6	.4455	.5895	.7716	1.0000	1.0926
8	.3856	.5132	.6753	.8795	1.1344
10	.3328	.4455	.5895	.7716	1.0000

j/k	4	8	12	16	20
6	.3150	.4700	.6904	1.0000	1.1348
8	.2563	.3855	.5707	.8324	1.1974
10	.2077	.3150	.4700	.6904	1.0000

j/k	4	8	12	16	20
6	.1768	.3222	.5737	1.0000	1.2089
8	.1298	.2394	.4311	.7594	1.3103
10	.0946	.1768	.3222	.5737	1.0000

2
Multipliers at i=5%

Approximate : $\left(\frac{1+k-j}{1+i}\right)^n$

j/k	4	8	12	16	20
6	.3553	.6474	1.1528	2.0093	3.4335
8	.2608	.4810	.8663	1.5259	2.6329
10	.1901	.3553	.6474	1.1528	2.0093

greater (or smaller) than the general inflationary rate are enlarged (deflated at the rate $k' = (1+k)/(1+j) - 1$. Note that the present worth is identical to that calculated using Methods 1 and 2. But, the method is simpler.

A step by step procedure is given below for calculating the present worth in multiple inflation rate analyses.

1. Determine all component cash flows in "constant worth" dollars, except those for which $j \phi k$.

2. Project those cash flow components for which $j \phi k$

   using $k' = \dfrac{1+k}{1+j} - 1$

3. Discount to present worth using the interest i.

Approximate Approach

Rather than explain the rationale and bring the modified inflation rate k' as derived in the Appendix, some would prefer to use the modified rate $k'' = k - j$. This is easy to understand, and yields close results so long as j and k are not too different. For example, Table 1 compares k' and $k-j$ with a series of multipliers, These multipliers not only provide the modified (or approximate modified) inflation factor k' (or k''), but the discount factor i as well.

As can be seen, the error definitely increase with increasing n and increasing difference between j and k. In Table 2, the multipliers are calculated for $i = 5\%$ and $n = 15$. For the interest rates used, the value of i makes little relative difference in the comparison of the approximate to the correct approach.

Even though the approximate method is not bad, the reader is encouraged to use the correct approach. This is due to its theoretical justification as well as its comparable case of use.

After Tax Analysis

After tax cash flow analyses under inflation are highly similar to those assuming no inflation. For example, expenses and depreciation allowances are subtracted from incomes and/or savings. Therein lies the difference. Depreciation is set up on the first cost of an asset. The depreciation, therefore, does not inflate. The savings and costs are free to increase as described by the analyst. Following is an example of an after-tax present worth analysis under inflation.

Example 3 : Reconsider Example 2, modifying it to include sum-of-the-years'-digits depreciation and a tax rate of 50%. The after-tax interest rate i is 5%. While this value seems quite low remember that it is an after-tax rate and it is exclusive of the inflationary component j=8%.

Once again, the present worth of the cash flows are negative. This indicates the project is not cost effective at the rates considered.

Tax Incentives

The National Energy Act and many state legislations have provided for tax relief on energy related matters. A prudent energy analyst will become aware of all these opportunities and will stay up with this rapidly changing arena.

At the onset, it is necessary to distinguish between a tax credit and a deduction. A credit is a reduction in the income taxes of the credited amount, whereas a deduction (such as depreciation) is a reduction in the taxable income from which the taxes are calculated. Dollar for dollar then, a credit means considerable more.

For example, if the $10,000 investment in Example 3 qualified for a 20% tax credit, then taxes at the time of purchase are reduced by $2,000 (20% of $10,000) making the effective cost $8,000. This tax credit could be applied against other six liabilities in the company or carried over or back in

End of year	Investment	Then Current Savings	Then Current Maintenance	Depreciation SYD	Taxable Income	Tax 50%	After tax "Then Current" Cash Flow	Present Worth After Tax at i=.05 J=.08
0	10,000						—10,000	—10,000
1	—	2,400	−1,080	2,500	−1.180	−590	1,910.00	1,684.30
2	—	2,880	−1,166.40	2,142.86	−429.26	−214.63	1,928.23	1,499.45
3	—	3,456	−1,259.71	1,785.71	410.58	205.29	1,991.00	1,365.51
4	—	4,147.20	−1,360.49	1,428.57	1,358.14	5,679.07	2,107.64	1,275.51
5	—	4,976.64	−1,469.33	714.29	2,435.88	1,217.94	2,289.37	1,220.82
6	—	5,971.97	−1,586.87	714.29	3,670.81	1,835.41	2,549.69	1,198.97
7	—	7,166.36	−1,713.82	357.14	5,095.40	2,547.70	2,904.84	1,204.57
								−552.07

years. That same piece of equipment would still qualify for depreciation, deductible as a business expense, based upon the entire $10,000 investment. Thus, the net present worth would suddenly jump from −552.07 to + 1,447.93, making the project attractive.

The National Energy Act allows for an *additional* 10% tax credit for investement in* :

—Equipment using geothermal energy

—Equipment using solar energy

—Equipment using wind energy

—Combustors using coal or other alternate fuels

—Equipment to produce alternative fuels

—Equipment for handling and storage of alternative fuels

—Pollution control equipment

—Equipment improving energy efficiency of existing processes (including waste heat recovery)

—Equipment for extraction of geopressurized methane and shale oil

—Equipment for recycling waste materials

—Equipment midifying existing equipment for alternative fuel use (must use at least 25%)

—Automatic energy management systems

---

* Drawn in part from ***The Systematic Energy Conservation Management Guide***, (1) p. 7.

At the same time, the Act denies accelerated depreciation schedules or any investment tax credits for new oil or gas fired boilers or air conditioners and portable oil or gas fired space heaters. It also allows for early retirement (faster depreciation) of oil or gas boilers.

Finally, there are some miscellaneous items that might affect company *plans*. They include :

—A 10% tax credit for employers providing vans or buses to and from work

—Exemption of van pool benefits from an employee's taxable income

—Removal of excise tax on buses and bus parts

—Gas guzzler tax

—A depletion allowance for geothermal deposits

Another important item with strong pay of potential is that in many states, companies do not have to pay sales tax on energy *used directly in the production process*. The key here is recognition. If the energy becomes a recognizable part of the product, then no sales tax need be paid on that energy. For example, the energy used to bake paint on a product should not have sales tax imposed while the energy required for lighting of the plant would have a sales tax.

Department of Energy Document

The Department of Energy recently published a document intending to provide a basis for life cycle costing analysis of energy related projects. The document is entitled. *Life-Cycle Cocting : A Guide for Selecting Energy Conservation Projects for Public Building*. (2) This section examines that document.

On page 3, the document states : "......the LCC (life

cycle cost) estimates are not appropriate as budget estimates because they are expressed in constant dollars (excluding inflation)......". Obviously, the book is using the constant worth approach.

On page 8, the document expands into problems where some costs inflate more rapidly than the underlying rate of inflation. Basically it proposes that *these costs be adjusted to include the differential* thus implying the recommended procedure presented earlier in this paper. Although the booklet does not elaborate on how to obtain this differential rate, it implies simply subtracting the general inflation rate from the energy inflation rate and using the result to inflate energy costs (k" earlier). In fact an example on page 16 uses a 6% differential rate of escalation." This, of course, *is not theoretically correct but the accuracy is probably greater than the analyst's ability to estimate anyway.*

Procedures examined in the booklet include Present Value, Annual Equivalent, Savings to Investment Ratio (SIR, the ratio of present or annual dollars of saving to present or annual dollars of cost), rate of return (annual savings investment—so not internal rate of return) and a discounted payback method. Forms are given with several examples. Discussions include such subjects as selecting from interdependent projects (page 28). The usual federal discount rate of 10% is recommended.

Short of the normal problems of rate of return (as used here) and payback, the procedures all appear correct and the document does a very good job of presentation. Some intresting forms and monographs are provided.

Finally, it should be noted that the discount factors given on page 46 don't appear to match those of White, Agee and Case (3). The difference is that White et. al. uses A1 as the cash flow at the *end* of the year 1 while the booklet assumes that A is the cash flow in constant worth dollars (i.e., beginning of year 1). The key is that

$$A1 = A\,(1+j)$$

when this factor is applied, the figures do agree.

Summary

This paper has examined the problems involved in the economic analysis of energy related projects. Basically, those problems include 1) how to handle energy cost that are increasing faster than the general inflation and (2) how to incorporate the special tax benefits presently being applied to energy related projects.

To handle energy inflation, the paper shows that it is probably easiest to use constant worth dollars (i.e., ignore general inflation) and to escalate energy costs at a "modified rate." The theoretically correct modified rate is derived and used; but examples are given to show that a straight approximation of subtracting the general rate from that of energy and using the result as the differential rate yields results pretty close to the theoretically correct procedure.

A special section is devoted to discussion of unique tax benefits available to energy projects. Probably, the most interesting or attractive is the use of investment tax credits.

The paper ends with a survey of the Department of Energy's book of Life Cycle Costing.

Appendix

Derivation of Modified Energy Inflation Rate

Assuming Method 1 gives correct results and we are trying to simplify the method, then the present worth for each of the years must be equal for the two months. That is,

Method 1 *Method 2*

$$(CFn)\,\frac{(1+k)^n}{(1+i)^n\,(1+j)^n} = CFn\,\frac{(1+k')^n}{(1+j)^n}$$

where

k = Energy inflation rate

i = Interest rate

j = General inflation rate

CFn = Cash flow in year n

k' = Unknown incremental equivalent energy inflation rate

$$\frac{(1+k)}{(1+i)(1+j)} = \frac{1+k'}{1+i}$$

$$k' = \frac{1+k}{1+j} - 1$$

8

An Exploratory Study on Buying Decisions in the General Engineering, Chemical and Pharmaceutical Industries in India

Thomas Mathew, P.C. Benjamin***

Abstract

This study explores a few aspects of industrial buyer behaviour. The focus is towards an analytical investigation of the composition of the 'Decision Making Units' for a few selected companies in the General Engineering, and the Chemical and Pharmaceutical industries in India. For new purchase decisions, the variation in the degree of influence exerted by the purchase executives in the decision making process is analysed, and external sources of information are identified. Finally, the study analyses the relative importace of several supplier evaluation factors.

* Professor, NITIE, Bombay.

** MICO Ltd., Nasik.

Introduction

Modern organisations owe much of their success to the effective implementation of the marketing concept, namely, "Profits are the rewards for creating a satisfied customer." It is crucial for every company to have a strategy which focusses attention on its customers needs and wants : thus a thorough understanding of "Buyer Behaviour".

Historically, the first few attempts to analyse buyer behaviour were for consumer products. Research in this area developed largely from the information needs of sales and marketing. The rapid increase of competition in the industrial product market led to the need for reseach in industrial buyer behaviour. In the last two decades siginficant contributions have been made in this area—primarily in the industrialized world.

In some segments of Indian Economy, the relevance of Industrial Marketing itself may be in question, partly due to the existing 'Sellers Market' environment for some products. However, the situation is changing fast. Realizing this, many companies in India have recognized the importance of a professional approach to Industrial Marketing. Hence, the need for research efforts in industrial buying is an urgent one.

'The Decision Making Unit' in Industrial Buying

The 'Decision Making Unit' (D.M.U.) in industrial buying consists of those individuals, or groups of individuals who make decisions at various stages of the purchase process. The identification and analysis of the D.M.U. is of crucial importance to the industrial market; it will focus attention on a selected section of the organization on whom marketing effort is to be directed. In identifying the D.M.U., it is essential to include all personnel generating alternatives and making recommendations in addition to those making the final decision, i.e. all "Buying Influence" are to be considered.

In the Indian context, the culture and basic management

philosophy of organizations play a major role in determining the type of D.M.U. composition. In family owned companies, D.M.U. members are likely to be individuals with a high degree of concentration of power. At the other end of the spectrum are professionally managed companies, where decision making is essentially a group effort. Hence, the D.M.U.'s of such companies are likely to be composed of groups of individuals—both intra and inter-departmental. Possible D.M.U. candidates for the industrial purchase process are the board of directors, purchase managers, purchase officers, production engineers, industrial engineers, design engineers, R & D personnel, etc.

Field Research in Industrial Buying

The results of the first comprehensive field study in industrial buying were published in 'How British Industry Buys' (Brand, 1972). Using semistructured interviews, the study analysed the purchase process in 60 British Companies. The results showed that for the industry as a whole, the personnel most concerned with purchasing were :

For Plant Equipment :

Board of Directors

Operating Management

Production Engineers

For Materials and Components :

Buying Department

Design and Development Engineers

Operating Management

Since then, major contributions in this area have come from Scientific American (1970), Upah and Bird (1980), Bellizzi and Walter (1980), Erickson and Gross (1981), and Johnson and Bonona (1981).

In the Indian contex, Sarin (1982) adopted a 'Case Study' approach to analyse purchase behaviour in four Companies in Eastern India. The focus of this study was on the organization factors of industrial buying—tasks, structures, technology and people.

Objectives and Scope

The study attempts to achieve the following :

A. Identify and analyse the D.M.U. composition in :

(a) The General Engineering Industry for the following types of purchases : (i) Capital equipment, (ii) Raw material for production, (iii) Finshed components for production.

(b) The chemical and Pharmaceutical Industry for the following types of purchases : (i) Capital Equipment, (ii) Raw material for production.

B. Analyse New Purchases to :

(a) Measure the influence of the purchase executive at various stages of the purchase process for the companies studied and examine the differences between large and small companies.

(b) Identify the external sources of information at the awareness and interest stages of the purchasing process.

C. (a) Identify, and rank supplier evaluation factors.

(b) Compare supplier evaluation ranking of General Engineering with the Chemical and Parmaceutical Industry.

The boundaries of the study are as follows :

A. Only 'task' factors of buyer behaviour are studied.

B. The study consider only the Intra Company or the Corporate buying process. Inter-Company and individual buying processes (Hill and Hillier, 1977) are beyond the scope of the study.

C. Only Purchase personnel—Managers and Executives are interviewed in the survey.

D. The choice of the sample restrict the study to the following target group boundaries : Private Sector; Chemicals, Pharmaceuticals, and General Engineering industries; Sales Turnover not less than Rs. 1 crore.

The Research Design

The Target Group

The achieve the objectives of the study an appropriate target group was chosen. Companies were selected from the General Engineering and Chemical and Pharmaceutical industries in a manner ensuring a fair representation of the industry as a whole. Size was the main criterion in the choice of the sample; Seles turnover was considered as an appropriate measure of a company's size. A cut-off level of Rs. 40 crore turnover was used to classify organisations as either "large" or "small". Other factors influencing the final choice of the Companies were proximity to Bombay and the case of accessibility of company personnel.

The Method of Data Collection

To carry out the study, in-depth semistructured personnel interviews were conducted of Purchase managers and Purchase executives of the sample consisting of 10 general engineering companies and 10 chemical and pharmaceutical companies chosen. A detailed questionnaire (Appendix A) formed the basis for conducting these interviews. Questionnaires were sent to several companies by mail in an attempt to supplement the study.

Analysis and Evaluation of the Results

D.M.U. Composition Analysis

Two major observations can be made from the results for the industries studied as a whole, viz. (a) A large variation in the D.M.U. Comoposition between capaital equipment and other types of purchases—a higher involvement of top management in capital equipment purchases. The cause for this is fairly obvious : The higher level of investment and the long-term nature of the capital equipment purchase decisions. (b) A high degree of concentration of power with purchase personnel. This could be due to two reasons : The essentially commercial implications of most purchase decisions; The presence of an increasing number of technical personnel in Purchasing, making interactions with other engineers in the company.

General Engineering Vs. Chemical and Pharmaceuticals

(*i*) *A Comparison of D.M.U. Composition*

Need recognition and technical specification stage.

For capital equipment purchases a concentration of purchasing power at the lower levels of the management hierarchy is observed in the Chemical and Pharmaceutical Industries. A possible explanation for this lies in the differences in the nature of industries and their organization structure. In chemical industries where technical decisions are more often related to chemical technology, mechanical engineering related problems are tackled by personnel in operations management or project management. Hence, decision making shifts to a relatively low level in the management hierarchy.

A second observation is the differences in the functional natures of the D.M.U.'s between the two types of industries for raw material purchases. This could be because of the basic difference in the distribution of functional authority in the organization structure of the two industries.

Another interesting observation is the wider spread of decision influencers in the General Engineering Industry. A possible cause for this could be the higher variability of purchase requirements for this industry as compared to a process type of industry. The frequent changes in material and component specifications, which result as a consequence of these varying requirements, call for a high degree of expertise and specialization in several fields of knowledge; hence, the need for the involvement of a larger number of functional areas, such as design engineering, research and development, value engineering, etc.

(ii) Commercial Evaluation and Performance Monitoring Stage

A close similarity in the D.M.U. composition is observed at this stage of the purchase process between the two types of industries. This is probably because of the essentially commercial nature of the decisions involved at this stage. Purchase personnel have a predominant influence in all decisions at this stage.

Comparison with the British Industry

The major D.M.U. areas identified in this study coincides with those identified in the research project undertaken by Industrial Market Research Ltd., and the Institute of Marketing (Brand, 1972). Significant differences between the results of the two studies are :

(i) The 'Spread' of the decision influencers

—A wider spread of the functional areas involved is observed in the British Industry;

(ii) The degree of concentration of buying power with Purchase Personnel

—The industries covered in this survey showed a far higher concentration of buying power with the purchase department.

Analysis of New Purchases

(*a*) *Influence of the Purchase Executives*

The result indicates an appreciable difference between small large companies in the influence exerted by their purchase executives in buying decisions. This observation is confirmed by statistical tests. The average scores of the purchase executive's influence at the purchase stages for the companies were ranked separately for the small and the large firms. The rank correlation coefficient between the two sets of ranks was used as the basis for comparing the two classes of Companies. The relevant statistical parameters computed are shown below :

Coefficient of Rank Correlation	*t-Statistic*	*Degree of Freedom*	*Level of Significance*
0.524	1.508	8	0.05

The results indicate a significant difference (at a significance level of 0.05) between the ranking of the purchase executives influence at various stages of the purchase process between the two categories of companies. Hence, it can be inferred that there is a considerable difference between small and large Companies in the variation of influence exerted at various stages of the Purchase process.

(*b*) *Comparison with Previous Work*

Variations of the Purchase executives influence across the stages of the purchase process were analysed by Bellizzi and Walter (1980) and Bellizzi (1981). The results of these studies are found to be considerably different from those of the current study. The variation could be attributed to the wide differences between the characteristics of the sample units chosen.

(*c*) *External Sources of Information*

The results show that for new purchases, most popular sources of information for purchase personnel are manufacturers, salesmen and trade journals.

Supplier Evaluation Analysis

The depicted results indicate that three of the factors considered, viz.—quality, price, and delivery are considerably more important than the other factors.

Comparison Between General Engineering and Chemical and Pharmaceutical Companies

The rank correlation coefficient between the average ranks of supplier evaluation factors for the two types of industries was used as the basis of comparison. The following statistical parameters were computed :

Coefficient of Rank Correlation	*t-Statistic*	*Degree of Freedom*	*Level of Significance*
0.098	5.292	8	0.05

The t-statistic value computed is 5.292. Hence, General Engineering and Chemical and Pharmaceutical Industries are considerably similar in their evaluation of suppliers, using the factors considered as the basis (at a level of significance of 0.05).

Limitations

The most severe limitation of the study was that only 'Task' aspects of buyer behaviour were considered. Non-task (emotional) factors such as ego enhancement, personal risk reduction, previous experience, etc., although difficult to measure, are crucial determinants of industrial buyer behaviour.

Only a simplified classification of purchases, from a seller's viewpoint were considered. Classification from the customers frame of reference would give a better insight into buyer behaviour. Moreover, a broad division of industrial purchases as being either 'Buyer Specified' or 'Seller Specified' would present a more realistic picture of industrial purchase behaviour.

The reseach methodology involved interviews with purchase department personnel only. A thorough understanding of the buying process requires interactions with all relevant D.M.U. members. A deeper probe into buyer behaviour will be possible with the use of 'Snowballing' interviews, or a case study approach.

Concluding Remarks

The study was an attempt to understand purchase decision making in the Indian Industry. It was exploratory in nature, with no evidence of any earlier work in the area. Hence, the results of this study may be considered as a starting point for a full-scale research project of descriptive nature.

Great care has to be exercised in interpreting the results of the study; they should be viewed in light of the limited scope of the study. No generalized conclusion can be drawn from it.

Implications for Industrial Marketers

In the worlds of Hill and Hillier, (1977) "...industrial marketing executives will never provide the company with the best profit opportunities unless they have a thorough understanding of tactical and strategic customer behaviour at both macro and micro levels". A thorough understanding of buyer behaviour requires knowledge of the following : The key buying units in an organisation; The exact composition of individuals in the buying units; The time phasing of decisions made by the buying units; The variety of influences which the members of the buying units are subjected to; Inter-buying unit inter-actions.

Scope for Future Work

This particular study is a simple demonstration for some Indian industries. However, the methodology explained can be extended as well to similar types of situations. Purchases could be classified according to the customer viewpoint to make the analysis more meaningful. Little work has been done to analyse the 'Task' variables in indstrial buyer behaviour. A study in this area would give valuable insight into purchase decision making.

'The Interactive dimensions' of the buying centre (Johnston and Bonoma, 1981) could be an interesting area for further research work. A study on the effect of environmental conditions on purchase behaviour would be relevant in the rapidly changing industrial scenario of today.

9

Bank Cost Accounting System Design

*K.A. Lifson, Ph.D.**

Bank cost accounting is uniquely difficult and has been subjected to many criticisms by lending officers and operations officers. We have interpreted frequent criticisms into requirements for useful cost accounting concepts. Priority of cost and profitability information is : asset deployment, customer profitability, operations efficiency, non-asset product costs, overhead justification, analytical decisions, simulation. Significant cost measurement concepts are discussed as : standard cost system, bill of materials usage, modified marginal transfer costs, the identification of manageable, committed, and assigned costs, the measurement of officer controlled profit contribution, and the establishment of targets for customer profitability to sum to bank profit goals.

I. Criticisms

From the biased viewpoint of the consultant called in to

* Lifson, Herman, Blackmarr & Harris.
Reprinted with permission from Proceedings 1979 Fall Industrial Engineering Conference, AIIE.

evaluate and revise bank cost accounting information, the first topic we discuss this afternoon should be some comments on why the cost accounting function has been perceived as unsatisfactory.

It certainly is easier to talk about what's wrong with the results and use the cost accounting information than it is to design a system that produces the desired results. Our experience in designing and implementing cost accounting system, however, invariably begins with the senior officers of the bank describing what they are getting in the way of cost information and why they can't or don't use it or believe it. It is much easier for them to express the negatives than to state what they would really like to have. I have taken their comments and put them into more operational terms :

A. The Emphasis is on Precision Rather than Usefulness

For example, the conclusion that one lunch in the officers' dining room costs $ 32.84. Nobody is going to close the dining room, or reduce the cost to $ 30.68 by serving beans instead of ribeye. What they will do is take customers elsewhere (or not have working lunches) if they are transferred $ 32.84 charges for each meal.

B. The Detail of Reporting is Based upon the Detail that is Available Rather than on What's Important

For example, I have had a real estate department officer show me an exquisite allocation of the cost of his floor space to the various kinds of loans that his department makes, but he could only guess at whether his spread on lending money to small builders of single family residence was a profitable use of assets considering the cost of administering and monitoring the loans and the higher credit risk and surveillance required.

C. The Emphasis of the Reporting has been on Historical Accuracy and According Procedures Rather than on Providing Information as to What will or Should Happen with Regard to Costs

Detailed analyses and assignments of depreciation to

products is an example. Depreciation is usually reckoned based on tax considerations. It is an approximation and the effort to assign precise quantities of this approximation to historical unit product costs does not have much meaning for current decisions.

D. Costs are Frequently Summed up without regard to Personal Responsibility

This occurs when the reporting emphasis is focussed on functional profitability and functional costs rather than on a profit center concept of organisation. An example would be chastising the head telephone operator because bankwide telephone expenses are too high. Another example would be focusing emphasis on the profitability of the "demand deposit function". Almost everybody in the bank has something to do with this profitability but there is no one individual responsible for the waiving of service charge fees, float costs, compensating balance requirements being enforced, etc.

E. Emphasis on Line Item Expense Reporting and Line Item Transfer Costs

Gives the operations center manager the feeling that he really is not responsible for managing anything. He is not permitted to make the compromise decisions (without criticism and review) of overtime expense versus regular payroll costs. Or regular payroll costs versus float cost, for example.

F. The Reports are too Voluminous

Management by exception principles are not employed and the accountants tend to report everything they know. Examples are reporting on a line item basis how much costs have been transferred into the Metropolitan Division for FICA, cafeteria subsidy, allocated firstaid cost, etc. All the head of Metropolitan needs to know is that it costs $ 38 per month in indirect support costs for every employee he has. The only thing he can control is his number of employees. He cannot control any apportionment of the cafeteria subsidy, and complaining about a $ 60 increase in this item than he will a $ 60,000 swing in cost of funds.

G. *Information Dilution*

A corollary of the lack of management by exception is the inclusion of arbitrary assignments of costs or the assignment of costs that can't be managed during the time period. This dilutes the emphasis on what the profit center manager or operations manager should do and has done on the cost and profit elements that he *can* manage during the time period. An example is the manager of the wire transfer department who has succeeded in reducing the unit labour cost of repetitive transfers by 10%, only to have this favourable trend wiped out during the month because he has absorbed his share of his boss's travel to the BAI Conference. Another example is the uniform allocation of the amount that the bank chooses to take into loan loss reserve. This can obscure the real world appearance of the relative profitability of different asset uses.

H. *Goal Incongruence*

The reporting of costs and profitability is such that certain actions which the officer takes which he knows in the real world favourably affect the condition of the bank, show up as bad decisions on the report of the profitability of cost of his department. Examples are being charged for CD's of his customers at an interest expense rate greater than the transfer value rate he receives. Another example is selling, at a deep discount, item processing which will be performed at off-peak load hours. If he is charged the average cost for item processing, the cost will exceed the revenue he has derived.

I. *No Predictive Ability*

Senior officers frequently complain that they cannot predict, from the cost figures available to them, the effect of additional volume of depository services on profit.

J. Line Officers Frequently Complain that Transfer Costs of Support Services are Averaged Over too Broad Groupings

For example, an average transfer cost of $ 30 per lock-box item would penalize the account executives who mainly sell retail lock-box services. Another example would be an average cost for item processing that averaged in both on-us and transit items.

K. Transfer Costs for Support Services that are Based on Units Meaningful to Operations may have no Controllable Meaning for the Line Officer

For example, if data processing services are charged to the line officer on the basis of CPU seconds, he does not feel he can control them. He does not know how the services required to support him and his customers affect the charges he gets for data processing costs.

L. No Target Profitability

In most cases targets have not been developed which relate, for the line officer, cutomer or product profitability relative to the total goals of the bank.

M. Line Officers Suspect that they are Absorbing Inefficiencies

(Which they cannot control) in the operations and support functions.

N. Operations Officers Suspect that they are Being Held Responsible for Underabsorption of their Fixed Costs

Despite the fact that they cannot control the volume fed them by the line officers.

O. Percentage by Historical Usage

When costs analyses are made to determine the historical usage of support facilities by profit centers or functions, the allocation of costs is then not responsive to changes in user demands. For example, assume that a historical cost study is done and it shows that vault services spends 18% of its time on handling coins and currency for Metropolitan accounts. Then assume that during the next year, 18% of the total cost of vault service is attributed to that function for that group of customers. It would not respond to the possible doubling of the requirements by Metropolitan customers for that service during the year.

P. No Efficiency Measures

Cost information frequently does not provide either for measures of operational efficiency or trends in unit costs.

Q. When Cost Accounting Systems become Sophisticated the Reporting becomes Cumbersome

There is a tendency to report on a routine basis complete analytical results that are really needed only when decisions of new product introduction or closing a branch or buying a new reader/sorter are to be made. The compromise is in the direction of completeness rather than conciseness.

R. Occasionally, Expenses are not Associated with the Revenue or Balances that Justify the Expenses

A frequent example is international services were fee revenue on letters of collection get logged in one department and the collection expense gets charged to another department.

II. Banks are Different

In defence of bank cost accountants, they do have a difficult task. Following are some reasons that a cost accounting system for a manufacturing or distribution company cannot be applicable to a bank.

A. Customer does not Buy Operations

The operations that are performed (and create expenses) in the "factory" of the bank are not always apparent in the product that the customer thinks he is paying for, or the account executive considers he is "selling".

B. Operation Frequency Irregularity

The "factory operations" (and their cost) do not necessarily have a one-to-one relationship, a regular frequency of requirement, with delivered products. Costs of many operations that are measured and used for factory cost control must be transferred to products, and thence to customers on a probabilistic frequency basis. Examples would be useless telephone calls in balance reporting, number of authorization calls for credit cards, or percentage of reject items.

C. Operations Not Countable

Many cost-creating operations are incurred in units that are not easily countable or would be difficult to attribute to specific customers, and approximations must be used both for cost accounting and customer profitability measures.

D. Work in Process is Money

Because "work-in-process" or the "factory" is money, some "factory" operations generate positive or negative float which must be accounted for and attributed to products and customers.

E. Volatility of Raw Material Cost

The measured profitability of products or cutomers over a short period of time will appear quite different from a measure over longer durations because of the volatility of cost of funds. Operational costs that include positive or negative float generation will also experience this variation.

F. Balance Justification Indeterminate

The keeping of nostro and vostro balances is frequently partially justified by operations and partially for funds sources and uses reasons. The assignment of the cost or imputed income of these balances to customers and operations requires some conceptual decisions, and the difference is significant.

G. Profit Versus Liquidity

Some banking activities (purchase or sale of participations, or issuance of large CD's for example) are identified with specific customers, but may spuriously reduce the measure of customer profitability; they were engaged in as sources of liquidity.

H. Definition of Support Centers and Profit Centers is not Clear-cut

Some support centers log in fee income (and it is accounted for in those support centers) which really was generated by a customer-oriented profit center, and for which the expense is accounted for elsewhere.

I. Some Operations Centers Perform Support Activities for a Fee

(Or sometimes balances) for banking customers, correspondent banks, non-customers, and other banking departments. A conceptual decisions as to the transfer value of the services of these centers to other departments at cost or price influences operational cost and customer profitability measures.

J. Capacity Costs are High

Conceptual design of the assignment of the costs of maintaining capacity to perform operations, of common support functions, and of the basic expenses of the bank influences both customer and operational cost measurements, to a larger degree than in most non-banking corporations.

K. Critical Ratios are Changing

As banks continue the trend toward "unbundling" prices, the traditional ratios used in measuring relative customer profitability, relative profitability of asset usage, and relative profitability of services becomes inappropriate. Changes in the ratios used require some conceptual decisions, and these should be consistent for the different dimensions.

III. System Priorities

What are we really trying to accomplish with a cost accounting system? The following list represents my interpretation of the usual order of priority of accomplishments required of cost accounting information.

1. Measure the relative profitability of different asset uses, funds sources, and customer groups.

2. Evaluate and assist account executives with regard to the profitability with which they develop and manage customer relationships.

3. Evaluate and assist operations managers with regard to the efficiency with which they manage their organizational units.

4. Evaluate the profitability of specific non-asset product and services, and provide information as to how the profitability could be improved.

5. Predict and evaluate cost of certain overhead functions.

6. Provide more informed bases so as to make analyses and influence specific decisions. The kinds of decisions involved are: pricing, product, design, production and delivery methods, capacity development and capital expenditures, cost component trade-offs of labour versus float, etc., initiations or terminations of products, services or locations.

7. Provide a basis for projecting the financial plans of the bank and for simulating financial results under diverse conditions.

IV. General Specifications

Some general management information system design specifications have been pertinent to the design of cost accounting systems. They are :

A. Management by Objective

Actual results should be compared with a credible, committed standard.

B. Management by Results

Profit components of income, funds, expense should be accumulated and combined at the lowest level at which an individual officer is responsible for profit results.

C. Dynamic Management

The mechanics of the reporting system should accommodate quick and frequent changes in the aimed-at-results.

D. Management by Exception

The mechanics of the reporting system should accommodate input of definitions of "what is remarkable" and the highlighting of special reporting of "remarkable" conditions of absolute values, changes, differences from a standard, or remarkable trends.

E. Simplicity

A compromise is required between precision of the reporting and the complexity of developing and understanding the figures reported.

F. All Figures Must be in Record

Totals will be precise, and must cross-foot across dimensions of customers, departments, products, operations. All systems should derive input from compatible data bases.

G. Transfer Rates for Funds and Support Services Must be Simple and Credible

The cost objects by which transfers are made must be in terms meaningful to the user as well as the provider, and the rates must be understood. Transferred costs must be known on a priori basis.

H. Fixed and Variable Components

Should be understood to permit flexible budgeting and price versus volume considerations to be made on a more informed basis.

I. Controllable and Committed Components

Should be understood to permit focus on the components that are manageable in the given time period at each level of authority.

J. Simulation Modelling Should be Accommodated

By the system, so as to enable predictions of costs and profits under different anticipations of future conditions, as assistance in budgetary planning, and as assistance in planning with customers for rates, balances, fees and services.

K. Variance Analysis

Variance of costs or profit performance from standard or budget should be identifiable in terms of cause : rate, volume, spread, service expenses, operations costs, balances, fees and other components.

L. Immediacy

Reports must be available in time to take action. A compromise between precision and detail versus immediacy may be required.

V. Dimensions of Cost

We have found it useful to think of cost information as being reported along four dimensions.

All of these dimensions must be derived from a common data base in order that everything cross-foot, the totals jibe with the financial records of the bank, and everybody is dealing with the same set of numbers. The major feature requires that every credit to a cost center for an operation performed be balanced by an identical debit to a product, directty to a customer or to an organisational entity.

A. By Cost Center and Operations within Cost Centers

This dimension is essential to operational budgetary control, cost planning, considerations of cost and volume relationships, methods and equipment considerations, and other concepts affecting operational efficiency and the management of operations officers in their control of efficiency.

B. By Product

This dimension sums up the cost of operations, funds usage, and support; across organizational lines. It is essential to pricing structure, negotiations, and merchandising strategy.

C. By Customer

Some costs are to be accounted for by product and then product costs are attributed to the customers for whom the products are provided. Some costs are directly and specifically attributable to the development and service of specific customers, independent of product usage. This dimension, which must mesh in general design with the customer profitability reporting system, is essential to pricing and negotiations, and other considerations affecting merchandising strategy and the management of account executives.

D. By Line Organizational Entity (Profit Centers)

To measure the profitability of a profit center, the cost

accounting system must assign to the center all of the costs associated with the generation of revenues or balances which are attributed to the profit centers. Some of the costs will be accounted for in the direct administration of the profit center, some will be attributed based on product usage, and some will be attributed based on general or customer support.

VI. Operations Cost Concepts

The major mechanical difficulty with most accounting systems has been the treatment of operational costs of depository services : item processing, lock-box, etc. The association of interest expense, real or imputed, with the revenues derived from the use of the funds; the assignment of risk expense; and the apportionment of general bank basic expenses have been conceptually difficult but mechanically easy.

With regard to operational costs, the following features have been important :

A. The Use of a Standard Cost System

Which credits the cost center with a reasonable determination of what the operation "should" cost permits us to accomplish two significant objectives :

The cost of operations inefficiencies should not be passed to the profit centers.

The cost of under-absorption of fixed costs should not reflect as inefficiencies of the operations centers.

Thus, if we do not have the correct machinery or our operators are not as skilled as they will be, or our volume is in the early stages of expansion, by charging the standard cost, we can assign the variances to the organizational entities that have justified incurring the unfavourable variance or the start-up cost. The establishment of cost standards—the determination of what operations "should" cost involves a large one-time effort and continuing updating of standards but it will meet the bank's needs far better than attempting to track actual costs by operation or customers. In the long run, it will also require less cost accounting work.

B. The Use of a "Bill of Materials" Concept and Assembling

The costs of operations into the transfer cost of a product. It is easier to measure costs of operations than costs of products and it is easier to catalog a relatively few operational standards than a relatively large number of product standards. However, it is easier to count product output. For example, in lock-box, we might have standard costs associated with each operation. The cost accounting system would then pick up the quantity of lock-box items processed for Customer "A" and multiply that by the assembled standard costs for each of the operations that need to be performed for Customer "A". This will simplify the cost assignment—by assuming that each deliverable product has a standard set of operations attached to it, the cost is then assigned on a basis of products rather than operations. This logic will prevail in instances where the operational count is not definite—for example, a normal reject rate in check processing, or a normal percentage of useless phone calls in balance reporting. The bill of materials concept facilitates having transfer costs that are in terms of products which the account officer understands and can discuss with his customers.

Some products incur costs they are different not for each customer, but different because of operational requirements of the items themselves, for example, customers' deposits of items with different end point costs. The standards for sets of end points, receiving methods, transmission methods (and for peaked operations time of day) will be applied to items "on-the-fly"—as they are processed. A similar procedure can be used to capture and record, for each customer, the standard operational float associated with the items processed for that customer.

C. Transfer Costs Should be Reasonably Close to Marginal Costs

The use of marginal costs for operational services jibes

with the use of marginal opportunity value for a funds transfer rate. We feel that the use of a "modified" marginal transfer rate is the best compromise for :

Pricing decisions

Measure of efficiency

Cross-footing profit center and cost center reporting

The concept of what is marginal has been modified for convenience and simplicity, particularly in : the definition of processing labour as variable, the relating of labour-supporting expenses to labour cost as variable, and the treatment of machinery expense.

The use of marginal costs suits the expressed requirements of senior operations officers, in terms of measuring processing efficiency. It is acknowledged that the "factory" must provide staff capacity to handle peak loads, particularly in instances where a queuing up of work to smooth out workload has a float cost that overwhelms any labour saving. However, it has been evident that the management of labour costs, and the reporting of the level of excellence of that management, would be better based on unit labour standards than on a comparison of actual costs with a forecasted budget. Senior operations management believes that measuring actual labour cost against "what it *should* cost to turn out the work" will effect consideration of efficiency improvement by changing shift schedules, bringing in more part-time help, and reducing work force if anticipated requirements do not materialize.

In the short run, a transfer price that was strictly incremental would make the profit center appear to be acting prudently when it sold services at any spread above out-of-pocket expenses. However, in the longer run, some capacity costs or committed costs will increase in order to accommodate any significant expansion in volume and thus should be accounted for in the transfer price.

With regard to machinery expense, we have found it

most practical to allocate small machines (typewriters, etc.) based on labour dollars within a cost center. For machinery as expensive as reader/sorters that have a fixed capacity, we have found it most practical to divide the cost by realistic operational capacity and assume that charge to be marginal. This has appeared to be the best compromise between two conflicting goals of the cost accounting system.

D. Manageable, Committed and Assigned Costs

In terms of measuring and managing operational efficiency, we think that the identification of costs as manageable, committed, and assigned is more meaningful than the distinction between direct and indirect.

Manageable costs are almost by definition marginal. Our definition of manageable costs are those costs which the center manager can affect either up or down during the year. Some of these manageable expenses are traditionally direct which he controls by approving purchase orders, authorizing salaries and turning in expense vouchers. Some he manages by creating more work for the Personnel Department and other support facilities.

Because these expenses are the ones which are manageable, it is these that we should focus on in reporting whether or not he is managing them well, and that distinction is more important than whether they are direct or indirect or fixed or variable There may be a one-to-one relationship between "manageable expenses" and "variable expenses" but that depends on our definitions of manageable rather than the definition of variable.

Committed expenses are those which are manageable by the cost center manager but on a longer term. We arbitrarily use a one-year term. If he must commit to a space allocation for a year, his occupancy cost is committed, for example. The cost center manager should be held accountable that his actual committed expenses are in line with what he budgeted.

Assigned expenses are those which, while logically

attributable to the functioning of his cost center, are those over which he has no control. For example, an allocation of the salary and travel expenses of his boss. Another example would be the occupancy cost of the operation function of a foreign office. There is no reason not to attach the assigned expenses to the cost center to which they are assigned but variances in them should not be reported as though they were under the control of the cost center manager.

VII. Customer Profitability Concepts

We have found certain cost accounting concepts appropriate to the measurement of customer profitability.

A. *Meaningful Transfer Units*

For the account officer's control, it is essential that the costs reported to him be in terms of elements he can discuss with the customer—number of deposits, timing of deposits, number of lock-box items, etc. rather than the operational tasks composing or supporting the countable units. Ideally the countable elements would have a predetermined standard cost.

B. *Controlled Profit Contribution*

We think that the account officer should be held responsible for the marginal profit contribution of the total customer relationship, independent of fixed costs and of assigned costs. We have frequently called this the controlled profit contribution as it represents the bottom line of the relationship in terms of that which the account officer can negotiate, maintain surveillance and control.

C. *It is Necessary to Establish Targets of Customer Profitability*

Establishment of the spreads required between revenues, balances, and standard costs so that the fixed or assigned costs will be covered and the goal of bank profitability will be achieved.

The assigned overhead will include institutional expenses that are independent of specific products, services or customers the maintenance of nostro accounts that are neither volume nor customer related and other such items. Credit for capital may be included in general bank overhead which will materially reduce the size of the target.

One way or another, we must make an assessment of whether, if all of the bank's resources were priced out in a fashion similar to the way in which this specific customer received them, would the bank make its targeted return ?

D. Significant Customers

Most banks institute profit center profitability reporting before they attempt customer profitability reporting. However, most application systems identify loans, deposits, interest income and interest expense by customer number so that the original entry for most of the data is at the customer level. We have found it practical to report, on a routine basis, the profitability of only those customers who are so significant that they are important enough to track (and possibly to plan for) on an individual basis. Others can be grouped by officer, SIC code, etc. We see no value in devising a system to routinely report the profitability of individual household customers. In the retail area, we would rather report them by the function they use, such as savings accounts, regular checking accounts, etc., or by branch.

E. Credit Versus Service Cost

It is essential to separate the costs of producing non-asset using services from the profitability of the credit relationship.

F. Service Cost by Customer

We must be able to develop, for each significant customer,

or group of customers, the cost of providing each non-asset using service.

G. General Support Costs Separation

It is essential to separate general support expenses from the cost of specific products.

H. Customer Expenses

We must provide the ability to log and record expenses directly incurred on behalf of a certain customer, either for maintenance of the customer relationship or on a specific product.

I. Accounting far Service-Generated Balances

We must provide the mechanics to treat balances required to pay for non-asset using services as a reduction in funds supplied, or an increase in net funds required for credit relationships.

VIII. Product, Officer, and Market Reports

By accumulating data at the customer or customer group level, and by accumulating data on the cost and profitability of each product used by the customer, we can then summarize in one direction so as to report on the total cost and profit attributable to each product bankwide. In the other direction, if we code each customer to an officer, we can summarize to provide officer and departmental profitability. By properly coding customers, we can then do special (non-routine) analyses as to costs and profitability by SIC code, size, geography, whether or not we are their lead bank, whether or not they use lock-box or international services, or other such analyses.

Dr. K. A. Lifson, Chairman of Lifson, Herrmann, Blackmarr & Harris, Management Consultants, Dallas, Texas.

Dr. Lifson is the founding member of this practice, established in 1954. With degrees in Engineering, Business Administration, and Industrial Psychology, his areas of specialization are Organizational Analysis, Mathematical Modeling of Businesses and Management Information Systems. He has been the principal consultant of Management Information Systems and Cost Accounting studies for First National Bank of St. Louis, Banco Nacional de Mexico, Birmingham Trust Co., First National Bank of Denver, Bank of Cyprus, Republic National Bank of Dallas, Marine Bank of Tampa, The Bank of Indiana, and many non-banking organizations. He is Chairman of the Board of Directors of the Federal Home Loan Bank of Little Rock. His professional associations include Tau Beta Pi and the World Business Council.

10

Performance—Evaluation of Purchasing Functions in an Engineering Organisation

*Parth Sarathi**

Introduction

Purchasing can be critical to profitability. Business operations can be thought of beginning with the procurement of materials, supplies and services needed to produce a product to sell. The influence of purchasing depends on the percentage of value added to the product. In big Industries 60-70% of the product cost is the material cost, so reducing even a small percentage of this cost will add substantially to the profits. An efficiently organised purchase department staffed by a band of competent professionals helps a lot in fulfilling the company objectives—has been agreed upon the conceived by all major companies. Performance evaluation of the purchasing function is for the purpose of gauging the effectiveness of different functions and discovering the opportunities for improving them in the interest of efficiency, economy and better control.

* Sr. Engineer (Systems), BHEL, New Delhi.

Purpose

The purpose of appraisal of the functions of a department or organisation is primarily to determine whether the department or organisation is working towards the objectives as laid down in the plans. Thus the purpose of evaluating the purchasing function is to find out whether the purchasing objectives are met maintaining its overall relationships with and obligations to other departments/agencies.

Some reasons for evaluating performance are :

(1) It is human nature to work better if work is to be evaluated.

(2) For future planning and control reliable and systematic data must be available.

(3) In the absence of an appraisal system, the management may not be aware of many real problems faced by the purchase department, and the results will mark only dissatisfaction.

(4) Cost control and cost reduction is achieved by appraisal system,

(5) An appraisal system helps to find out whether the production holds up reported due to lack of material are real or false.

(6) Reasons for vendor dissatisfaction are highlighted and removed.

(7) Defects in systems relating to puchasiag and allied functions are highlighted—some other reasons are—

(8) To know to overall purchase climate.

(9) To find out the man power requirements.

(10) To feel the need and effect of introducing modern techniques like requirement Planning Standardisation, values Engg., Codification etc.

Problems in Evaluation

Organisational Setup

All organisations are unique in their organisational setup, tasks to fulfill and manpower. The responsibility and function is not identical in all organisations. Thus a standard Evaluation programme cannot be applied everywhere.

Not So Clear Objectives

In many organisations the objectives of purchase department are not defined clearly. Without having the clear predetermined objectives for the year, how the performance during the year can be evaluated ?

Absence of Procedure-manual/Systems

In many organisations, there is no well laid out procedure manual/system. As a result the records and data available are not uniform and consistent. This makes the evaluation difficult.

Absence of Integrated Management Systems

The functioning of Production shops, Sales deptt., Maintenance deptt., Production planning & control etc. is greatly effected by the purchasing functions. In the absence of an Integrated Management systems it becomes difficult to correlate the information available to evaluate the effectiveness of various measures and also the consequences.

In the light of the above it is clear that any one method of evaluation shall not be perfect and suitable for all organisations.

Prerequisites

For a successful evaluation, some of the important prerequisites are given below :

1. A thorough 'Q & M' study should be conducted in various areas of material management and a rational system of Indenting, procurement, storage and accounting of materials be designed and installed.

2. A purchase manual be completed and distributed to all concerned persons.

3. Modern Inventory Control techniques be introduced with codification etc.

4. Various reports to reveal the working of various sections and departments be generated and cricu-lated.

5. Professional persons with good understanding of materials management should man the purchase departments.

6. The objectives for various functions for the year be fixed every year in the light of the production programme, budgets etc.

Purchase-Elements

A glance at the purchase elements given below will help in framing the scheme of evaluation. These parameters are not independent and isolated, but many a times are related or dependent on one or other.

1. Right attitude—Training

   SWOT (Strength weakness, opportunity and threats) Analysis. Material intelligence.

2. Right Material—Value engineering, Standardisation.

3. Right quality—Specifications, Inspection and S.Q.C.

4. Economic order Qty.—Inventory models.

5. Right price—Negotiation, Vendor development, Price comparisons.

6. Right Time—Reordening levels, Lead-time analysis, Followup.

7. Right transportation—Cost analysis of transportation logistics, Modes.

8. Right Source—Vendor analysis.

9. Right place of delivery—Communication price.

10. Right contracts—Legal aspect.

What to Evaluate

Before starting the evaluation the elements to be evaluated are to be identified. These elements should be the triggering elements for their identification the system and documentation should be thoroughly examined. These may be termed as check elements. The check elements may be identified from the following broad functions :

1. Information—various records, files, reports etc.

2. Procurement—requisitions, quotations, vendor selecting, mode of purchase, collecting information from vendor, negotiation purchase schedules and deliveries invoices followup etc.

3. Research/Innovation—Studies for substitution of material cost analysis.
   Vendor investigation product development.

4. Disposal—Surplus identification, disposal, salvage.

5. Source development—Exploring new supplies.

6. Import substitution—Exploring indigenous supplies, Comparison.

7. Inventory Control—Ordering cost, Carrying cost, Inventory holding.

Who Makes Appraisal

The appraisal can be made by either by internal review and appraisal personnel or by an outsider (consultant).

Evaluation by Internal Agencies

This is a continuous process of evaluation in which the experating results are compared with the predetermined Objectives for the purchase activities, plans, budgets, previous performances etc. Access to various documents and authorities is easy. The organisation and functions are well known to the evaluator, thus, a very realistic evaluation can be done in some of difficult areas like :

(i) Adherence to policies and procedures.

(ii) Purchase departments relationship with other departments.

(iii) Work load allocations.

(iv) Vendors attitude towards the company.

For the work of appraisal the company may use a suitable executive who will perform this function on part time basis along with his normal duties or full time basis. A committee may also be constituted for this purpose comprising of the persons from departments like Engg., Production Planning & control, Industrial Engg., systems, finance etc.

Evaluation by External Consultants

Consultants may also be engaged for this purpose. The appraisal by the consultants is supposed to be unbiased. But he should have a thorough knowledge of the organisation and working of the organisation. He may have to face non-co-operation and resistance while collecting data. So he will have to proceed systematically and spend much time before starting the actual work.

Preparations

1. Study the organisation, the products, processes etc.
2. Study the purchasing functions and relationship with other functions.
3. Collect and Study the procedure and policies manual systems reports etc.
4. Make an action plan for the investigation.

Evaluation

The evalution has two aspects.

1. Qualitative.
2. Quantitative.

Qualitative

Qualitative appraisal will give an overview of the status of the functioning of purchase department in the company. This will show the strong and weak areas. It will also show whether a rational infrastructure for efficient functioning exists or not. For this check lists are prepared covering the activities of all the areas. Small objective type questions are prepared such that answers are short (YES/NO) etc. This will help the evaluator know :

(i) Whether a rational system exists to cover various activities.

(ii) Whether the people adhere to the system.

(iii) Salient features of the system and purchasing functions.

The check list is circulated to different agencies for answering the questions from their areas and the answers are studied and a summary is prepared. The status of the broad activities will be highlighted by this.

Conclusion

The scope of the purchasing function these days is not limited to the procurement only. It is very closely related to all the functions of the organisation. Thus a very close watch over the functioning of purchase department with a view to highlight the areas of improvement is a must for a progressive organisation. The plan and strategies of 'evaluation of the performance may not be the same in all the industries.

In this paper, an effort has been made to help the organisations start performance evaluation and certain key areas have been highlighted.

11

Group Technology : Some Managerial Implications

Mr. Dhiraj Sharma, Prof. R. P. Mohanty***

Abstract

This paper explains the managerial implications for applying GroupTechnology (GT). GT has evolved over the years as a powerful manufacturing strategy particularly for batch production and job order production systems. This technology, if properly understood, planned and implemented within the existing framework of manufacturing systems, can bring enormous benefits economically, technologically and socially. The objective of this study is to clarify the following pertinent issues :

---

* Dhiraj Sharma is presently a post-graduate student in the Division of Industrial Engineering and Management, Asian Institute of Technology, Bangkok 10501, Thailand. He is on study leave from Ms. Larsen & Toubro Ltd., Bombay.

** Visiting Professor, Division of Industrial Engineering and Management, Asian Institute of Technology Bangkok 10501, Thailand.

1. What are the principal advantages of Group Technology as a manufacturing strategy ?

2. What are the methodological mechanics involved for applying GT ?

3. What constitutes the conditions for successful applications of GT ?

The study goes on to present a comparison of GT with a contemporary manufacturing system. Apart from these issues some implications have also been put forth as to how GT can facilitate Industrial development in developing countries.

Introduction

Several definitions exist in literature for Group Technology. Most simply stated, GT is a philosophy holding that managers should exploit similarities and achieve efficiencies by grouping like problems (Hyer and Wemmerlov, 1984). This definition is appropriate for a production system. This explains the internal arrangement with reference to the inputs, outputs and the various control functions.

There are variety of production system used in practice which can be classified as :

1. Continuous production system,

2. Mass production system,

3. Batch production system,

4. Project production system.

For mass production, high productivity levels can be achieved through specialised machinery, designed on a product specific basis. In the case of jobbing or small batch production due to the wide variety of products manufactured, standardisation in equipment and methods is difficult to achieve and flexibilities are required to respond to changes that generate from product design specification. Group Technology (GT) can be understood as a manufacturing arrangement for products within a set of production facilities to aid in the process of variety reductions of product components through standardisation of manufacturing methods; to permit the use of more efficient production methods by eliminating unnecessary repetitions of operations and above all providing information to guide the decision makers to achieve cost reductions and other allied benefits like job enrichment, reduction work-in-process inventories etc. Thus, the objective of GT is to enhance the productivity of a manufacturing organisation engaged in the production of a variety of products as per the customers' requirements. However, the application of GT requires some premises such as :

—Similarity of dimension

—Similarity of shape

Technological Similarity

This paper does not deal with the operational issues as faced in the shop-floor situations but tries to address the managerial issues involved in successful planning and implementation of GT. It has been observed that many managers do require an understanding of the potentials and limitations of GT (Edwards, 1971). Sometimes, without clarifications GT has been applied, but, ultimately, the diffusion of GT in the reorganisational milieu has created problems of acceptability. The whole purpose of this paper is oriented to explain the implications of GT within the overall perspective of a manufacturing system.

Principal Advantages of GT Application Economic Benefits

The economic advantages accruing from the implementation of Group Technology as sumarised by Knight (1973) are :

—Reduced throughput and resetting times

—More ordered workflow

—Lower levels of work-in-process

—Higher machine utilization

—Increased ability to meet deliveries

The implications of applying GT vis-a-vis conventional system costs is now explained in terms of Capital costs. Pre-production costs and Annual running costs.

Capital Costs

An index for the number of machines required under the conventional system and the GT system can be obtained by productivity factor given by Knight (1974) as :

$$\text{Productivity factor} = (S_1 + M_1) / (S_2 + M_2) \quad \ldots(1)$$

—where S_1 = set up time under conventional production system.

S_2 = set up time under GT production system.

M_1 = machining time under conventional production system.

M_2 = machining time under GT production system.

Knight reports the achievements of productivity factors of upto 2 due to the reduced set up times of the GT system. Hence for some output about half the number of machines would be required by a GT approach than with the conventional method.

On the other hand, when machines are arranged in a

cellular formation a lower utilisation results. But this is generally true for machines performing secondary operations, whose capital costs are not so high. But with the GT system a higher degree of labour utilisation is possible, partially compensating for lower machine utilisation.

However, perhaps the major savings in capital costs arise from the finer degree of machine specification possible with the GT method. This arises from the assignment of specific parts to machine cells. Whilst in the conventional system greater latitude is kept in equipment specification to permit manufacture of wide variety of parts, resulting in the purchase of larger and more costly equipment. Thus considerable capital cost savings results from using the GT system.

Pre-productian Costs

This cost category covers Planning, Data preparation, Jig and Tool Design and Production. The reduction in pre-production costs occurs as a result of the similarities of parts in a Group. Thus for items within a group similar process planning needs to be carried out with only slight modification for individual members, resulting in considerable saving in time and labour. Similarity of parts also permits the development of common jigs and fixtures and toolings for the group. The benefits are two-fold. Firstly the resetting times are reduced. Secondly lesser number of jigs and fixtures are needed with appropriate inserts for individual parts. Knight (1974) quotes 50% saving in jig and tooling costs by using GT over the conventional methods.

Annual Running Costs

The impact of GT on Annual Running costs is explained in detail in Table 1.

Table 1

Effect of Group Technology on Annual Running Costs

Cost	*Increase or Decrease*	*Explanation*
1	*2*	*3*
Direct Labour	Decrease	1. Higher labour utilisation. 2. Less skilled labour may be used if jigs & fixtures are properly designed.
Indirect	Decrease	1. Group tools & fixtures reduce the number of setter required. 2. Less expenditure required due to faster processing times. 3. GT layout provides for reduced transportations.
Maintenance	Increase*	Reduced setup time leads to machines cutting material for most of the time. Machining similar parts leads to high wear and tear in narrow zones due to limited side movements.

(*Contd.*)

1	2	3
Consumables	Increase*	Machines spends more time winning material.
Tools & Fixture Maintenance Storage & Interest	Decrease	Less number of tools needed in a GT system due to use of group tools.
Fixture & Material Preparation	Decrease	Less number of tools needed due to use of group fixtures.
Tool Preparation & Setting	Increase*	More Intensive machine operation gives rise to higher tool wear.
Space Occupied	Increase/ Decrease	1. Decrease : Due to less number of machines required with GT. 2. Increase : Within each cell extra material handling eqipment is required for transportation within the cell.
Inspection Cost	Decrease	By using a Travelling inspector & group inspection equipment.
Insurance	Decrease	Due to reduced capital costs.
Scrap and Re-working costs	Decrease	Precise are still to be determined.
In-process Inventory	Decrease	1. Reduced through-put times. 2. Ability to produce parts quickly lead to reduced batch sizes.

*The cost per production unit produced remain unaltered.

Thus we see that substantial savings in manufacturing costs are possible by GT. These should be compared vis-a-vis the costs of installing such a system, such as parts coding. family development, planning, altering layout etc. before actually going in for Group technology.

Technological Benefits of Group Technology

The Group Technology philosophy has far reaching consequences than those that might appear at first sight. The benefits of a GT program ripple down to practically all departments of an organisation. In this section some of the benefits that are accruing by a GT program, but which are not readily apparent are discussed.

Production Planning and Control

The integration of GT and a PPC technique as MRP is one of the areas of recent research interest. The "marriage" of the two methodologies produces a synergetic effect. The scheduling process occurs in two stages.

Stage I:

The master production schedule would indicate the demand for an item. The MRP would indicate the date of realease of part for production.

Stage II:

The GT system would now evaluate on criteria whether to release an order for an economic number of parts in the group for some periods ahead or to release an order of the lot size of the item required.

The trade off of increased production efficiency against increased inventory costs must be considered for GT and MRP to work in harmony.

Process Planning

Hyer and Wemmerlov (1984) report that substantial productivity improvements have been reported in process planning through a GT system implementation. GT is used here in conjunction with computer aided process planning (CAPP) to build process plans CAPP and GT enable the standardisation of process plans, reduce the number of new ones and store, retrieve, edit and print them out very efficiently.

There are two methods available for using of CAPP, namely the variant based planning approach and the generative planning approach. KT & CAPP are combined in the former approach. In this method a master plan is made for each part family and stored. Thus when the user feeds in the GT part code the computer furnishes the best process plan. In the event that no plan exist, the computer then fetches the process plans for similar components.

GT can also aid in the preparation of codes for operation of numerically controlled machines. Hyer Wemmerlov (1984) report the case of an engineering firm where a GT program reduced the time to produce an NC tape form 8 hours to 30 minutes.

Parts Design

The GT code serves two important functions in part design. First it allows for quick storage and retrieval of part design and secondly it permits part design standardisation. Both factors lead to shortening of the design process and limit the design proliferation.

The benefits of standardisation need to be emphasised here as they not only involve the designer but also the material manager as well. Standardisation of parts, it has been claimed (Tersine, 1982), leads to substantial reduction in raw materials inventories. This is no small achievement considering that in some cases material from more than 60% of the total cost.

One of the reasons that lead to wide variety of parts instead of standardisation in the inability of designer to locate a similar part designed earlier. This time consuming process is carried out with the touch of finger by employing the GT part code. Once the part code is enteled the computer lists on CRT similar components already designed. The designer can suitable "edit" the drawing to design the new part. In terms of money, Hyer and Wemmerlov (1984) repart savings of upto U.S. $10,000 for a single component.

Other Spheres of GT

GT can be used by both the procurement wings as well as the sales wing of the same organisation. In purchase, the variety of purchase can be reduced by determining products that serve the same function, thereby increasing the purchase of few products. This would enable the firm to secure quantity discounts from the suppliers. Sales dept. can use the GT coded part to locate substitutes, in case they are unable to meet the demand for a certain product. Companies that bid for orders can use GT for cost estimation purposes. The GT codes of components that make up the product are fed into the computer which furnishes the costs of the items. GT can also be employed to determine the effects of changes in raw material costs. Thus if cost of a material changes, GT code can be used to list all components using that material and thereby assess the implication of the cost alteration on the total manufacturing cost.

Social Benefits

The gains in productivity achieved by implementing group technology arise not only by the factors discussed earlier but also by its social implications (Fazakerly, 1974).

Benefit 1 : Removal of delay=Removal of frustration

In traditional batch manufacturing there are considerable

delays involved in production times through the intervening set-up periods. The delay leads to considerable worker frustration. Fazakerly (1974) puts the gains by removal of such delays by using GT as quite substantial as it prevents the breaking up of momentum of work and thereby dissolving the frusration of the worker.

Benefit 2 : Job Satisfaction

Job satisfaction results from the following :

1. The cell formation in GT gives rise to complete parts being formed within the bounds of each cell, resulting in the establishment of responsibility by workers for their work and a sense of pride and accomplishment. Responsibility can be tapped by encouraging workers to solve day-to-day technical problems on their own, leaving the foreman with more time to devote to managerial activities instead of trouble shooting.

2. GT permits flexible manning i.e. the shifting or assignments of operators to differing types of works from [day-to-day, thus breaking the monotony in his routine and increasing his job satisfaction.

3. Workers are generally given the liberty to arrange the layout of their own machine cells and the methods to complete the job. This involvement in decision making further enhances job satisfaction of the workers.

Benefit 3 : Improved payment schemes for worker motivation

GT offers the scope of payment schemes based on group bonus which motivate worker instead of merely satisfying them. It is found Fazakerly, (1974) that GT based payment schemes are fairer and more effective than conventional schemes. However when implementing group bonus systems the management should take care that it protects the interests of other wings of the organisation by providing suitable schemes for them also. Failure to do so may lead to inter-organisational conflict.

Methodological Mechanics of GT Application

GT requires two distinct but mandatory activities, namely parts coding and cell formation or grouping of parts and machines. Several methods exist for performing both the tasks. A comparative study on contemporary coding scheme serves no purpose as parts codification is a situation and requirement dependent feature. However, a flexible coding scheme does create synergistic effect throughout the organisation. This aspect is also examined. The other equally important activity, which follows part condification, is group formation. A multiple of techniques have been developed for cell formation, ranging from manual methods to sophisticated computer routines. The paper critically evaluates the contemporary techniques in use and comments on the strengths and weakness of each method.

Parts Identification

Parts identification procedures have been in existence since the early days of organised manufacture. However, in the earlier days there was more reliance on using the part name directly. But the complexity of final products have led to the requirement of more and more unique parts which in turn has resulted in the adoption of number codes. With the advent of the numerical part codes, the next logical step was the computerisation of the parts data base. The computer assists in two ways :

(i) Application of the code to the data base of parts.

(ii) In the sorting of parts into groups based on commonality.

Dunlap and Hirlinger (1983) have suggested two factors on which decisions have to be made prior to developing and implementing a coding system :

1. *Planning* : Before commencing codification, management must decide on the objectives that the codification is likely to achieve e.g. will it be used by design department for parts design, by manufacturing for cell formation, by purchase for parts procurement, by stores dept. for inventory control purposes etc. The plan for codification will therefore include what the codification should accomplish and how to go about accomplishing the objectives set.

2. *Flexibility* : Relates to a multiple objective situation where in the code system has to satisfy the part infromation requirements of several departments. Each department has specific parts data needs which has to be incorporated into the code. Such systems have to be very flexible and compromises have to be made.

Coding Schemes based on System of Information Interpretations

Graphics classification system : This system is based on the physical characteristics and geometrical shape of the part. The inherent assumption is that such attributes would indicate the manufacturing process needed for producing the part. These systems are typically easy to implement in the design department but information indicated by their resulting numbers is not derived from the actual manufacturing needs.

Manufacturing oriented classification system : Such systems are based upon the exact manufacturing needs and are more informative but, because of the extra information generated are more costly to implement.

Coding Schemes based on Method of Partitioning the Code

The hierarchical format : This format applies the code in groups of two digits. As the name implies it is hierarchical in nature, so that "code pairs" in a long list, or string of code, have meanings that are determined by what code pairs preceded them.

The non-hierarchical format : This does not depend on a hierarchy in the code. Thus a part code will always have the same information stored in its location, regardless of the preceding codes' value. Digits of code in this format are usually added one at a time, but also can be paired as with the hierarchical code.

Specific Systems

There are a combination of the two major systems described above. They permit interactive coding of a part at the computer terminal and are intended for use with CAD/CAM systems. The systems are user specific and therefore a detailed discussion is omitted. The interested reader can refer to Opitz and Wiendahl (1971) for a parts coding exercise.

Classification by Filters

To sort out the coded parts on some selected characteristics and thereby enable the formation of groups requires the aid of "filters". Filters define a classification and represent groups of features upon which part families are based. The problems which crop up with the use of filter are two fold. Firstly, two sets of family filters may overlap to some degree. This may result in a part matching the requirements of two or more separate filters each of which defines a separate part family groups. Secondly due to the large variety of parts hundreds of unique individual filters will be required for a workable family size. This is a very time consuming process.

Layered Filters

This is an alternative to the individual filter approach described earlier where a single part family was created at a time. Layered filters are created by first taking the parameter types that are covered in the code and listing them according to their level of importance, or influence, in the area for which the filters are to be created. Second, groupings are created using only top parameter. Each parameter may be subdivided to include any and all codes that could be applied at that level. Next grouping is based on the second parameter of importance. It is essential that all possible codes be covered at each parameter level. When all parameter levels have been addressed, part sorting is initiated.

The advantage with layering is that different families can be obtained at different levels by changing the order of layers although ultimate families remain unchanged. Thus parts can be split into finer groups without creating a new set of individual filters of each family. In addition this approach assures a unique position for each part.

Synergetic Effect of Part Coding

A firm can be spilt up into three major sections, namely, Business, Manufacturing and Engineering. Whenever an order is received from the customer then the three units intercast with each other and the business sector with the customer on the basis of part number.

Thus with a marginal increase in effort and planning it is possible to create an evolutionary path to much broader productivity improvement opportunities throughout the enterprise.

Cell Formation Methodologies

The next stage in the development of GT, after part codification, was the formation of machine component cells. Research in this area began in the early 70's and is still in progress. In this paper we briefly examine the techniques developed to date. Table 2 outlines the various methodologies available and presents their respective strengths and weaknesses. The table will serve to illustrate how the techniques have evolved over the years from simple manual methods to complex paradigms involving sophisticated computer codes.

Conditions for Successful Applications of GT

Group Technology, like every other technique, has certain applicability zones, that is to say that a conversion from the conventional system to the GT system is not a valid proposition under all circumstances. When to apply GT ? That is the question which is answered in the part of the paper. The sole criterion generally evaluated by management before plunging into GT is typically an economic one. The economic analysis to be performed when making the "go-no go" decision is explained in detail. However, feedbacks from the field suggest that another important parameter dipping the balance in favour of or against GT is an information system within the production department. The paper therefore, also outlines the information requirements of a GT system at its various stages.

Economic Analysis of Group Technology

Knight (1974) has aptly described the problem of Group Technology facing the Engineering Economist as "Application or GT methods in a batch production concern can result in substantial savings in manufacturing costs, with 30-40% reduction being possible. This saving must of course be weighed against the investment in installing the new manufacturing system." However, very little work has been carried out in the area of Engineering Economics of Group Technology to determine the precise cost benefits accruing from GT implementation. The analysis procedures herein, stem from the work of two teams : Singh and Kumar (1978) and Boucher and Muckstadt (1985). The latter pair concentrate on a broader framework of manufacturing costs whilst the former have carried out a more elaborate analysis but restricted it to machining costs only.

Manufacturing cost reduction arise from the following factors :

1. Reduction in Setup Times

Cost reduction are achieved from reduced setup times in two ways namely increased labour and capital productivity and reduced inventory carrying costs.

2. Reduction in Production Lead Times

This affects the manufacturing cost by reducing work-in-process inventory, finished component safety stocks, the number of hot jobs and the difficulty of controlling the production process.

3. Reduction in the Number of Tools

In a GT system as parts are manufactured in groups having similar characteristics, generally a set of group tools with adaptors are employed instead of separate tools for each component. Accordingly the machining costs are reduced.

4. Reduction in System Support Functions

This arises due to the elimination of many of the functions relating to monitoring of components. Such reduction in support functions result in reduced overhead costs.

The impact of the above parameters on Inventory cycle stock, safety stock, work-in-process inventory, allocated costs and machining costs has been investigated by the above mentioned teams. Table 3 presents their results.

Management Information Systems for GT

Edwards (1971) highlights the importance of a MIS for GT implementation when he states that "success or failure of any GT plan and subsequent implementation depends upon whether or not certain information is available at various stages in the process". The stages in the GT system implementation alongwith the information requirements of each stage are discussed in Table 3.

Table

Cell Formation

Methodology/Authors	*Description*
Composite Component Approach Edwards (1971)	A composite component which includes all or most of the shape & design features of a family of similar parts is developed. Machine cells are formed to cater to the machining requirements of such composite components.
Production flow analysis Burbridge (1971)	The method involves breaking up the problem into smaller manageable sub-systems. Stage 1, termed Factory flow analysis seeks to arrive at simple inter departmental material flows. In the second stage, Group analysis, a route card analysis of components is carried out to form groups. Finally in Line Analysis, the best material flows within the groups formed is determined
Component flow analysis El-Essawy (1972)	A three stage analysis similar to PFA is involved. The objective of the first stage is to sort the components in order of machine require-

2

Methodologies

Strengths	*Weaknesses*
1. The composite component once formed aids in the development of tooling layouts on machines.	1. Composite components are rarely found in practice. 2. Family formation leads to low utilisation of certain machines. 3. It is more difficult to form families during the latter stage of the analysis.
1. System approach to cell design. 2. Problem is partitioned into smaller segments to provide ease in handling.	1. Approach involves subjective judgements requiring substantial local knowledge (situation specified). 2. Method is cumbersome for large no. of components and/or machines. 3. Back tracking of components is not considered.
1. Flexible methodology which can also be applied to facility layout and work flow problems.	1. The method of determining combination of different machine types to process different components is cumbersome for large num-

(*Contd.*)

1	2
	ments. In the second stage group formation is performed using the list of the previous stage and the local constraints imposed. Third stage is detailed analysis of intercell flow to ensure acceptable design.
Single cluster analysis McAuley (1972)	The similarity coefficient defines as the ratio of the number of components which visit both machines to the number of components that visit atleast one of the machines, are determined. Machines with highest S.C. are clustered. Entry level into groups is lowered in steps of equal magnitude. Single linkage cluster analysis is used to transfer machines from one group to another.
Bond Energy Method McCormick (1972)	This is basically a matrix clustering technique. A machine-component matrix is formed, where the entries, called bonds, represent the degree of association of machines and components. Maximisation of the sum of products of adjacent elements by row & column operations is sought. McCormick has developed a sub-

3	4
	ber of machines and components.
	2. Cell formation is not transparent and requires subjective judgment.
1. Permits manual calculations for	1. Method aims to form machine disjoint cells, which is not true in practice.
2. First method to use clustering technique for cell formation.	2. Does not consider processing times, quantities of components and their loading sequence on each machine.
	3. The threshold values for the similarity coefficient used, requires considerable arbitration.
	4. Method does not consider the machine idle time and back tracking of components.
1. Simple logic is employed with consistently good results.	1. Algorittm is inferior in computational efficiency to ROC algorithm. Large problems therefore require excessive computer time.
2. Simple computations which may be done manually for certain cases.	2. Does not account for the no. of components to be produced. This leads to cell formations having low machine utilisation.

(*Contd.*)

1	2
	optimising heuristic to cut-down on the computation time for this quadratic assignment problem.
Numerical Tavonomy Carrie (1973)	A machine-component matrix is developed in the first stage. In the next stage this matrix is used for determining similarity coefficients between component pairs, defined as the ratio of set of all common machines needed for processing of the two components to the number of machines required for processing one or either of the components. Finally in the third stage, cluster analysis is performed wherein grouping is not permitted for a specified minimum value of S.C.
Graph theoretic Approach Rajagopalan and Batra (1975)	A three stage procedure is used. In stage 1 a graph with vertices representing the machines & the edges the inter-relationship between them is determined. Machines having strong relationship are recognised with the aid of graph theory and are grouped together by graph partitioning methods. Finally the compo-

3	4
	3. No upper limit on cell size with the result that large cells are apt to be formed.
	4. Effect of machine idle time and component back tracking are not considered.
1. Method lists separate components which not grouped and need separate examination	1. The min. cluster size to specified is arbitrarily fixed.
2. The method checks that groupings produced do not violate machine availability restrictions.	2. Level of similarity between component at which they may not be grouped together is arbitrary.
1. Cells formed are not machine disjoint cells.	1. Similarity coefficient used does not perform satisfactorily under all conditions.
2. Incorporates machine and the quantity of each component manufactured.	2. Threshold value of similarity coefficients are determined arbitrarily.

(*Contd-*)

1	*2*
	nents are assigned to cells by utilising certain heuristics.
Rank order clustering algorithm King (1980)	The method seeks to serve as a generalised procedure to reduce the machine-component matrix through row & column operations, in a finite number of steps, into a diagonal block form if one exists. The block structure obtained makes the cells transparent & visible.

3	4
	3. Machine graph is highly dense resulting in large no. of cliques of which many are not vertex disjoint.
1. Simple to understand, effective and efficient.	1. The end output is a function of the initial matrix, but no criterion exists for placing of rows and column in the initial matrix.
2. Simultaneous machine grouping and component allocation.	2. The machine component matrix does not use the concept of similarity of components
3. More computationally efficient than Bond energy algorithm.	3. Does accout for the no. of components to be manufactured.
4. No setting of a arbitrary values required.	4. Storage of 0-1 matrix limits the size of problems that can be handled.
5. Can handle exceptional elements also.	5. No means to provide constraints on cell size. Thus either very large or very small cells are possible.
	6. Effect of back tracking of components and idle time of machines are not considered.
	7. Output quality varies inversely with the size of the machine component matrix.

(*Contd.*)

1	2
ROC-II King and Nakornchai (1980)	Some modifications have been made over the previous version to make it computationally efficient.
Dewitte's Approach (1980)	This is another similarity coefficient based approach. It differs from those discussed above in two aspects. Firstly the machines have been classified into three categories according to number of machines available of a particular type. Secondly 3 similarity coefficient are defined which take into account operational similarity, number of machine type & total quantity of each component to be manufactured.
Direct clustering algorithm Chan and Milner (1982)	This is a heuristic procedure to obtain diagonalisation of machine-component matrix. The values are entered as x and are regarded as positive, blanks are treated as negative. The method sequentially shifts the rows with left-most positive to the top & the columns with top-most positive value to the left to

3	4
1. Quicker sorting than earlier version of the- algorithm.	Weaknesses no. 1, 2, 3, 5 and six of the parent algorithm still remain.
2. Reduced complexity compared to the earlier version.	
1. Unlike single cluster analysis it also considers : no. of machine types; total quantity of materials produced; and permits different cells.	1. Selection of the threshold values of similarity coefficients are arbitrary.
2. Possible to analyse a great no. of routings.	2. Requires classification of machines into three eategories which is difficult in practice.
	3. Unable to handle situations where not all available machines are required or where additional machine procurement may be economically justified.
1. Computationally superior to ROC	Same limitations as the ROC algorithm.

(*Contd.*)

1	2
	achieve diagonal block formation.
MACE Waghadekar and Sahu (1984)	This another heuristic approach based on 3 similarity coefficients : adaptive type, product type and that based on total flow of common components. In the first machine groups are formed by utilising S.C.s. The next step involves grouping of cells on the basis of intercell flow S.C. Finally in the third step component replacement is carried out.
Ideal seed, non-hierarchical clustering algorithm Chandrasekharan and Rajagopalan (1986)	A bi-partite graph with one set of vertices denoting the components & the other set the machines with the edges representing the relationship between them is developed. The solution procedure involves clustering where a theoretical upper limit is placed on the number of groups. A concept of grouping efficiency is introduced to evaluate results. Based on the previous operations initial column clusters are generated. These are then used to obtain the final clusters.

3	4
1. Results contain min. no. of exceptional elements. 2. Cells with large intercell flows placed adjacent to each other, making mergers easier. 3. Computational storage limitation of ROC algorithm is avoided. 4. Three outputs based on the three definitions of similarity coefficients are available to check the consistency of the results.	
1. Ideal seeds remove the arbitrariness long associated with graph theoretic approaches. 2. Coucept of group efficiency permits the evaluation of solutions w.r.t. within cell utilisation and intercell movements.	1. Machine graph is highly dense resulting in high number of cliques of which many are not vertex disjoint

Table 3

Formulae for Economic Analysis of GT vis-a-vis Conventional Systems

Effect on	*System*	*Formula*
Cycle	Conventional	$Q_f = ((2\ S_f\ R_f\ D)\ /\ (i\ (M + m\ R_f)))^{1/2}$
Stock	GT	$Q_s = ((2\ S_s\ R_s\ D)\ /\ (i\ (M + m\ R_s)))_{1/2}$
	Benefit under GT	$f_{cc} = 1 - (Q^s\ /\ Q_f) = 1 - (S_s\ /\ S_f)^{1/2}$
Safety	Conventional	$r_f = L_f D + Z_p (L_f V_d)^{1/2}$
Stock	GT	$r_g = L_g D + Z_p\ (L_g V_d)^{1/2}$
	Benefit under GT	$f_{ss} = 1 - (L_g\ /\ L_f)^{1/2}$

WIP	Conventional	$W_{Af} = ((M + C_f) / 2) L_f D$
Inventory	GT	$W_{Ag} = ((M + C_s) / 2) L_f D$
Machining	Conventional	$C_f = C_1 U_{mf(i)} N(i) + n (C_1 T_{sf} + D_f)$
Costs	GT	$C_s = C_1 (U_{mg}(^s) N(_i) T_{ss} + (n-1) T_{sa}) + D_s$

The nations used are explained in the Appendix.

It is thus clear that at every stage the management has specific information requirements which have to be met to prevent the GT system turning into a "guessing game". Thus before proceeding with a GT policy, management must ensure that it has the necessary information system functioning to see the implementation through and provide smooth day-to-day operation.

Comparison between GT and FMS

GT also known as Cellular Manufacturing System (CMS) has grown to such an extent to warrant a comparison with the Flexible manufacturing system. This paper would therefore not be complete without a comparison of the two systems. Table 4 furnishes the characteristics of both systems.

FromTable'5 comparison it can be observed that the FMS is just the "latest model" of the same product. However, its high investment and negligible labour requirements make it an ideal towards which all CMS should tend towards. But till such time that conditions are favourable for a transition GT will continue to play a dominant role in industry.

Implications for Developing Countries

Several manufacturing systems are being transferred by the developed countries to the less developed countries and developing ones. But such systems invariably require large capital investment together with minimal and highly skilled labour requirements. Admitted that the fully automated factory is a goal to be sought by mankind for the future in order to save the humanbeigns from the discomforts of the shopfloor environment, however, the current needs of the developing countries, on the contrary, are the exact opposite with their low capital availabilities and abundance of man-power. Moreover, considerable capital evaporation would ensue as the conventional machines would become obsolete quickly. In order to overcome such problems, we turn to GT for some plausible answers. For example, it can provide a transition

Table 4

Information Requirements in a GT Programme

Stage No.	*Work Involved*	*Information Needs*
1	*2*	*3*
1.	Analysis of Component	Components information from production planning sheets.
2.	Rough determination of machine groups	Component-feature information within families demand; machine tool information
3.	Assessment of Component demand	Sales forecast information

(*Contd.*)

1	2	3
4.	Closer determination of machine groups	Information on constant requirement of components to marry demand to best machines for the volume of work
5.	Labour requirement balanced with machine utilisation	Information on calculation of man/machine load
6.	Planning the work program within the group, plus incentives plus foremanship	Information required to introduce effective disciplines and control within the GT unit.

Table 5

Characteristics of CMS and FMS

CMS	*FMS*
1	2
* Small to medium sized lots of families of parts (1200). A special set of parts or products.	Medium sized lots of families of parts (200 to 10,000 parts).
* One to 15 machines	Five to 12 CNC machines.
* Rapid changeover-single setup	Rapid changeover; no set up at machines.
* Significant reductions in inventory	Significant reductions in inventory

(*Contd.*)

1	2
* Greatly improved quality control through automation.	Greatly improved quality control through automation.
Unmanned :	
* Flexible/programmable machines.	Flexible/programmable machines
* Robotic integration for parts handling (1-5 machines)	Integrated conveyor system for parts and tooling.
* Network computer control	Networked computer control.
Manned :	
* A set or group of general purpose machines equipment laid out in a specific area.	
* A set of Multifunctional workers.	
* Enhanced worker input leading to job enlargement.	
* Job enrichment.	

from the functional set up of today to the automated factory of tomorrow. It requires the installation of systems which utilise the same conventional machinery under a different layout resulting in marginal investment compared to other systems. No drastic labour cuts are necessary nor are higher labour skills required. Moreover the systems setup under GT such as parts coding schemes etc., can be readily utilised by the other advanced manufacturing systems as and when they are installed. GT can thus provide the needed interface to aid the metamorphosis from the manual factory to an automated one. GT is the answer for developing countries to boost their productivity with the minimal of capital investment.

Conclusion

On the basis of the study carried out in this paper we may conclude that Group Technology is coming of age. From its modest beginnings in the 60's Group Technology has developed from a production related technique to an organisational philosophy that makes its presence felt in the functioning of most departments of the organisation. The benefits accruing from GT multiply over the years as it sparks of new application in the various branches of the organisation. Its benefits range from economic and technological to social. Over the years the mechanics of GT has developed at a rapid pace. The coding schemes have now matured and several commercial packages are now available for this purpose. Research is still in progress in the area of developing method for cell formation. Some of the problems that still remain unresolved relate to back tracking of components and the degree of arbitrariness involved in the initial stages of the algorithms. However recent work in this area using graph theoretic methodologies has been encouraging. The field of Engineering economics of Group Technology has not been deeply explored. Scope for futher research work exist in this area in determining the precise conditions under which it would be beneficial to implement a GT program. Clear guidelines are also available on the organisational changes such as retraining of personal, re-defining of organisation structure etc. needed for fruitful group Technology implementation. A crucial factor in deciding the success or failure of a

GT program is an information system. Strangely, there is hardly any research work undertaken to define the generic structure of such a system. Case studies reporting the information system aspect are few and lack direction. Scope therefore, exists to develop cases relating to the information systems and their associated computer hardware and software.

Finally the study shows that FMS though technologically superior to GT, as a concept or tool will take its own time in many developing countries to gain acceptance because of the reasons outlined. Group Technology therefore has a future.

12

Human Performance Approach to the Development of Standards for Manual Lifting Tasks

K. Krishniah, N. Sambandam**

Abstract

An experiment was conducted to determine the maximum acceptable weight of lift for an 8 hour work shift using Psycho-physical criterion. In this experiment fifty male industrial workers experienced in manual handling tasks participated. The lifting task with free style technique consisted of lifting a rote box from floor to a bench hights of 51 cm. at a frequency of 4 lifts per minute. The average maximum acceptable weight obtained in this experiment has been compared with those reported in the literature.

A predictive model for predicting the maximum acceptable weight of lift from physical measurements data and Job specific dynamic lift strength (maximum voluntary lift strength)

*College of Engineering, Anna University, Madras.

was developed. The model explains about 92 per cent of variation ($R^2=0.92$). Finally lifting capacities for Indian industrial workers in the form of lifting distribution are suggested.

Introduction

Manual Materials Handling activities are defined as unaided human acts of lifting, lowering, pushing, pulling, carrying or holding and releasing an object. In spite of the increased degree of automation in recent years, a large portion of the materials handling in industry is still carried out manually, especially where the product mix is too large to allow economical automated materials handling system. In countries like India, where cheap labour is available in abundance, much of handling is done manually.

A large number of work injuries arise from handling and/or mishandling of materials. These could result from slipping and falling, dropping of the load or strain and injury caused by lifting. Manual materials handling has been recognised as a major source of hazard to workers by many authorities on occupational health and safety. But occupational safety has been lacking in the area of materials handling by humans.

Out of all manual handling activities, lifting objects in an industrial context has been considered a problem for a long time in the field of occupational safety. The interest in this problem is growing in recent years because of the numerous compensation claims resulting from back injuries.

Mital (1984) reported that in the United States approximately 35 per cent of all compensation claims related to back injuries. From a small survey by Krishniah (1982) it was found that back injuries of varying degree were seen in 24 per cent of the cases interviewed. It is believed that the problem of low back-injury in manual lifting is more or less same in almost all countries. Thus manual lifting is one of the most hazardous tasks in manual materials handling.

An extensive research has been done in the area of manual materials handling to reduce the number, severity and the resulting costs of manual handling injuries. The National Institute for Occupational Safety and Health (NIOSH) of U.S.A. had published a work practice guide for manual lifting during 1981.

However in India, very little effort has been made by researchers and also by governmental organizations in the area of manual materials handling research. In industries most of the manual lifting work is done at low-levels. For example, movement of inprocess components (Collected in containers) such as bolts, cycle chain components, small machined components, small pallets, cartons etc. are loaded onto low-level platform trucks and moved. This type of work is done either by a single worker or two workers. In this paper a single man low-level lifting task is discussed.

Guidelines for manual lifting standards have already been developed in several countries except in India. These guidelines were established by using their own workers as subjects in experimentation. Since those workers are anthropometrically significantly different from workers in India and also their conditions of working are different, it is not clear whether such guidelines can be used in Indian industries.

The purpose of this research is to develop glidelines (how much to lift ?) for low-level manual lifting tasks by Indian Industrial workers, and also to develop a predictive model for lifting capability of an individual worker. Then we compared these results against the results reported in the literature.

Approach to the Problem

Many of the handling injuries are believed to occur because man exceeds or is asked to exceed his physical capabilities. So one must study systematically the influence of various variables affecting the manual handling capacity and design the handling task within the safe limits for the worker. Alternatively if the physical effort demanded by the handling task is known, then one can select and place a suitable person for the task. The first approach has been used in this study.

In the lifting task, the lifting capacity is influenced by various factors like the amount of weight lifted, frequency of lift, origin of lift distance (height) of lift, type of object lifted (its size, shape, handholds etc.) apart from the worker and environmental characteristics. Another aspect is whether the lifting activity is intermittant or repetitive.

However, it may not be possible to consider all the variables simultaneously and determine the lifting capacity of an individual because of the complexity in modeling and its solution. One approach is to control some variables and develop separate capacity norms under varying conditions.

Methods to Assess Lifting Capabilities

Several researchers used the following three different criteria to assess individual's capacity for manual handling tasks.

1. Psychophysical (Ayoub, *et al.*, 1978, Mital and Ayoub 1980, Garg and Saxena 1980, Mital and Manivasagan, 1983).

2. Biomechanical (Chaffin 1969, Chaffin and Baker 1970, Garg and Chaffin 1975, Garg and Herrin 1979, Leskinen *et al.*, 1983).

3. Physiological (Rodgers 1978, Garg and Hervin 1979, Givoni and Goldman 1971).

Psychophysical models combine objective performance measures and subjective assessments of the Perceived strain. Biochemical modeling is primarily involved in estimating the stresses imposed on the musculoskeletal system of the worker, especially on the low back and studying the effects of body segments on available muscle strength. Physiological models provide information on energy conversion and expenditure, measured in kcal/min and on the loading of the circulatory system (e.g. heartbeats/min.).

Psychophysical studies provide recommendations on the maximum permissible weight of the load for infrequent lifting as well as for repetitive lifting. Biomechanical studies in general, are for infrequent lifting tasks and metabolic energy expenditure rate and/or heart rate criteria are applicable to repetitive lifting only (Garg and Ayoub 1980).

Mital and Ayoub (1980), Garg *et al* (1980), Pytel and Kamon (1981), Mital and Manivasagam (1983), Mital (1983) have used psychophysical criterion for seeting safe limits and developing lifting capacity models. In fact, it was reported that the maximum permissible weight of lift based on psychophysical criterion was the result of the integration of biomechanical and physiological stress imposed by the lifting task (Ayoub *et al.*, 1983). The same approach has been used in this study.

Review of psychophysical models (Ayoub, *et al.*, 1980) for lifting capacity shows that all the models developed were based on static strength measurements. Garg *et al.*, (1980) developed simple linear regression equations for predicting dynamic lifting capability (maximum acceptable weight of lift) from job specific static strength measurements which had low correlations (0.48 to 0.79). Pytel and Kamon (1981), and Kroemer (1983) developed techniques for measuring dynamic strength of an individual. But the use of dynamic strength for lifting capacity modeling has received very little attention. In the current study, the authors decided to measure and use job specific dynamic lift strength for possible modeling of lifting capacity of an individual.

Procedure

Subjects

Fifty male industrial workers participated in the study. All of them were judged to be physically fit for the lifting task under consideration. Their physical characteristics and strength data are shown in Table-1. The method to measure the maximum voluntary lift strength (MVLS) is discussed below :

Table 1

Anthropometric and Strength Data for Fifty Industrial Workers

Measurement	*Mean*	*Standard Deviation*	*Range*
Age (years)	25.44	6.704	17—55
Body weight (Kg)	51.26	7.349	38—78.5
Body height (cm)	164.92	6.543	153—175
MVLS (Kg)	49.87	6.517	35—54

Measurement of Strength

The measurement of the strength was based on Psychophysical approach. Since the actual conditions of the lifting task will be used for its measurement, it is called job specific dynamic lift strength. Each subject was instructed to lift as much as he could from origin (floor) to the destination (51 cm. high shelf) using a metal container (45.5×25.5×26 cm) with two side handles and with free style lifting technique. These are the simulated conditions of the actual lifting task under study. The subject was encouraged to adjust weights randomly and allowed not more than one minute rest between trials. The maximum weight lifted by the subject was taken as the job specific dynamic lift strength. Since this strength corresponds to the maximal exertion of the subject, it is referred as maximum voluntary lift strength and is denoted by MVLS throughout.

Determination of Maximum Acceptable Weight of Lift

Psychophysical approach was used to determine the maximum acceptable weight of lift for an 8-hr work shift. The lifting task was performed in the Sagittal plane and it was to lift a rectangular container (45.5×25.5×26 cm) with two side handles from floor to a height of 51 cm at a frequency of 4 lifts per minute using free style lifting technique (the posture that the subject feels comfortable). The size of the container and height of lift selected are representative of those used in Indian Industries especially for the inprocess components movement (Krishniah, 1982). It would be possible to compare our results with that of Garg and Ayoub (1980) as they have also used the same height and frequency in their experiments.

The subject was allowed to subjectively adjust the amount of weight that a worker could lift repetitively for an 8-hr work day, based upon the estimate of his working capacity fatigue and endurance. The subject was instructed to adjust the work load to the maximum amount he could lift without strain or discomfort and without becoming tired, weakened, overheated or out of breath.

To arrive at the acceptable weight, each subject started the first phase of the lifting task without knowing the exact weight in the box and subsequently adjusted the weight of the box to continue the lifting for about 20 minutes. Then the subject was allowed to take about 10 minutes rest. The subject started the second phase of the lifting task without knowing the amount that he finally selected at the end of the first phase of the study. The initial weight of the container at the start of the second phase was either heavy or low whichever was not used in the first phase. The order of the initial weight was randomized for different subjects.

The maximum acceptable weight of lift was determined by averaging the weights selected at the end of the first and second phase of the lifting task. If the difference between the acceptable weights selected at the end of the two phases of the study was more than 15 per cent, that observation was discorded and the subject was asked to repeat the study at a later date.

Results

The mean and standard deviation of the maximum acceptable weight of lift for industrial workers have been calculated and are shown in Table 2.

Table 2

Maximum Acceptable Weight of Lift for Fifty Indian Industrial Workers

	Mean	*Standard Deviation*	*Range*
Maximum Acceptable Weight (Kg.)	21.42	2.334	16—27

Lifting Capacity Prediction Model

Operator characteristics such as worker's age, height and lift strength the lifting capacity of individuals. Multiple regression analysis was used with the maximum acceptable weight of lift as the dependent variable. Data from 41 subjects were used to develop the model and remaining 9 data were used for verifying the predicting capability of the model. The predictive model obtained is as given below :

Max. Acceptable Wt. of lift = 21.54 + 0.71 (Age) 0.131 (Body Height) + 0.391 (MVLS)

The model explains about 92 per cent of variation and the standard error of estimate is 0.68 Kg.

Model Validation

A prediction error which is defined to be the difference between the acceptable weight calculated using the model and the observed acceptable weight for a subject is taken as the measure to check the validity of the model. The predicting capability of the model based on this measure can be seen from Table 3.

Table 3

Predicting Capability of the Model

S.No.	*Observed Acceptable Weight*	*Predicted Acceptable Weight*	*Prediction Error (Predicted-observed)*
1.	18.5	19.91	1.41
2.	27.0	25.79	—1.22
3.	21.0	21.69	0.69
4.	23.75	23.25	—0.50
5.	22.00	20.71	—1.29
6.	20.00	18.83	—1.17
7.	23.00	20.61	—2.40
8.	22.50	20.77	—1.73
9.	22.00	21.76	—0.25

It is found that there is a very high correlation (0.867) between the predicted and observed acceptable weights. The predicting capability in terms of the prediction error is :

Minimum error	=—0.25 Kg.
Max. error	=—2.4 Kg.
Average error	=—0.72 Kg.
Mean squared error	=1.78

Discussion

Examination of the predictive model shows that the lifting capacity is a function of age, body height and the maximum voluntary lift strength. The model is comparable with the models reported in literature (Ayoub, *et al.*, 1980) and similar to the model developed by Krishniah and Balasubramanian (1985). However it is to be noted that all the models reported in literature are based on static strength as against the current model wherein the whole body dynamic strength is used. And also the application of the current model is very easy since all the variables are easily and quickly measurable without any instrumentation. However it is to be noted that the model underestimates the lifting capacity in most of the cases and it is good from the safety point of view.

The mean maximum acceptable weight obtained in the current study is 21.42 Kg. Comparison of this mean acceptable weight with some of the previous research results reported in literature is shown in Table 4.

Examination of Table 4 shows that there are large variations in the acceptable weights obtained by different reserchers. The variations could be due to differences in subject populations used in terms of age, size and nationality; experimental condititions and differences in the methodologies used in obtaining maximum safe loads. Also the variations could

Table 4

Comparison of Mean Max Acceptable Weights of Industrial Workers

Researcher	*Acceptable Weight (Kg.)*			
	Lifting Height	*Frequency (Lifts/min)*	*Mean*	*Standard Deviation*
Snook (1978)	Foor to 51 cm.	4.3	26.0	...
Ayoub *et al* (1978)	Floor to 51 cm.	4	25.81	...
Ayoub, *et al* (1980)	Floor to Knuckle	4	23.83	6.70
Ciriello and Snook (1983)	Floor to 51 cm.	4.3	31.0	6.70
Mital (1984)	Floor to Knuckle	4	15.42	4.52
Present study	Floor to 51 cm.	4	21.42	2.33

be due to the differences in the height of lift, variation in frequencies, box sizes and sample size. This confirms the hypothesis that the results obtained elsewhere cannot be used as guidelines for Indian Industrial workers.

Finally the lifting capacity for male Indian Industrial workers is suggested below. These capacities are in the form of the lifting distribution based on average and standard deviation of the maximum acceptable weight of lift. The distribution is assumed to be normal.

Table 5

Lifting Capacity of Male Industrial Worker (Kgs)

Per cent Population	90	75	50	25	10
Acceptable Weight	18.5	20	21.5	23	24.5

This distribution can be used as guidelines in the design of lifting tasks. This indicates that 90 per cent of the workers can perform tasks involving lifting 18.5 Kg. or less and only 10 per cent of the workers will be able to lift weights 24.5 Kg. or more.

Conclusion

1. The lifting capacity predictive model is of great help to the personnel managers of industries to predetermine the lifting capability of individuals and decide about their selection and placement for manual lifting tasks. This model can also be used for periodical testing of the lifting capacity of workers engaged in normal lifting tasks.

2. Currently no standards are available for manual lifting tasks. The results obtained in this study could serve as guidelines in this direction.

3. The results obtained in this study are applicable only for sagittal lifting tasks performed at 4 lifts per minute in the height range of floor to 51 cm. height. However multiplier factor could be developed to determine the guidelines for varying conditions of the lifting tasks and also lowering tasks. And the same approach could be tried for other lift heights.

4. The method suggested for measuring MVLS and its use for lifting capability modeling proved to be a useful technique. This method would be especially useful for studying two-men lifting tasks, which is currently under progress.

13

The Role of Industrial Engineering in Banking

*Roger C. Guarino**

Real economic growth during the current business cycle has been stagnant due to three principle inter-related factors :

1. low rate of innovative capital investment

2. labour costs rising faster than productivity gains

3. effects of government regulation

The consequent adverse impact on productivity and corporate well-being are quantified in economic terms. One aspect of the solution lies in a needed commitment by the industrial engineering profession to significant productivity gains. The role of government in adopting realistic public policy and the need for more enlightened long-term self-interest by labour unions are also discussed.

* Sr. Executive Vice President, Federal Home Loan Bank of New York. (Reprinted with permission from Proceedings 1979 Fall Industrial Engineering Conference, AIIE).

Industrial Engineers, back to the days of Taylor and Gilbreth, have been concerned with improving the methods of production so as to increase the *efficiency* of the production process. The old guard term "efficiency" was always understood by the practicing professional as meaning increasing productive *output* at a rate greater than the consumption of productive resources, i.e., *input*. As an undergraduate industrial engineer it was endemic in my education some twenty five to thirty years ago that the *economics of alternatives* must be exhaustively identified so as to be in a position to recommend that combination of methods, site selection, shop processes, materials, machine tools, etc. that would yield the highest rate of return for an existent or future venture, product, or service. Indeed, it was this attribute of the educational process and *modus vivendi* that set industrial engineering quite apart from the other engineering disciplines.

Has anything changed in the intervening years ? In principle, no, but of course there have been innumerable developments as to techniques (the digital computer comes to mind) and the economic environment in which business and industry must now operate is certainly significantly more complex. For one thing, ours is primarily a *service economy* whereas not so many years ago we would have characterized the environment as a manufacturing or industrial economy. Obviously, banking is a part of that service economy. Another all-too-evident perturbation today that we were only vaguely aware of twenty five years ago is the great uncertainty caused by double digit inflation and unstable (and high) short and long term interest rates.

But the principle remains inviolate that efficiency is directly related to the ratio :

Output/Input

Even so, this is the era of the macro economist who has defined *Productivity* (in the aggregate of course) roughly in terms of :

$$\frac{\text{Private Sector GNP}}{\text{Private Sector Labour Hours}}$$

It is evident that industrial engineers and economists are talking the same language with a twist because the measure of productivity (efficiency) relates to the same Output/Input equation. Whereas the macro economist is concerned with productivity in the American economy-at-large (thus GNP as the measure of Output), the industrial engineer is concerned, typically, with productivity at the level of the firm. Thus, as practitioners you know that the day-to-day activities of the I.E. are often described with such terms as cost reduction, work simplification, standards, incentives, cost accounting, information systems, organisational planning, work measurement—in other words, those activities designed to either increase Output or decrease Input.

I am convinced that the application of sound industrial engineering techniques such as are going to be discussed at this Conference by many eminent and highly qualified speakers would result in improved productivity—and thus profitability at your institutions. In fact, you *must* achieve higher levels of productivity just to keep even in the competitive sense as well as to preserve and hopefully improve on that "net of all nets", your return on Assets (ROA).

My immediate concern is the possibility that you may not be aware of how bad the current environment is for *real* productivity gains and thus how vital your efforts on behalf of your firm really are. It's one thing to stay abreast of the competition but quite another under a very difficult economic scenario to improve ROA and profitability because I am frankly a bit pessimistic about the productivity outlook given the current climate of government regulations and the apparent position of organized labour. I grant that there is a practical limit to what engineers (and management) can accomplish in this climate short of organized political action which by and large has been anathema to most engineering societies (although this hasn't bothered the doctors too much).

Nevertheless, I think it is useful for I.E.'s to understand a bit about the current national economic situation as it impact productivity and as it is impacted by public policy and labour. I would hope, then, to convey to you a perspective of the problem that you face in your financial institutions. Then, I would like to return to a general discussion of some of the opportunities for industrial engineers to improve their banks' productivity although I will be content to leave detail descriptions of techniques to subsequent speakers who are much more competent than I as I.E. practitioners.

A starting place would be the President's Economic Report to Congress this past January (1). This message devoted an unusual amount of space to Productivity highlighting the Administration's concern over a very unhealthy national picture. Whereas national productivity rose in 1978 only 0.4% the President said "The slowdown was concentrated in the nonfarm nonmanufacturing sector, whereas productivity *actually declined 0.3 per cent* during 1978 (emphasis added)...If we ignore the realities of slower productivity growth—if governments continue to press forward with unabated claim on resources, and private citizens continue to demand large gains in money incomes—our inflationary problems will worsen." Abont one week after submittal of the Economic Report to the Congress, as reported by the Wall Street Journal on January 29, 1979, the President also stated that he was "confident that the economy's performance in the year ahead will match the administration's forecast of *gently slowing growth without a recession*" (emphasis added).

This later statement of the president was at odds with even a sophmoric analysis of the accurate depiction of the Productivity scene contained in his congressional message. Indeed, as reported by *Business Week* on September 3, 1979, "For the quarter ended last June, the productivity gap stood at 13.1 – a 9.3% increase in compensation per man hour combined with a 3.8% *decline in productivity* (emphasis added).

This term "productivity gap" is crucial as it has been demonstrated [12] that inflation can only decline when and if labour's wage demand less the real productivity gain *is less than* current actual inflation, i.e., inflation will decrease when :

Wage Demand—Productivity Gain

<Actual Inflation

To drive the point home more forcefully, actual inflation will be zero when wage increases *exactly equal* productivity gains. Nothing less will do so it is perfectly obvious why the inflation rate has been exacerbated by the double whammy of higher wage demands coupled with lower productivity—indeed, *negative* productivity gains, i.e., the productivity gap previously mentioned.

I'm not terribly optimistic that much can be accomplished with regard to wage demands as it has been kind of a rule of thumb of labour negotiators to bargain for an increase equal to current inflation plus one half of the *long term* productivity gain. But the longterm gain in this country has been approximately 3%, a far cry from the rapidly decreasing trend in recent years. Thus recent wage settlements seem mathematically designed to further stimulate the upward inflationary spiral.

Your guess is as good as mine as to whether organized labour really understands the underlying economic principles or whether we are merely observing a manifestation of aggressive competition with management, and public policy for that matter. In a mid-summer pronouncement concerning government restrictions on the export of computer hardware, the AFL-CIO. Executive Council stated, "One ironic aspyct of the massive buildup of Soviet military might is that it has been aided by profit-hungry U.S. corporations selling America's most critical technology......Lenin's statement that the Western democracies would 'sell us the rope for their own hanging' seem like a prophecy......" Regardless of where one stands on the issue of export restrictions, the union rhetoric is frightening because it seems to reveal an underlying lack of understanding of the capitalistic system—of which labour is a beneficiary—and which *most certainly* is motivated primarily by profit, although not out of the bounds of articulated public policy.

As pragmists, we probably are left with the challenge of increasing productivity gains both nationally and at the level of the firm. But, first, why is productivity at its current low level ? There's an old story that attributes to Harry Truman the prayer for a one-handed economists—one who could not hedge by saying "but, on the other hand." Nonetheless, as a banker, I have been reviewing many sources of economic thought regarding the low ebb of productivity and believe it or not, there seems to be a consensus. At the risk of simplistic conclusion, let us say that primary negative impact on productivity falls into two categories :

1. low capital spending for R&D and plant and equipment

2. non-productive government regulations

Referring again to the President's Economic Report to Congress, he displayed perceptive insight in stating that the "......growth in the capital-labour ratio...has dropped to 1.3/4 percent per year (from 3 percent......analytical studies estimate that it would well have reduced productivity growth by up to one-half of a percentage point per year from earlier trends." The President further stated

> "......important indirect costs are generated by social regulation...... Moreover, some regulations specify or suggest the technology to be used to meet new *standards, rather than prescribing a level of performance to be attained* (emphasis added). As a consequence, innovations that could meet the standards at lower cost are not encouraged ......It has already been noted that the output measures generally used to calcutate productivity do not include environmental improvements and other benefits of

regulation.*

Nevertheless, the magnitude of the productivity effects does highlight two facts : Regulation is very costly; and *benefits should be closely compared with costs in the design of regulatory legislation and specific regulations*" (emphasis added).

Converting the President's posture to action seems problematic at this writing. The department of Commerce has concluded that a two percent increase over the long term trend in the share of GNP dedicated to business capital investment would merely increase capital per worker at the same rate as in the previous decade in view of programmed costs of energy, environmental and safety programmes and other "benefits" of government social regulation—public policy, if you will. Being neither an economist or a tax expert, I would still suggest that as matter of self-interest public policy must be galvanized towards abetting productivity by (a) creating a tax climate that fosters R&D, innovation and risk capital and (b) significantly scaling down regulatory expenses in the private sector (e.g. environmental improvements), which have been estimated to aggregate 10% of all capital investment so as to divert these funds to productivity-improving investments. [14]

I said earlier that I felt it useful to provide you with this economic perspective on the productivity problem as a kind of umbrella for your individual efforts on behalf of your financial institutions. Although not a pessimist by nature, I would say that the rather bleak productivity outlook at least underscores the importance of your role as industrial engineers in implementing such innovative programmes as will have maximum leverage on the previously discussed Output/Input equation. Let me outline at least a few opportunity areas.

Cost-effective automation is possibly the tool with the

---

* Environmental improvements as a *benefit* of regulation is hardly a universally held view.

highest potential for productivity improvement in banking if it is done right. When I was in manufacturing, I came to understand that the only productive computer applications were those that directly related to the metalchopping process—and only then when the net marginal benefit of the application provided a return on investment (ROI) greater than the firm's general internal ROI. Thus, in banking, computer applications should be directed towards increasing revenue flow (new services) and decreasing the utilization of labour. More to the point a computer application which at the margin does not increase stockholder's earnings per share is suspect, as far as I am concerned.

I don't have to tell you that another opportunity areas and one which has received minimal attention in banking, is the establishment of production standards. Data is very sparse, but I have a suspicion that labour efficiency in banking is rather low in absolute terms. Unlike manufacturing, heretofore there hasn't been the incentive to tighten up employee performance because the competitive pressures weren't as apparent. Of course, I'm referring to work measurement and standard setting for such typical banking operations as Proof and Transit, teller transaction volume, check processing, microfilming and so on. Unfortunately, the Bank Administration Institute reports that overall labour productivity declined by four percent in 1978. So, whether the solution lies in better training, improved work methods, automation, or just plain happier workers—and what that implies—the challenge is facing the industrial engineering profession. In any event, I earnesty believe that well-conceived and executed work improvement programmes can achieve minimum tangible labour reduction in the range of 20%. But senior management must be willing to make the emotional and ethical commitments clearly involved.

Another notion I have is that cost accounting in Banking is not all that good. I really believe that in many cases banking product managers don't know what their costs are when they package and price services, particularly new services such as NOW accounts, telephone transfers and automatic transfer accounts. Generally, industrial engineers are better prepared to develop cost accounting systems than accountants so I would urge you to explore this area. Obviously, improved costing will lead to more strategic and profitable pricing of a bank's total service package, which in turn will result in improved revenue flow at least expenditure of productive resources.

I pointed earlier to ROA as the "net of all nets" for financial institutions. A west coast consulting firm that specializes in Savings and Loans did some interesting work in relating SEL productivity to ROA and discovered an essentially linear relationship* based on a sample of 91 institutions. While not statistically significant, or perhaps not even salient to all classes of financial institutions, nonetheless this is a possibly fruitful area of investigation in your own bank. Incidently, in the same analysis, the consultants observed that the ROA of S&L's using EDP service bureaus was greater (.815) than for those having In-House EDP (.768). A not surprising result to me as automation projects typically encounter excessive slippage and are accomplished best by "bare bones-plain wrapper" for profit, experts.

Surely, I have failed to mention any number of significant opportunity areas for industrial engineers in banking. I expect that the subsequent speakers with whom I have the honour to share this platform will remedy this oversight. However, I have tried to provide you with an economic backdrop for America's pervasive productivity slide as an added incentive for your own innovative undertakings and I hope that, to some degree, I have succeeded. As you can tell, I am concerned about capital disincentive and excessive governmental regulations as impediments to your progress. So, I am encouraged when a distinguished spokesman of the Federal Reserve System stated to a recent assembly of bank directors that the longer-term success

---

* While I don't have their rata available, crudely speaking the relationship was found to be :
  ROA=0.2 [Productivity Ratio],
where the Productivity Ratio was defined as :
  Dollars of Gross Margin/Payroll Dollars.

of the economy and of banking is dependent on a revitalization of the free market place and that the best results will be obtained when "......we simply let the market do what it does best—allocate resources where and to whom they yield the greatest return." [7]

Bibliography

1. "Economic Report of the President" transmitted to the Congress, January 1979.
2. Tilford Gaines, "Might the Worst Happen ?" *Economic Report*, Manufacturer's Hanover Trust Co., February 1979.
3. Leon Greenberg, "A Practical Guide to Productivity Measurement," The Bureau of National Affairs, Inc., Washington D C., 1973.
4. "Improvements in Productivity and Staffing Produce Increased Profitability. *Asset*, June 1979. The Newport Group, Irvine, California 92714.
5. Louis Kohlmeier, "Organised Labour has no Place to go," *Financier*, September 1979.
6. Robert H. Long, "Productivity Impact Studies," *The Magazine of Bank Administration*, date unknown.
7. Robert P. Mayo, "The Economy and the Banking system," *Economic Perspectives*, Federal Reserve Bank of Chicago, July/August 1979.
8. "Measuring Department Productivity," Bank Administration Institute, 1965.
9. Merrill T. Miller, Jr., "On Line Terminals Boost Productivity, Improve Service," *The Magazine of Bank Administration*, March 1975.
10. Robert E. Nolar, "Approaches to Improving Staff Productivity," paper presented at Bank Administration

Institute National Convention, Philadelphia, October 18, 1976.

11. *Payment System Newsletter*, February 1979.

12. *Payment System Newsletter*, April 1979.

13. "Priority for Productivity," *Financier*, p. 3, March 1979.

14. "Reaching a Higher Standard of Living Office of Economic Research, The New York Stock Exchange, January 1979.

15. D. Raymond Riddle, "Automation and Productivity in Commercial Banking—What it Means," 1978 Fall I.E. Conference.

16. Dale W. Sommer, "Low Productivity Gains Abet Inflation," *Industry Week*, April 2, 1979.

17. "1977 Survey of the Check Collection System," Bank Administration Institute, 1978.

18. Joseph C. White, "Building Toward Worker Productivity," *The Magazine of Bank Administration*, June 1975.

14

Optimum Selection of Heavy Earth Moving Equipments for Surface Coal Mining Projects Through Systems Modelling

*M. Mandal**

Introduction

The advantages of large opencast mechanised mines have gradually been felt by the different sectors of coal industry in order to have faster rate of extraction and meeting the increased demand of coal. To evaluate the equipment sub-systems, designed capacity of individual equipments has to be accounted for HEM equipment programming and still being in use. This leads to a gap in achieving the target production by an individual equipment. This occurs because it does not corelate the real life situation as happened in an opencast project.

Systems modelling is essential to integrate the corporate

* Industrial Engineer, Tata Exports Limited.

objectives ensuring right equipment programming. Only sub-system equipment planning will mislead and cause to create bottlenecks in the operational system.

This paper emphasises the selection of Heavy Earth Moving Equipments for various levels of coal production (I.M.T. to 10 M.T./annum). For this purpose Dynamic programming approach has been utilised to make the decision of choosing different capacity/model of Heavy Earth Moving Equipments in stages. Here the stage refers to the selection of particular set/type of equipments.

Evaluatian of Sub-system Equipment

The management decision process can be rationalised by scientific analysis of the equipment sub-systems and formulation decision rules on the basis of techno-economic mathematical models of different key sub-systems and that of the total system. Such approach will first analyse he operations of existing sub-system and assess scientifically the capacity, production of coal and overburden, face advancement and other techno-economic indices that could be achievable. The system will then be subjected to a techno-economic audit to discover the bottlenecks in the operation, pit geometry and management procedures which could be overcome duction, productivity and other indices will be aswith practically at cost, and fresh capital investment can be ensured easily. The resultant increase of processed, corresponding which will be the first phase of implementation of the study. Different operational and management sub-systems will be used to develop techno-economic mathematical models incorporating most of the quantifiable decision variables with their interaction with the system of the operation. The optimum solution of the systems model will be realized through the use of computer which would indicate the optimum level of equipment planning for a predetermined target production. The plan of implementation should be supported by an action network graphic where results to be achieved at different stages will be highlighted.

Having the knowledge of achievable capacity of different HEM equipments, the equipment programming can easily be done linking it to the production programming. To achieve the target production, phasing of equipments is also done to meet the production. Here also, the optimization of equipment plays a vital role for stagewise equipment programming based on the techno-economic evaluation of each sub-systems of equipment. For different levels of coal production numbers of individual equipment have been calculated using the computer programming.

Evaluation of Total Cost

The purpose of cost estimating system presented here is to establish a relative comparison between two or among the more earth moving equipments. The system of estimating hourly ownership and operating costs presented here should be used for planning purposes as a basic guideline only. For the evaluation of ownership cost of individual equipments, the total cost of purchasing one equipment is divided by its working capacity. This standard has been developed based on the working hours of the engined fitted in the equipment. This then has been estimated on cost of ownership per tonne/cu. m. material handling linking to its achievable capacity. It may, however, be mentioned here that the cost as evaluated above also includes depreciation cost, customs duty, etc. for the imported items as the case may be (Annexure II : Table No. 1).

Different opencast projects prepare their monthly cost sheet showing the production versus different costs on different equipments. The cost elements have been identified to evaluate the cost of a particular equipment per tonne of material handled. For different types of equipment; consumption rate of fuel, oil lubricant and other consumables were being noted and based on individual equipments handling capacity, cost/tonne of material handling are evaluated whose summation leads towards the level operating cost/tonne of material handling.

Having the knowledge of individual equipments investment, i.e. ownership and operating cost per tonne of material handling, the summation of these two gives the total cost of owning and operating cost/tonne of material handling. These cost figures are multiplied by the annual achievable production to calculate the cost of individual equipment.

Establishment of Cost Capacity Replacement

The cost figures as enumerated above have been compared against the different production level and generalised empirical formulae have been established. The co-efficients of these parameters are shown below. Here, 'Y' has been considered as cost while 'X' as capacity of equipments.

Shovel : $Y = A_0 + A_1X + A_2X^2 + A_3X^3 + A_4X^4 + A_5X^5$ ...(1)

Truck : $Y = A_0 + A_1 + X \quad A_2X^2 + A_3X^3$ ...(2)

Drill : $Y = A_0 + A_0 + A_1X + A_2X^2$ ...(3)

To explain the cost capacity relationship as enumerated above are given below for a target production of 3 M.T./ Annum.

Shovel : $Y = 56.79 - 33.16X + 20.98X^2 - 5.47X^3 + 0.66X^4 - .2X^5$ ...(4)

Truck : $Y = 191.79 - 5.07X + .138X^3$ ...(5)

Drill : $Y = 2.22 - 0.0193X + 0.00015X^2$ ...(6)

Model Formulation

Methodology

The decision making in respect to a particular size and capacity of HEM Equipment involves a process that takes place in several stages (multi-stage process) in such a way that at each stage the process is dependent on the strategy chosen.

To meet the increased level of coal production, it is essential for the managerial planners, with the complexity of operation, to select a specific type of HEM Equipment, to encounter more flexibility in the equipment system of operation. For a target coal production one type of specific bucket size of shovel will be more useful rather than considering it for all the levels of target production in different opencast projects. Accordingly, the dumper/truck capacity is also affected resulting in bottlenecks in the equipment system.

Dynamic programming is a mathematical technique for making a sequence of interrelated decisions. Here, of course, the decisions are in respect of selecting Heavy Earth Moving Equipment system in a specific target production which minimizes the overall cost, resulting in total system effectiveness in the conventional mining operation. Mathematically, a Dynamic programming problem is a decision making problem in n-variables, the problem being subdivided into n-subproblems (segments), each subproblem being a decision making problem in one variable only.

Decision Making Process

Here the stages are being identified as different Heavy Earth Moving Equipment subsystems and States are defined as the different capacity/models of the individual equipment subsystems. It may be mentioned that dozers and drilling equipments do not have any restrictions in respect of other types of equipment in the system and/or from production point of view. But each shovel has its restrictions with the matching capacity of the trucks.

To define the actual model formulation for the decision making of various types of Heavy Earth Moving Equipment for a target production of I.M.T./annum to 10 M.T./annum, the ingredients are enumerated below :

Stage	*States*	*Decision Variable(s)*	*Solution*
1	7	Shovel capacity	Sub-optimum for shovel
2	2	Shovel in combination with truck	Shovel-truck combination Sub-optimum solution for
3	4	Shovel in combination with truck and drills	Sub-optimum solution for shovel-truck-drill combinations
4	5	Shovel, truck, drill & dozer	Optimum solution for HEM equipment.

Optimum Solution

The computer output gives the optimum cost on Heavy Earth Moving Equipments for different level of coal production as shown in Table 2, stagewise optimum cost on Heavy Earth Moving Equipments (Table 3), optimum number of Heavy Earth Moving Equipments (Table No. 5) and minimum cost of individual Heavy Earth Moving Equipments sub-systems (Table 4).

Sensitivity Analysis

The effect on changing a particular equipment sub-system in the total equipment system can be studied, when a particular size of equipment termed as 'states' is changed. Based on the calculated data as outlined above, the stage optimum value is calculated. It may be mentioned here that the minimum value of cost towards transportation is minimum among the five individul capacity of trucks, while optimizing this minimum values gives a guideline to choose the optimum value in second stage inclusive of the shovel. This is a searching method of possible combination shovel and truck capacity and each time it compares with the previous one and stores the minimum value in the memory of the computer. This process similarly extends through different possible combinations of 5 states of truck, 7 states of shovel, 4 states of drill and 2 states of dozer and subsequently stores the minimum value comparing each other individual path. The computer output gives the minimum cost for different levels of coal production (1 M.T. to 10 M.T.) and also the minimum cost of individul equipment sub-systems. The cost figures as mentioned above also give a clear picture showing the sensitiveness of choosing a particular capacity for equipment sub-systems Vs not choosing it for a target production level.

The stage optimum value as found in the first stages changes considerably with a particular combination of loading shovel and truck. When the process works backward, then the stage optimum value decreases considerably and the decision on selecting a particular equipment sub-system is optimised. For a target production of—M.T. per annum, the minimum value of individual equipment sub-system, i.e. shovel is Rs. 12.12 lakhs, whereas the value of rises to Rs. 13.92 lakhs following the minimum path.

Again, because of the technological constraints, it is not feasible to deploy low capacity equipments for bigger projects. On the other hand, all the individual equipments cannot be used with each other, because of mismatching in the equipment sub-system. One 85 T truck will incur much more loss on idleness if it is forced to work with a loading shovel of 0.9 or 10.91 m^3 bucket capacity. It is also true in reverse case when a bigger bucket capacity shovel (i.e. 4.6 or 6.3 cu.m.) is deployed in combination with a small capacity of truck, say 15 T.

Therefore, the above situation reveals that individual project demands for evaluation carefully considering the haul distances of the project from different loading stations to the respective dumping yard, equipments availability for the target working hours, matching of equipment sub-system to the total system of mining operation, etc.

In this dynamic programming approach as enumerated above, the decision making process becomes a successful one for equipments planning and it leads towards corporate objective of any organisation through optimisation techniques in stages for the tactical, strategic and corporate planning.

Conclusion

The following conclusions can be drawn as indicated below based on the solution achieved through dynamic programming methodology for the selection of Heavy Earth Moving Equipments.

Any drilling equipment can be selected which is best matched to the working environment irrespective of the other equipment sub-systems being chosen.

More emphasis can be laid on EQC-4.6, cubic metre, HEC make shovel instead of EKG-4.6, EKG-6.3, and EKG-8 shovels presently being imported from Russia. Licensing capacity of these types of shovel should immediately be increased to meet the bigger capacity shovels, avoiding there by the need to import equipments. It is found from the data that the optimum cost on shovel is achieved through 0.9 m^3 shovel in the production range up from 2 M.T. to 4 M.T. when the production increased beyond 4 M.T. the ideal shovel size is 4.6 cubic metre bucket capacity. For convenience, it is always advisable to have smaller capacity shovel rather than introduce giant size shovel in smaller projects.

In respect of trucks it has become an universal method of coal transportation in India. In general, 35 T and 50 T truck capacity are found suitable at all production levels. But the cost figure reveals that 15 T truck is matched to the low capacity shovel, i.e. 0.9 and 1.91 cubic metre bucket capacity in the production ranging upto 2 M.T., whereas 25 T and 35 T trucks are suitable for the production levels from 3-5 M.T., and 50 T trucks are best matched with 4.6 cubic metre shovel beyond 5 M.T. production per annum.

Appendix I

Computational Algorithm for Selection Equipments

(*A*) *Selection of Drilling Machine*

$$T=\left(\frac{13790\ PcT}{n\sqrt{Q^3}}+\frac{12\ PcT}{\sqrt{Q^3}}+17.8\right)(1+0.0055\ \sqrt{a})\ KaKb \qquad \ldots(7)$$

where t=drilling time per metre of borehole

q=actual thrust in kilograms

n=spindle rotation in r.p.m.

pa = contact strength (kg/mm^2)

a = abrasiveness (mg)

Kd = coefficient representing the derivation of the actual diameter of hole from the standard diameter.

Kb = coefficient which represents the geometry and wear resistance of the bit.

The steps are as follows for the computational algorithm :

Determine and specify the condition under which the machine will be used; such as service factors, labour, site whether, etc.

— State the objectives for the rock breakage phases of the production cycle of operation considering excavation and haulage restrictions, crushing capacity, production target, pit geometry in terms of tonnage, fragmentation, throw/pull, etc.

— Based on blasting requirements, design the drill hole pattern, i.e. the hole size, its depth, inclination, burden and spacing.

— Determine the drill ability factors and for the kind of anticipated, select the drilling method(s) which appear feasible for the operation to continue.

— Specify the operating variables for each systems under consideration, considering the drill, rod and circulation fluid factors, etc.

— Estimate the performance parameters including cost and compare. Major cost items are bits, drill depreciation, labour maintenance, power, etc.

— Optimise the drilling system which is best suited at a predetermined level of production satisfying the above requirements and has the minimum overall cost of operation in the system of geomining environmental conditions.

(*B*) *Selection of Loading Equipments*

$$QDS = \frac{(Tsh - Tad)}{(QT/Bs)Tsc} \times QT \text{ Cubic metre/Shift} \quad ...(8)$$

$$QAS = QDS\ (Tsh - Trs)\ (1 - ksc)\ Kr \text{ Cubic metre/Shift} \quad ...(9)$$

where,

QDS = Designed capacity of shovel

QAS = Achievable capacity of shovel

Tsh = Duration of shift in hours

Tad = Duration ancillary delay

Bs = Bucket capacity of the loading shovel

Tsc = Cycle time of the shovel in Hrs.

Trs = Time of interruption of work in Hrs.

Ksc = Standstill factor

Qt = Capacity of truck in cubic metre.

The factors for standstill of loading equipment due to irrigular performance of technological operation, can with sufficient accuracy for practical calculations, be taken as functions of the members of the excavator in a load flow working in the system of operation in accordance with the regression equation.

$$Ksc = 18.66 - 154.47 K^2 - 738.90 K^3 \text{ for shovel} > 4.6 \text{ m}^3 \quad ...(10)$$

$$= 47.20 + 4490.16K^2 + 6919.45K^3 \text{ for shovel} < 4.6 \text{ m} \quad ...(11)$$

where, k = No. of shovels.

The value 'K' can be evaluated as mentioned below :

$$K = \frac{Qc + Qob}{(Tsh \times 2 \times 300)QAS} \quad ...(12)$$

where,

Qc = Output of Coal in tonne

Qob = Output of overburden in tonne.

(*C*) *Selection of Transportation Equipment*

For transportation of coal and overburden materials to the destination from its pit configuration can be dealt with the various modes in the system of mining operation :

— Truck (off-highway) in combination with excavator.

— Truck (articulated) in combination with escavator.

— Belt conveyor in combination with truck and excavator.

— Conveyor in combination with railroad transportation.

— Direct casting by draglines.

(*a*) ***Computation of Duration of a Transport Cycle***

$$T_P = T_L + T_M + T_M + T_M \quad ...(13)$$

where, T_L = Loading time

T_M = Maneuvering time

T_W = Waiting time for loading and unloading

T_R = Running time with load and empties.

Again, $T_L = TCE \times NK \times T$ ...(14)

where, TCE = Cycle time of excavator

N_K = Co-efficient of unbalanced nature of operation.

T_Q = Time taken to move from place of waiting to the excavator.

(*b*) *Computation of Working Capacity of Truck*

$$QAT = QT \frac{(Tsh - Tad)\, Bl}{\frac{L}{VXB_2} + TD} (1 - Kset)\, Krt \; m^3/shift \qquad ...(15)$$

where, QT = Load capacity of truck (m^3)

L = Transport distance (KM)

V = Average technical speed (KM/Hr)

B1 = Utilisation co-efficient of truck machine maintenance shift

B2 = Utilisation co-efficient of truck running

TD = Total delay time in a cycle in hours (Loading, unloading, maneuvering etc.)

Kset = Standstill factor of the track due to non-uniformity of the process.

Krs = Factor for technological readiness of the truck.

The following relationship were being arrived at for the truck.

$$Kset = 69.39 - 972.45\ T + 4855.45\ T^2 - 8272.56\ T^3 \quad ...(16)$$

(*c*) *Computation of Number of Trucks*

Required number of trucks per excavator can be obtained as follows :

$$NTE = QAS/QAT \quad ...(17)$$

where,

QAS = Hourly achievable capacity of excavator

QAT = Hourly achievable capacity of Truck.

Appendix II

Table 1

Evaluation of Total Cost/T of Material Handling

Type/Capacity of equipment	*Manufacturer*	*Total Capital Cost including taxes depreciation etc. (Rs.)*	*Life of Equipment (Hrs.)*	*Fixed Cost/T (Rs.)*	*Operating Cost/T (Rs.)*	*Total Cost/T (Rs.)*
1	*2*	*3*	*4*	*5*	*6*	*7*
Shovel :						
10 Cubic Metre	Imported	224.00	36000	33.77	0.86	34.63

(*Contd.*)

1	2	3	4	5	6	7
EKG-8	HEC/Russian	140.28	36000	29.75	0.86	30.61
EKG-68	HEC/Russian	93.76	36000	15.72	0.84	16.56
EKG/EQC-4.6	HEO	62.40	30000	7.80	0.82	8.62
2.29 Cu.m.	Tata P & H/L & T Poclain	38.62	21600	6.00	0.96	6.92
1.91 Cu.m.	TELCO/HM	24.48	16000	4.00	0.96	4.96
0.9 Cu.m.	L & T Poclain	22.80	16000	3.80	0.96	4.04
Front end loader :						
6.0 Cu.m.	BEHL	28.76	12000	5.74	1.36	7.12
4.74 Cu.m.	TEREX	36.05	10000	7.50	1.32	8.82
Drill :						
SBSH 269 mm Dia	Russian	30.50	20000	3.20	0.74	3.94

RBH drills	RMT	28.80	16000	3.70	0.74	4.44
IDM-30	Ingersoll-Rand	22.20	14000	4.80	0.76	5.56
IDM-45	Ingersoll-Rand	22.20	12000	4.67	0.82	5.49
Trucks						
85 T	Haulpack	73.20	30000	14.64	1.68	16.32
50 T	BEML	37.20	21600	7.20	1.66	8.66
35 T	BEML	19.56	16000	3.91	1.94	5.85
25 T	BEML	13.80	12000	2.50	1.40	3.90
15 T	TEREX	10.80	12000	1.68	1.48	3.16

Table 2

Optimum Cost on Hem for Different Levels of Production Per Annum

(*Lakh Rupees*)

Production (M.T.)	*Truck*	*Shovel*	*Drill*	*Dozer*	*Total*
1.0	47.70	13.92	3.94	10.14	75.70
2.0	89.70	27.84	3.94	13.52	135.00
3.0	128.70	41.76	4.44	16.90	191.80
4.0	175.50	65.68	4.44	20.28	255.40
5.0	222.30	86.20	5.49	23.66	337.65
6.0	257.40	112.06	5.49	23.66	398.61
7.0	327.82	129.30	10.98	27.04	495.14
8.0	345.54	146.54	10.98	30.42	533.48
9.0	372.12	163.78	16.47	37.18	589.55
10.0	409.56	181.02	21.96	40.56	653.10

Table 3

Stagewise Optimum Cost of the Equipments

(Lakh Rupees)

Product (M.T.)	*First Stage*	*Second Stage*	*Third Stage*	*Fourth Stage*
1.0	47.70	59.82	65.76	75.70
2.0	89.70	114.50	118.44	135.00
3.0	128.70	168.38	172.82	191.80
4.0	175.50	223.98	228.42	255.40
5.0	222.30	291.60	297.09	337.65
6.0	257.40	347.88	353.37	398.60
7.0	327.82	432.22	443.20	495.14
8.0	345.54	463.86	474.84	533.48
9.0	372.12	504.36	520.83	589.55
10.0	409.56	555.72	577.68	653.10

Table 4

Minimum Cost of Individual Hem Equipment Sub-System

(*Lakh Rupees*)

Produc-tion	*Truck*		*Shovel*		*Drill*		*Dozer*	
(M.T.)	*Capacity (T)*	*Cost*	*Capacity (Cum.)*	*Cost*	*Capacity (MM Dia)*	*Cost*	*Model*	*Cost*
1.0	15.00	47.70	0.90	12.12	100.00	3.94	D80-12	13.52
2.0	25.00	89.70	1.91	24.80	100.00	3.94	D80-12	10.14
3.0	25.00	128.70	1.91	39.68	150.00	4.44	D80-12	16.90
4.0	25.00	175.50	0.90	48.48	150.00	4.44	D80-12	20.28

5.0	35.00	222.30	2.29	64.64	269.00	5.49	D80-12	23.66
6.0	35.00	257.40	2.29	90.48	269.00	5.49	D80-12	23.66
7.0	50.00	327.82	4.60	129.30	269.00	10.98	D80-12	27.04
8.0	50.00	345.54	4.60	146.54	269.00	10.98	D80-12	30.42
9.0	50.00	372.12	4.60	163.78	269.00	16.17	D80-12	37.18
10.0	50.00	409.56	4.60	181.02	269.00	21.96	D80-12	40.56

Table 5

Optimum Number of Heavy Earth Moving Equipment (Units)

Production (*M.T.*)	*Truck Capacity* (*I*)	*Number*	*Shovel Capacity* (*Cum.*)	*Number*	*Drill Dia* (*M.M.*)	*Dozer* (*Model*)	*Number*
1.0	15.00	09	2.29	02	100.00	D80 12	03
2.00	25.00	14	2.29	04	100.00	D80-12	04
3.00	25.00	20	2.29	07	150.00	D80-12	05
4.00	25.00	27	2.29	09	150.00	D80-12	06
5.00	35.00	26	4.60	10	269.00	D80-12	07

6.00	35.00	30	4.60	12	269.00	D80-12	07
7.00	50.00	23	4.60	14	269.00	D80-12	08
8.00	50.00	27	4.60	17	269.00	D80-12	09
9.00	50.00	30	4.60	19	269.00	D80-12	11
10.00	50.00	33	4.60	20	269.00	D80-12	12

15

Materials Cost Estimating

Phillip F. Ostwald, Patrick J. Toole***

Abstract

Recently years have witnessed various inflation rates for processed raw materials, shortages of key materials, and difficulties due to substantial material lists have complicated the once relatively easy task of materials cost estimating. Standard cost schemes, which are the primary management plans for estimating raw materials, have been woefully inadequate. This paper reports on eight methods that are useful policies for picking a material cost. Categorized into point-in-time, contractual, and out-of-pocket costs, the methods lead to different results with an identical problem. One method is introduced for the first time and widespread consideration by industry is encouraged.

* Professor of Mechanical and Industrial Engineering Department of Mechanical Engineering, University of Colorado.

** Bell Telephone Laboratory, Homedel, New Jersey.
(Reprinted with permission from Proceedings 1979 Fall Industrial Engineering Conference, AIIE).

Introduction

This paper summarizes eight policies for assigning a cost to a particular material used in the job estimated. The complexities of this problem are first reviewed. The policies or methods are previewed, and a specific problem having costs, requirements, and inventory levels is formulated. Each method is discussed within the context of this problem. The last method presented is new and widespread consideration by industry is encouraged.

Background to Problem

The initial problem in cost estimating materials is to separate the problem into two steps, i.e., (1) find the shape requirements and (2) multiply that by the cost per unit shape. The term shape or mass, or area, or length, etc., implies various engineering dimensions. There is variety in the ways to calculate shape along with an allowance for scrap, waste, and shrinkage, but the focus of this paper is on the second step : that of finding the materials cost per unit shape.

Uncertainty in price has been a factor of increased importance since 1972 due to higher rates of inflation. Some companies have encountered financial losses after seeing their raw material costs escalate rapidly. For years, the inflation rate for materials has been considered "acceptable at three per cent or less", but during the 1972-73 period many companies watched their materials cost escalate approximately 30%. The standard cost plan used for product pricing was unable to keep pace, and because of a materials variance profits plunged. In some companies standard costs are used because of inter-divisional transfer pricing which requires prices to remain constant for a fiscal year or some other appropriate accounting period. Reliance upon standard cost procedures designed for more stable periods of inflation is the uncomfortable lesson of these experiences.

The material costing problem is important in other aspects.

When considering bills of materials, finishes, standard and non-standard designs, and recalling the size of inventories of direct and indirect materials, it is not surprising to find companies that have an active material list of many millions of part numbers. Inventories are extensive, thus complicating the finding of costs for materials in an estimate.

A vertically integrated company, i.e., copper ore to wire, has the problem of identifying ore and inter-mediate values of processed material. Because of the commodity behaviour of the cost of raw materials, a cost estimating policy can become complicated. Few models exist to select a material cost estimate for companies of this type.

Billing practices for materials have undergone a change in recent years due to inflation and outdated techniques in cost estimating. For instance, materials are estimated with a provision for potential billbacks. Some governmental contractors use a "quote or price in effect" method due to various regulations. Provisions exist for covering material cost increases.

Many estimating functions have been unable to cope with the problem of picking a cost value for a material. Cost estimates using accounting systems, engineering code classifications, vendors, government indexes, and shared professional, consulting or association information can add to the bewilderment of picking a cost value. The purpose of this paper is to provide a taxonomy of methods for the materials estimate problem, i.e., what is the cost per unit for the material.

Distinctions between Manufacturing and Contracting Estimates

A manufacturing firm may build a product from a continuously replenished inventory, while a contracting firm may not order materials until the bid has been won. For cost estimation purposes, the differences between manufacturing and contracting firms are to some extent superficial. For example, a job shop firm or a contractor will often not order many of its materials until a particular job is won, and a manufacturing firm may special order materials in building prototypes even though the equipment may be unsold at the time. The methods that follow are intended to suit the needs of both manufacturing and contracting.

The horizontal axis is time. The time units may represent days, weeks, years, etc. The present is to be time 0 and is labelled "E" to designate it as the time of the estimate. Negative integers are past time epochs and positive integers are future time epochs. If the estimate wins material is purchased explicitly for tbe job in addition to other requirements for this materials. Point B is the buy time for the material knowing that the estimate wins. Point D is the delivery time for the product. The vertical axis represents units of quantity of the material. The three functions designated by TS, TU and JJ are defined as follows :

TS (t) = Total supply of the material time t

TU (t) = total usage of the material, time t

JJ (t) = job J usage of the material, time t

These step functions will be used to obtain different estimates for the unit material cost for Job J.

To the right of point 0, each of the functions represent estimates. The step sizes on each of the integers $t=0, \pm 1, \pm 2, \ldots\ldots$, for the functions TU and JJ represent the material used in production during the period (t-1, t). The step sizes on each of the integers t for the function TS represent the quantity of inventory arriving at time t. Hence the inventory at time $t=0, \pm 1, \pm 2, \ldots$ is the difference between the functions TS and TU during the period (t, t½1).

In this example it is assumed that the total usage curve, TU, is comprised of the job J curve, JJ, plus other jobs. For example, at $t=4$, job J uses 50% of the total for the period, and at $t=5$ job J uses 100%. Material estimates are made assuming job J is won because, as will be expanded on in the next section, quantity discounts are assumed to exist for material purchases.

The inventory supply curve TS does not follow a pre-established review and re-order discipline such as a recorder point system or a periodic review system. As customarily found in estimating it is assumed to depend on factors external to the information presented. A fixed lead time of one period is assumed for all order.

Projecting Unit Costs

Table 1 displays historical and projected unit costs the firm uses for purchasing the material. Price breaks are available for various quantity lots. Two methods will be reviewed for projecting units costs in each of the price break categories. The second of these methods is the one used to derive the projected unit costs of Table 1.

A moving average projection method establishes, as an estimate of the future cost of one or more periods, the average of the present plus a number of immediately preceding period costs. After a period has elapsed a new average is calculated by stopping the oldest cost and adding in the lowest. For example, at time -2, a three period moving average for the 1—2 purchase range would be

$(10.00+10.70+11.10)/3=10.60$, and at time 0 the same average be

$(11.10+11.25+12.00)/3=11.45$.

Moving averages are useful when the data does not show any forecastable trend.

The linear regression trend is used when a linear trend is

Table 1

Historical and Projected Material Unit Costs

		Quantity			
	Period	*1—2*	*3—4*	*5—6*	*7—8*
	−4	10.00	8.00	7.00	6.50
	−3	10.70	8.60	7.50	7.00
Historical		11.10	8.95	7.80	7.20
	−1	11.25	9.00	7.90	7.30
	0	12.00	9.65	8.40	7.85
	1	12.95	10.01	8.73	8.12
	2	12.97	10.44	9.10	8.46
	3	13.52	10.89	9.49	8.83
Projected	4	14.10	11.36	9.89	9.20
	5	14.69	11.84	10.32	9.60
	6	15.31	12.35	10.75	10.01

apparent from the data (for a more sophisticated analysis, see Ref. 3). After plotting the data in Table 1 for each of the price break categories for t—4, −3, −2, −1, 0, the following linear model is established.

$$\ln P(t) = a + b\,(t+4)$$

where P(t) is the unit material price projection at time t. This relationship is reasonable assuming a constant rate of inflation 1+a, because in that case

$$P(t) = P(-4)\,(1+a)^{t+4}$$

Using standard statistical techniques we estimate a and b using the five years of available data. The resulting projected material unit costs are given below the line in Table 1. While Table 1 is simplistic, the real situation will have only a few historical costs for various periods and quantity. For any time period, the company will consolidate all of its requirements into a single purchase order, and not have actual historical values for the other quantities. Moreover some periods may not require any purchase. More advanced methods than the one used here are able to complete all missing entries for Table 1.

A Preview of the Methods

The eight policies to be used for selecting a material cost may be categorical into three groups :

I. Point-in-Time Costs

(a) Original

(b) Last

(c) Current

(d) Lead Time Replacement

(e) Delivery

II. Contractual Costs

(a) Quotation

(b) Quote or Price-in-Effect

III. Money-out-of-Pocket

These eight methods deal with the class of "processed materials". Commodity, semi-processed, and normative materials are other classes. Processed materials are former commodities which have received substantial engineering conversion, iron ore to pigs to hot rolled and pickled A.I.S.I. 1020 48×120 in. steel sheets. Commodity examples are food-stuffs, precious metals, timber, and extracted ores such as iron or copper. Semi-processed and commodity materials have erratic price behaviour and accurate projection of these material costs is uncertain at best. The difficulties of predicting future prices of commodities are well known. Semi processed material, insofar as its cost value is concerned, behaves as either a processed or commodity material. Copper wire is an example, several years ago roller coaster prices on the world market were commonplace. Nowadays copper costs have flip-flopped from a commodity into the process material class, i.e., increasing cost at a near-constant slope. Certainly, South Africa, a major producer of copper ore and processed copper, have stabilized the price of copper, but dumping and a world-price war could once again resume. Neither do these eight methods deal with the normative class of raw materials. Best known examples of normative materials are oil, which is price-administered by OPEC, and price-fixing or price control of key materials by various governments.

Policies to Pick Cost of Materials

Some of these policies were developed by the accounting profession for the purpose of inventory valuation necessitated by tax and ownership laws. However, accounting practices have different goals than estimating and caution must be exercised. Furthermore, the many accounting systems, often called standard cost, job or lot or process costs, are procedures and are not necessarily deliberate policies to estimate a future cost for materials. The methods to follow do include as special cases many standard industrial cost procedures which emphasize a predetermined value for the material. The accounting methods involved in job, lot, or process cost systems are not discussed because their basic function is to assess the material cost after production, which is not the basic estimating problem. Remember estimating is concerned with the cost value prior to the spending of money; by simple contrast, accounting is concerned with the money actually spent.

Original Cost

This method assumes that materials are used in the order they are received and establishes as a cost estimate the unit cost of the oldest material in inventory. The oldest material sustained in stock at time E came from a lot of six purchased at time −2. From Table 1 the unit cost is $7.80. Commonly called FIFO, this method has been popularized by the accounting profession for inventory valuation purposes.

Last Cost

The Last Cost method assumes that the latest materials purchased are the first to be used and esablishes as a cost estimate the unit cost of the most recent material in inventory. The most recent material in stock at time E come from a lot of six purchased at time −1. From Table 1 the unit cost is $7.90. This method, also called LIFO, is frequently used by the accounting profession.

Current Cost

A unit cost at time 0 is used in this method as the value of the estimate and thus is time coincident to the establishment of the estimate. If price breaks exist, a lot size must be determined before an estimate is figured. For example, if the purchase lot is assumed to be 5 at time 0 the estimate from Table 1 is $8.40/unit.

Lead-Time Replacement Cost

This concept adopts as an estimate the replacement cost of the first lot of the material a the time it arrives. This is commonly called the next-in-first-out method (NIFO) even though this label is obviously an anomaly. Suppose in Figure 1 that the estimate is won and a lot of eight is ordered at time 1. Since there is a lead time requirement of one period, the order arrived at time 2 and the unit cost estimate from Table 1 is $10.44. This concept is used by product estimators where material renewable are significant.

Delivery Cost

The point in time at which the product is delivered to the customer establishes the value for the estimate. As in the above methods, a lot size must be assumed if price breaks in material purchasing are significant.

Quotation Cost

The Quotation Cost method is perhaps the most widely practiced by job shops and contractors. The cost of the material is established by a vendor. This method is similar to the lead time replacement cost given above, except that the vendor makes the forecasts, perhaps similar to Table 1. Then the unit price would be $8.46 for a lot of 8 at time 2. The delivery price quoted is considered fixed for a specified period of time.

Quote or Price-in-Effect

Known for many years, this concept has become increasingly popular during recent years of high inflation and rapidly escalating material prices. A collaborative legal agreement between the buyer and seller is usually established which allows for adjustment to the original price should the seller incur material costs in excess of those estimated. If any material costs fall below or remain at their estimate, the buyer agrees to the original price and adjustment is unnecessary. If at the time of delivery of the product the seller can prove that the material costs incurred were in excess of the original estimated value, the buyer will make up the difference via formula or full cost allowances. A simplification of the quote or price-in-effect contract exists. On published price sheets, the seller may state the exception footnote "Price subject to change without prior notice." The quote or price-in-effect method may avoid the often difficult problem of making accurate forecasts; however, competition and bidding may not allow the luxury of this policy.

Money-Out-of-Pocket Cost

Money-out-of-Pocket refers to a general class of techniques in which the overriding philosophy is to have the estimate reflect actual material expenditure. If the material is purchased in a single lot, the estimate would simply be the unit cost of the lot. If the material is taken from inventory, the estimate would be the original purchase cost of the material use. If the material is to be purchased in the future, a forecast of the unit price to be realized would be used. If the material for the estimate is used from several inventories where each renewal is at a different cost, a cost model is necessary. Our method is a specific implementation of the Out-of-Pocket concept. In the example of the material for job J is actually taken from a number of past and future inventory purchases. Our method accounts for forecasted usage of the material in as accurate a manner as possible. Suppose at time t we have n(t) lots of the material in inventory, which were purchased at times $t._j$; J=1, 2, ... , n(t). At time t define

$f(t_j)$ = the fraction of the material inventory coming from the time t_j lot

$p(t_j)$ = unit cost of the t_j lot

d(t) = number of units of the material used for job J at time t.

The estimated unit materials cost is

$$\sum_{t} \sum_{j=1}^{n(t)} p\,(t_j)\, f\,(t_j) d_j\,(t) / \sum_{t} d_j\,(t)$$

To demonstrate the use of this formula, consider and the data in the following table.

Table 2

Values Used for Problem Removed from Table 1

Time	*Units of Inventory Delivered*	*Unit Price of Inventory Delivered*	*Units of Inventory of All Jobs*	*Units of Inventory for job J*
−2	6	$7.80	2	—
−1	6	7.90	4	—
0	0	—	3	—
1	2	12.95	0	—
2	0	—	4	2
3	2	13.52	2	1
4	0	—	2	1
5	6	10.32	1	1
6	0	—	4	3

We see if the 4 units total usage of period 2, one unit can be considered as purchased at −2 time for $7.78/unit and 3 units purchased at −1 time for $7.90/unit. The dash horizontal lines of relate the time of inventory purchase to time of usage. Under the out-of-pocket cost method, the 2 units of Job J usage for the 2nd period would be costed as

$$\left[7.80\times\frac{1}{4}+7.90\times\frac{3}{4}\right]\times 2=\$15.75.$$

The remaining periods of production for Job J (t=3,4,5,6) are similarly costed as

$$(7.90)\times 1+\left(7.90\times\frac{1}{2}+12.95\times\frac{1}{2}\right)\times 1$$
$$+(12.95)\times 1+\left(13.52\times\frac{1}{2}+10.32\times\frac{1}{2}\right)$$
$$\times 3=\$67.04$$

Lost cost for Job J is $82.79 and for the lot quantity of 8, unit cost=$10.35.

Conclusions

Table 3 summarizes the estimated unit costs of raw material. The out-of-pocket cost method is, we contend, superior to other methods.

Table 3

Unit Cost Estimates Depending upon Method

Method	*Value Adopted for Estimate*
Original	$ 7.80
Last	$ 7.90
Current	$ 8.40
Lead Time Replacement	$ 10.44
Delivery	$ 12.35
Quotation	$ 8.46
Quote or Price in Effect	
Money-out-of-Pocket	$ 10.35

*Cannot be established without further assumptions.

16

Methods to Keep Energy Expenditure Within Bounds

*N.N. Apsingekar**

Introduction

In spite of introduction of modern, mire sophisticated machines and automation in today's industrial age, manual labour at various level is predominant. At operator/worker has to perform his job either in push button environment, such as operating a control panel board, or he may have to do manual and clerical job. In this situation, man is a dominent factor in design of job. Any job, either manual or clerical, should be so designed that it best suits the operator, taking into account physiological and psychological factors. Physiological characteristics, which relate to Anthropometry, is vital in producing least effort, more confort to operator and in turn resulting in less energy expenditure. Energy which a man spreads in doing his job has a direct bearing on the total output or production. Nevertheless, energy is expended in any work situation, but the important point is that, in a man-

* Asst. Indl. Engineer, HAL, Nasik.

machine system any equipment, layouts, design of work place are so designed that they best suit the operator, i.e. they take full advantage of man's capability and his potential talent. The benefits possessed by such a man-machine system are : (a) Analyse work situation in order to optimise the physiological cost of performing operation. (b) Minimise the time required to carry out the operation. (c) Maximise product quality per rupee of cost. (d) Maximise business profit. (e) Strive for continuous growth of the concern. (f) Optimise, welfare safety and comfort of the employee. (g) Minimise the operating cost.

Measurement of Physiological Stress

When the physiological cost of doing the work exceeds the reasonable limits, result is some undesirable cost to, or reaction upon the individual. These sources of stress may be physiological, such as heavy work, noise, vibration or may be psychological, such as information overload, sleep loss, etc. Measures of physiological stress are—chemical-blood content, oxygen consumption, etc. Electrical-electromyograph (EMG), physical-blood pressure, heart rate, etc. measures of psychological stress are—activity—work rate error, etc., attitude-boredom, etc.

Energy Possessed by a Man

It is estimated that a normal man can give a maximum energetic output of 4800 cal. per day, out of which he requires nearly 2300 cal. per day, for basal metabolism and leisure, which leaves to him, a 2500 cal. per day for performing his work, taking normal value of 2000 cal. per day (4.2 K cal. per minute). Any work activity should be kept below this value for effective performance. For instance, when a brush painting a ceiling, the arm held over the head soon tires, because of insufficient blood flow into the contracted muscles. One should stop periodically in order to overcome fatigue and to allow flow of blood into the contracted muscles, while at work, the oxygen which comes either from blood or chemical compound within muscle fibre, if one's ability to supply sufficient oxygen during work, to these muscle fibres to prevent the bi-product of metabolism is termed as 'Aerobic' and if the job which prevents the reserve of blood into muscle or muscles the assignment is termed as 'Anaerobic'. The ill effects of this An-aerobic are, muscle pain and phychological fatigue and muscle weakness.

In order to give numerical values of energy expenditure for different physical activities, it is necessary to present physiological cost of performing every activity, such as sleeping, sitting and walking. For example, to walk a distance of 1.6 kilometer at a speed of 8.1 km. per hour, increases the heart rate and requires a period of recovery of 3 minutes. The heart rate and recovery period increases substantially with higher values of speed in km. per hour. This shows that physiological price of work per unit of work is greater at high rates than the moderate rates.

The factors which influences energy expenditure are: (a) Type and magnitude of load to be lifted. (b) Design of equipment. (c) Design of seating. (d) Strength of arm and muscles—grip strength, turning strength, etc. (e) Work place layout (f) Design of controls, displays, etc. (g) Rest pauses and allowances (h) Physical environment, such as temperature, lighting, thermal conditions, etc.

Methods to Overcome Energy Expenditure

It has been stated that a man requires about 4.2 K.cal. per minute of energy to do his work. At any time, if the work level exceeds this given value there must be rest to compensate for excess. In this connection Murrell presents a formula for total amount of rest required for any given activity depending on its average energy cost.

$$R = \frac{T(K-S)}{K-1.5}$$

Where R = Rest required in minutes.

T = Total working time.

K = Average K.Cal. per minute of work and

S = Kilo Cal. per minutes adopted as standard.

The value of 1.5 is an approximation of the resting level in K.Cal. per minutes.

Table No. 1 shows the amount of energy expenditure required in cal. per minutes and oxygen consumption in litres per minutes for different levels of activity.

Table No. 2 shows energy expenditure in cal. per minute for different postures of picking a light object from the ground level.

Design of Working Area & Seatings

Many of the assembly work, clerical work and other operations are performed on the table, either in sitting-standing position. To reach beyond this area involves trunk movements. For repetitive operations these trunk movements are fatiguing and require more energy. All the tools supplies, materials, etc. are arranged within this working limits to avoid fatigueing.

The seat design is of utmost importance for any manual or clerical operations. For best results the table height should be 7.5—8 cms. below the elbow. Chair and table are so designed that they can be adjusted in relation to the elbow. The seating design should permit maximum comfort and minimum fatigue to operator without cutting into flesh. This is necessary to prevent contraction of muscles and stoppage of flow of blood. The design of seating will depend on height, length, width and shape of the seat and on the height of back-rest. Following points have to be kept in mind while designing a seat : (a) Seat should not be too high. (b) Avoid cutting into flesh. (c) Avoid unsatisfactory posture.

Strength and Forces of Body Movements

These are essential in designing machines and tools,

where the operators do not require abnormal strength causing him to be soon tired. If the rate of contraction of muscle and muscle group is low enough, it can work indefinitely, but at higher rates it can become fatigued and should be avoided. Other factors, such as (a) load to be lifted by different age group should be within the specified limits, for example, male in the age bracket of 14-16, 16-18, 18-20, 35-50 and over 50 should lift 15 kgs., 19 kgs., 23 kgs., 20 kgs., and 16 kgs. respectively in order to avoid fatigueing. (b) Work pace and energy cost in lifting (c) grip strength (d) turning strength (e) pushing and pulling (f) lifting action (g) sex (h) age, etc. should also be considered.

Design of Equipment

Any equipment design should start from an operator who has to operate, control the equipment around him and can see what is going on. An ergonomic check list given below will help in designing any equipment :

(a) What role is the operator expected to play ?

(b) How will equipment suit the operator ?

(c) Whether operator can sit and stand properly in doing the operations ?

(d) Whether the equipment is likely to be handled partly or fully by women ?

(e) What type of information does an operator need, in doing his job ?

(f) What physical work will the operator have to do ?

(g) What are the conditions affecting his work ?

(h) What type of controls does he need ?

(i) What form of communication will have to take place between operators ?

Design of Controls

Control is a mechanism by means of which an operator conveys his instructions to machines. All controls, such as, hand wheels, cranks levers, pedals, push buttons, joy sticks and other control devices should be readily accessible to the operator and so designed as to give him maximum mechanical advantages and to utilise strongest muscle group and manipulate them with great proficiency, confort and with least fatigue. The type of controls to be used in particular situation is influenced by its relation to the body. The movement which an operator to called upon to make should be in the direction following the free movement, which a limb will make.

Rest Pauses & Allowances

These are essential in recovering from physiological and psychological fatigue, as they : (a) increase the amount of work without exhausting more energy. (b) They break-up the monotony. (c) Reduce the amont of time off taken during working operations. (d) Reduce rest pauses and allowances, the fatigue on operator and decrease variation in output and tend to maintain the optimum level.

Physical Environment

This has a significant impact not only on operators's performance but also on the reliability of the process. The major environmental factors that influence the productivity of personnel and dependability of the process include visual environment, noise, vibration, humidity, temperature and atmospheric conditions. Defective illumination and ventilation have long been recognised as important factor responsible for operator fatigue, poor quality of product, low output, etc. It is pointed out that failure to provide lighting will increase consumption of body energy. Table No. 3 shows recommended values of illumination for difierent tasks. When an operator is subjected to thermal, environment, his performance deviates substantially. Three types of temperature of working environment are : (a) convection, viz. conduction from hot or cold floor or tools, the radiation exchange from floor, walls, ceilings, etc. (b) Effective temperature—which includes temperature, air movement, humidity. (c) Operative temperature, viz. body temperature.

In fact, man's heart rate, oxygen consumption and body temperature are co-related to energy expenditure. When an operative is subjected to heat load, measurement of environment and person is necessary. Measurement of heat on person involves heat rate, oxygen consumption and body temperature. It should be seen that heat load should not cause an increase in the pulse rate of 15 beats per minute and combination of work load and environment should not cause an increase in pulse rate of 45 beats per minute above normal rate. An increase in body temperature should not be more than normal which is 37.1°C (98.6°F). The other methods, such as principles of motion economy, use of right type of display and comparability of equipment should be taken into account.

Conclusion

In short, man has to work in the (a) general environment —light, heat, cold, humidity, noise and vibration. (b) The immediate surroundings—control, display, design, comparability, layout, etc. and other factors—age, training, motivation, duration of work and rest activity are all important in keeping energy within bounds. These are important ingredients of successful work design, and any one who sets out to study a particular situation should take them into account.

Table 1

Energy Expenditure req. in cal/min. & O_2 Consumption for Different Level of Activity

Level of Activity	*Energy Expenditure req. in Cal/min.*	*Oxygen Consumption Ltrs/min.*
A. Unduly heavy (Carrying mortar upstairs @ 16.45 mtrs/min.)	Over 12.5	2.5 and above
B. Very Heavy (Shovelling charge into furnace)	10—12.5	2.0—2.5
C. Heavy (Carrying Load Upstairs @ 8.22 mtrs/min)	7.5—10	1.5—2.0
D. Moderate (Wheel Borrowing Sand @ 67 mtrs/min)	0.5—7.5	1.0—1.5
E. Light	2.5—5.0	0.5—1.0
F. Very Light (Bench work)	0—2.5	0—0.5

Table 2

	Activity	*Energy Expenditure cal/min.*
1.	Bending—Arm Supported by thigh	2.5—3.0
2.	Bending—No arms Support	3.0—3.5
3.	Kneeling—Hand Supported by floor	1.5—2.0
4.	Kneeling—No hand Support	2.0—2.5
5.	Squatting	1.5—2.0

Table 3

General Recommended Values of Illumination

	Task	*Foot Candle on Service i.e. on tank or 75 cms (above floor)*
1.	Most difficult seeing tank	200—1000
2.	Very difficult seeing tank	100
3.	Difficult critical seeing tank	50
4.	Ordinary seeing tank	30
5.	Casual seeing tank	10
6.	Rough seeing tank	5

Table

General recommended values of illumination

		[illegible]
1.	[illegible] seeing task	[illegible]
2.	Very difficult seeing task	[illegible]
3.	[illegible] critical seeing task	[illegible]
4.	Ordinary seeing task	[illegible]
5.	Casual seeing task	[illegible]
6.	Rough seeing task	[illegible]

17

Forest Movement for Food, Fodder, Fuel, Fertilizer and Fibre

*K. Chandramouli**

Perhaps the first Forest Movement (Green Movement) against the indiscriminate felling of trees was fought in India in the year 1730. The leader of this movement, like the Rani of Jhansi in the war of Independence, was a woman but not a queen. Amrita Devi with her 362 followers, both men and women, resisted the felling of Khejori trees in Jodhpur area. The contractor/businessman with his band of workers, enraged at the resistance, fixed the 363 people to death. It was only later on that the ruler of Jodhpur ordered that no green trees should be cut. In the recent few years, a big 'mela' is held every year near the memorial for these first martyrs. It may also be noted that the Bishnoi sect in Rajasthan treat the trees as their own children.

In recent times, the first of such organised movements was

* Superintendent, Indian Aluminium Company Limited, Belgaum.

started in December 1972 in what has now become famous as "Chipko Movement" (Cling to Movement). Strangely enough it was once again the women who took the lead in the movement which started in Tehri-Garhwal district of U.P., in the foot-hills of Himalayas. Whenever the forest contractors/businessman came to the hills to cut the trees, the local women would run around and cling to the tree trunks and embrace them. Then they would throw a challenge to the tree fellers by shouting "You will cut the trees only after cutting us off." These simple rustic folks had a simple argument to which no direct answer was possible : "You have not planted the trees. These trees are natural growth and are here because we spread them while cutting grass. These trees are protecting us against landslides. You have no right to cut them". Contractors took up the fight to the legal chambers in Lucknow but the movement continued under the leadership of Sri Sundarlal Bahuguna and became famous as the "Chipko Movement". The same movement has been continued since 1972 in various villages, like Advani (in 1977), and Budhekar (1980) of Tehri Garhwal.

Believe It Or Not

It may be surprising to note that many of the deserts that we see today were greeneries or thick forests a few centuries back. The following facts look stranger than fiction and can easily go into Riplev's "Believe it or not" book

> There is evidence that the Harappans laid waste many forests to expand their pastures and Farm lands, a factor which might have led to the floods and hastened the decline of the Indus Valley Civilisation.
>
> The bald hillocks of Syria and Lebanon were once having a thick growth of green forest cover.
>
> Persians were conducting water in underground canals about 400 Kms in length to fertile wheat fields now have become parched deserts.

In the recent past nearly one crore sq. cms. of land (an area larger than the whole of Brazil) has been turned into desert It is feared that in the next 20 years nearly thrice the above area will be converted into desert.

Only 12% of the once lush island of Java is left with tree cover and that in Philippines, forest cover is today less than 20% of the country's land area and not 33% to 50% as in commonly assumed. In Northern Thailand forests are being decimated at the rate of 5% to 7% a year. In Pakistan although 8.2 million hectares are classified as forest only 2.6 hectares are actually wooded.

According to FAO and UNESCO, during the last 30 years the destruction of forest in Latin America has been 36.6%, South East Asia 38%, Africa 52%, India, Srilanka and Burma 63.3%.

Nearly 30% of forest cover in the foothills of Himalayas, particularly in Nepal, have been denuded. People from Nepal are migrating towards Western U.P.

Cherrapunji, once the place with the heaviest rainfall in the country, is showing signs of becoming a desert with the receding tree cover and increasing baldness.

Presently India retains only 20% of its forest cover which it had about a century back. In the last 25 years (1951-76) India has lost 4.1 million hectares of forest area. (Details of Forest Area Appendix-I).

Reasons for Deforestation

Reasons for large scale deforestation are mainly three :

(i) Over the past several centuries, there has been an ever increasing pressure of human and animal population on forest and pasture lands in search of fuel and fodder.

India consumes nearly 135-170 million tonnes of firewood annually and 10-15 million hectares of forest cover is being stripped every year to meet the minimum fuel needs of urban rural poor.

Consumption of non-commercial fuel (firewood, animal dung, vegetable wastes, etc.) in India has come down from 67.6% of the total energy needs (1953) to about 35% in 1980. However actual firewood consumption has gone up from 86.3 million tonnes in 1953 to about 135 million tonnes in 1980, indicating the pressure on forests.

(ii) Indiscriminate clearing of forests normally goes unnoticed and when noticed it is branded as the most justified human need.

In the past 20 years (1951 to 1971) forests have been indiscriminately cut to give way for agricultural purposes (24.32 lakh hectares), river valley projects (4.01 lakh hectares), industrial purposes (1.24 lakh hectares), construction of roads (0.55 lakh hectares), and for other miscellaneous purposes (3.88 lakh hectares). As a total 3.4 million hectares of forests were lost between the years 1951 and 1971. Details of the State-wise forest area lost in 25 years are shown in Appendix-I.

(iii) There has been an over-exploitation of forests by commercial interests.

Nearly 42% of the annual recorded wood production goes for industrial uses and the rest is used as fuel.

Industrial wood requirement, which in 1970 was 15.9 million cub. mts. is estimated at 25 million cub. mtrs. in 1980 and 40 million cub. mtrs. in 1990. To meet this demand it would be necessary to convert nearly 100000 hectares into new plantations annually.

Against a requirement for industrial wood at 15.9 million cub. mtrs. in 1970, the production recorded was only 8.92 million cub. mtrs. Obviously the difference was met by imports and unrecorded sources.

Demand for fuelwood from 2000 AD is estimated at 225 million cub. mtrs. whereas the availabiliiy is estimated at only 33.5 million cub. mtrs. Therefore the gap would be 192 million cub. mtrs. (152 million tonnes) and afforestation required to bridge this gap will be 20 million hectares per year.

As a result of indiscriminate cutting of forest nearly 1% of the land surface of the country is being laid bare every year. 23% of the land surface (about 75 million hectares in 1976) is supposed to be covered by forests. But out of this area nearly 42 million hectares have been almost completely denuded of tree cover and these areas are forests for the name sake only. Actually only 12-15% of the land surface is under tree cover.

Effects of Deforestation

Effects of deforestation can be put in the following simple terms easily understandable by everyone.

(i) Deforestation leads of uncontrolled wing erosion.

Studies have indicated that one of the possible reasons why moisture-laden clouds pass over western Rajasthan withont precipitating their burden on its is the fine dust suspended in the air over the desert. This dust is, of course, the direct result of wind erosion caused by deforestation.

In the Himalayan ranges annual rainfall has declined by 3 to 4% due to deforestation.

(ii) Deforestation leads to erosion of the top soil by water, which undoubtedly constitutes the most serious threat to our land resources.

Quantity of topsoil displaced by water erosion alone is estimated at 6000 miliion tonnes every year. "The Wealth of the Himalayan is disappearing to the Bay of Bengal" according to Sri Sundarlal Bahuguna leader of "Chipko Movement".

6 million tonnes of soil nutrients are being swept into the sea along with the top soil due to floods mostly caused by denued forest area. This figure is 12% more than all the fertilisers used in the country. It was estimated in 1972 that soil nutrients swept away to the sea represented a loss (in terms of NPK alone) that would require 5.37 million tonnes of inorganic fertilisers to replace at a cost of Rs. 700 crores.

Ravines and gullied lands are the direct sults of water erosion. It is estimated that there are 3.7 million hectares of ravines and gullied lands in our country. It is also estimated that nearly 8000 hectares of land is degenerating into ravinces every year.

Waterlogging an increased salinity are mostly the outcome of poor drainage in areas covered by massive irrigation projects. It is estimated that 13 million hectares are affected by waterlogging and salinity.

(iii) Water erosion, due to deforestation, has a number of extremely deleterious side effects apart from reducing the fertility of the land directly affected by it. Thus it leads to the situation of reservoirs and tanks, the chocking of estuaries and harbours, the occurence of floods and finally to the loss to the sea of a great deal of priceless sweet water.

The premature siltation of our 5 lakh odd tanks and of the 487 reservoirs of our major and medium irrigation and multipurpose projects, on which the community has invested over Rs. 10000 crores during the last three decades, is a particularly serious matter.

Average rate of sedimentation in most of the reservoirs is 4 to 6 times as high as the rate which was assumed at the time of design. Hence, life expectancy of these projects is being reduced significantly by soil erosion. In most cases three will be no alternative sites for dams once the existing once are rendered useless. This means that even if we have the money to build fresh projects we shall not have the physical lands to do so.

Flood can be treated as a direct consequence of deforestation and water erosion. Floods occur because a great deal of the soil which is washed down from water-sheds gets lodged in the beds of rivers and reduces their carrying capacity.

Flood damages cost the country Rs. 21 crores in 1951 and increased to Rs. 1130 crores in 1977. Flood damage costs averaged at Rs. 126 crores per year during the decade 1960-70 and increased to Rs. 739 crores per year during the decade 1970-80. Out of the damages during the decade 1970-80, the crop damages accounted for Rs. 440 crores per year (59.5%) and non crop damages accounted for Rs. 299 crores per year (40.5%). In 1981, area affected due to floods was 3.07 million hectares. Area affected has doubled during the decade 1970-80.

If the problem of water erosion and floods is not tackled in time, it is not difficult to imagine a situation in which the increasingly frequent and intense floods may result in the rise in the level of river beds and large portions of the rich flat lands of the Ganga basin may be turned into undrainable swamps.

Soil erosion plays havoc with our water resources. This is so because the run-off of rain water from denuded surfaces is far greater than from slopes which are well-wooded and well-grassed. This means that a great deal of the water which would otherwise have been retained as subsoil or ground water is lost to the sea, often after causing a great deal of damage in the process. This is the reasons why springs and artesian wells dry up whenever extensive denudation takes place.

Fully recharged ground water aquifers play a most significant part in contributing to river flows during lean months. Both floods and droughts are thus in reality two sides of the same coin of poor land management.

In summary, it can be said that India's land resources have not been properly utilised and in fact have been badly misused by indiscriminate deforestation, inadequate attention to the environmental consequences of construction activities, poor land and water resources management and overgrazing and other biotic interference.

Appendix-II gives an idea of the present status of land resources of the country. It should be noted that this poor state of affairs is mainly due to lack of any Land and Water Resource Management in the past centuries.

Price TAG for Forests

It may be understandable if the common man does not realise the bad effects of deforestation but it is unpardonable if, even at the national level, there is not much of awareness about the price being paid by us for meeting our immediate requirements. An attempt is made as shown in Appendix-III & IV to attach a price tag for the forests in order to create an awareness of the calamity we are facing. As per this calculation total losses due to deforestation is estimated at Rs. 16400 crores per year and the price tag for forests at 10 times the looses can be taken as Rs. 164000 crores. However, it may be noted that the losses do not purport to be authentic as the statistical data are not fully available and whatever details available widely differ from source to source.

Therefore it is hightime that our planners, economists, ecology experts seriously view the effects of deforestation which is estimated to cause a hidden damage to the tune of Rs. 164000 crores a year.

What Other Countries Have Done

The problem of deforestration is world-wide and it is interesting to note what other countries have done or continue to do in order to overcome the problems of deforestation.

In Philippines a polybagged seedling of Subabul was distributed to each school teacher in 1976. The teacher planted the seedling and raised it with the assistance of her students. After a year, when seeds were produced, seedlings were grown again for a second year on the school premises. These seedlings were distributed to the students who raised them on the school premises or in their houses. In three years, the extension work was so successful that every house now has substantial trees in its compound.

The Philippines plan to support rural electrification with several wood-fulled power plants. In 1978, it planted an energy forest which will be used to fuel a 75 MW steam power plant. A study has identified 25 potential energy plantation sites with a total area of approximately 320000 hectares. If full planted, these could support 19 wood-fired power plants with an overall generating capacity of 1425 MW.

South area has solved its rural fuel problems by a grass roots programme. As part of the "Saumaul" or new community programme, a forestry schemes was launched in 1973 to mobilise villagers to plant trees in public and private lands, to produce mushrooms and valuable leaves and to establish firewood lots to meet local needs. Owners of suitable lands were given the opinion by the VFA (Village Forestry Association) officials either to reforest the area themselves or turn them over to the VFA in return for a tenth of the proceeds. The harvested wood from the wood lost is distributed among the households and any marketable surplus is put into a co-operatives fund for further community development projects.

In China and Indonesia, too, house gardens supply a good deal of family's fuel and in China about 4.5% of the population is believed to be engaged in social forestry.

For decades floods, droughts and famine were recurring calamities of Fukien Province in China, but in the five years since forests were reestablished in the hills and water-sheds, the inhabitants have lived free from all the three.

China has placed 55 million hectares (nearly 75% of India's existing forest area) under new forests during the last 30 years while in South Korea there is now hardly an acre of denuded land to be seen anywhere. These are the only two countries in the developing world that have been eminently successful in tackling their problems of deforestation, denudation and soil erosion on a wide scale.

For 25 years, steadily expanding fuelwood plantations of Calliandra (a small Central American tree that was imported as a shade and ornamental tree) have been established in Java, until they now cover more than 30000 hectares there. The wood, too small for lumber, is dense, burns well and is ideally sized for domestic cooking. It is also used for fuelling brick, tile and kilns and for copra and tobacco driers. Today Indonesian villagers make good living selling the firewood, earning more from it than from their food crops.

It is a well established Korean practice to plant Leapedeza species along ridges as a firewood crop.

8% of Sweden's energy an 15% of Finland's energy is generated from wood. In USA in 1974, more energy was generated from wood than from nuclear power. An electric generator designed to consume about 25000 dry tonnes of wood fuel each month has recently been installed at the Jari Project in the Brazilian Amazon to power a pulp mill, a saw mill and a township of over 10000 people.

What India Needs To Do

Following suggestions would greatly help in overcoming the catastrophical effects of deforestation : (For details of the various categories of land mentioned below please see Appendix-II)

(i) Increase the tree coverage in the so called forests declared in our statisticai figures.

Presently, out of a declared forest area of 83 million hectares only 35 million hectares are supposed to be having tree coverage. Balance area of 48 million hectares, presently devoid of vegetation, should be planted with trees at a rate of 25000 trees per hectare. This requires active involvement of Forests Departments in the country.

(ii) Convert the degraded land not useful for agricultural purposes into forest land.

Out of a total area of 87 million hectares demarcated as degarded agricultural lands, nearly 43 million hectares are not at all good for agricultural use. At least 60% of this area (25 million hectares) can be converted into forest area at the rate of 2000 trees per hectare.

This again requires the active participation of the Forests and Revenue departments of various States. About 12 million hectares of this area can be given to private institutions on lease for energy plantations.

(iii) Utilise the culturable wastes and fallow lands estimated at 17 million hectares and 23 million hectares respectively.

Estimates have revealed that India has approximately 4 million hectares of gullied lands, 7 million hectares of saline/alkaline lands and 6 million hectares of waterlogged lands. Special types of trees could be planted in these areas.

On a very conservative estimate at least 30% of the cultivable waste and fallow lands amounting to about 12 million hectares can be planted with trees at a rate of 1000 trees per hectare.

Private entrepreneurs, industrialists, companies, institutions and voluntary services organisations like NSS, Rotary, Lions, Giants, Jaycees and others can be given such lands on lease for development in a planned way within a targeted time. Even if each of 5000 and odd service clubs takes an initiative to plant only 10 hectares per year a total of 5000 hectares can be planted every year with trees.

(iv) Plant trees on roadsides, railway lines, canal banks and boundaries of farms.

It is estimated by the National Commission on Agriculture that the land available on the boundaries of farms is about 2.7 million hectares and the land along roadsides, canal banks an railway lines is about 0.9 million hectares. However all the land cannot be utilised effectively and assuming only 15% of the land can be utilised, nearly 0.54 million hectares will be available for tree plantation.

(v) Encourage planning of firewood trees in woodlots around villages, school yards, public buildings, church yards, cementries and market squares etc. Individual institutions, public or private, should be encouraged to take up such jobs. Similarly every household should be encouraged to grow at least 2 trees per house with the slogan "A Tree for Every Child". This can be done with less effort by active interest of the officials, individuals and even by Shramdan camps by students and villagers.

(vi) Test the growth in all the production areas and control the harvesting intensity to improve the forest productivity.

The Dehradun forests which have been scientifically managed get a yield of less than 0.2 cub. mtr. per hectare. The potential yield is at least 20 times this figure. Even with a very conservative increase of 4 times the present yield, the production by 1985 with only 83 million hectares of area can be increased from the present 10 million cub. mtrs. to about 40 million cub. mtrs. This requires not only scientific management but also lot of work by the Forest Departments.

(vii) Impose the present laws strictly to avoid illegal and indiscriminate felling of trees by businessmen/industrialists/rural population. Industries using wood as their raw material should be made to compulsorily plant 20-50 times the number of trees cut by them every year. If necessary they could be leased enough of available land for this purpose.

(viii) Search out and reduce the wasteful use of available fuel by ensuring that the existing wood resources are harvested and used without waste.

This requires testing and developing fuel efficient stoves, particularly ones that villagers can make themselves. Also we will have to seriously think of alternate energy source such as biogas and solar and heat.

(ix) Encourage energy plantation in the industrial and rural sectors.

In the rural sector, it has been estimated that using 18 tonnes of air dry wood it is possible to generate 20000 KWH of electricity daily, for a group of 15 villages. The land required for generating that much electricity would be 145 hectares. In our country, there are 567000 villages. Assuming one unit of fuelwood power generating capacity to be established for every 15 villages, a total of 37800 power generating units on decentralised basis would be required. Total area required for the whole country would therefore be 37800 × 145 or 5 5 million hectares of land.

For details on energy plantation please see Appendix-V. Summary of the suggested Action Plan is given in Appendix-VI.

It may be seen that the suggested action plan envisages a potential for afforestation of 91 million hectares of land and plantation of 36520 crore trees at an average rate of 4000 trees per hectare as against the modern approach of planting about 10000 trees per hectare. This plan may appear to be too difficult to achieve when we see that during the Fifth Five-year Plan only 0.52 million hectares were planted with trees and during the Sixth Plan it is planned to afforest only 1.52 million hectares. Our present plan targets for afforestation of 1.52 million hectares are not taking us anywhere when we realise that our forest cover is being depleted at a galloping rate of more than 1 million hectares every year. Hence it is essential to think of afforestation in a big way and not restrict ourselves to present conservative targets. In order to achieve the target within a reasonable time the entire afforestation of 91 million hectares of land will have to be spread over the next 20 years with an average of 4.5 million hectares per year. This suggestion of afforesting 4.5 million hectares per year is close to the UN report which calls for afforestation of 4 million hectares per year if India is to have the wood energy it needs by the turn of the century.

Investment and Benefits

Various agencies have estimated an expense of Rs. 3000 for afforesting one hectares of land. But in many areas, the saplings get only short time attention and later on goats and animals destroy them. If the saplings grow into trees, in spite of these destructions, then the rural poor will cut off the branches to meet their fuel needs. In order to give more protection that the sapling/trees deserve in a good afforestation scheme, it is essential to provide fencing etc. and the cost per hectare is therefore taken as Rs. 4000. At this cost, the investment per year for afforesting 4.5 million hectares would be Rs. 18000 millions Rs. 1800 crores.

Investment of Rs. 1800 crores per year for afforestation is only a small portion of the expected hidden losses due to deforestation at Rs. 16400 crores per year. Damages due to floods cost the country approximately Rs. 1200 crores every year and the request from the States to the Centre for financial aid for drought and flood relief has been around Rs. 1200 crores in the past few years. The total investment in afforestation will be about 1% of the price tag of Rs. 164000 crores calculated for the forests. Hence an investment of Rs. 1800 crores a year should not look as impractical.

The benefits of afforestation of 4.5 million hectares per year will be as enumerated earlier in various aspects like insurance against floods, droughts, soil erosion, loss of nutrients, creation of ravines and fallow lands, early siltation of tanks and dams, and its contribution to ecology and increased avail ability of wood for domestic, industrial and energy needs.

Our estimate gives the wood production as 10 bone dry tonnes per hectare per year from the fourth year onwards. With an area of 4.5 million hectares of fresh forest land the total production of wood would be 45 million tonnes per year and at a nominal rare of Rs. 500 per tonne this would mean a return of Rs. 22500 million a year which would be more than the yearly investment of Rs. 1800 crore for afforestation.

Another major benefit of afforestation is in the area of providing employment and minimising the poverty to some extent. It has been estimated that 0.25 million jobs will be created for the afforestation of 1 million hectare of social forestry. At this rate the new jobs created by planned afforestation of 4.5 million hectares per year would be approximately 1.1 million jobs a year in soil preparation, conservation, harvesting protection and other down-stream activities. This will from a major share of the 7 million and odd people entering the job market every year and will even surpass the half million jobs a year provided by the industry, trade and government. If the same investment of Rs. 1800 crores per year is made in industries instead of in forestry, the job opportunity will be around 0.18 million jobs, nearly 1/6th of the job that can be found in forestry. It may also be noted that in forestry nearly 40-50% of the cast goes towards the wages to the labour and therefore 1.1 million people would share about Rs. 720 crores a year. Each job, employing low level technology, would be paid an average of Rs. 6500 per year which would be nearly 16 times the average per capita rural income of Rs. 400 or less. This would help in greatly increasing the purchasing power of the people.

In conclusion, it is high time for all of us to arise from the deep wood slumber, awaken to the new knowledge and stop not till we reach the final goal of Afforestation.

Appendix—I

Statewise Forest Area

1976-77

States/Union Territories	*Forest Area 76-77* ('000 ha.)	*Forest as per cent of total land area*	*Potentially Exploitable* ('000 ha.)	*Other Forest Area* ('000 ha.)	*Per Capita Forest area* (Ha.)	*Area lost in 25 yrs. 1951-76* ('000 ha.)
1	*2*	*3*	*4*	*5*	*6*	*7*
Andhra Pradesh	6,437	23.25	1,661	1,665	0.13	202
Assam	3,081	39.24	165	229	0.17	73
Bihar	2,928	16.84	NA	225	0.05	67
Gujarat	1,959	10.00	NA	287	0.07	180
Haryana	146	3.30	30	104	0.01	—

Himach al Pradesh	2,177	39.11	202	1,000	0.56	—
Jammu & Kashmir	2,104	9.47	203	1,544	0.40	98
Karnataka	3,757	19.59	235	158	0.11	308
Kerala	1,133	29.15	172	236	0.05	189
Madhya Pradesh	16,230	36.67	4,009	2,048	0.34	1,810
Maharashtra	6,672	21.68	254	2,047	0.12	215
Manipur	602	26.92	311	NA	0.47	—
Meghalaya	637	28.32	565	NA	0.55	—
Nagaland	289	17.48	179	52	0.74	—
Orissa	6,793	43.61	1,042	68	0.28	109
Punjab	206	4.09	NA	106	0.01	—
Rajasthan	3,461	10.11	1,215	8,493	0.12	86
Sikkim	282	38.63	107	175	1.20	—

(Contd.)

1	2	3	4	5	6	7
Tamil Nadu	2,254	17.38	37	4,332	0.05	66
Tripura	603	57.54	48	198	0.33	—
Uttar Pradesh	5,075	17.24	599	2,003	0.05	221
West Bengal	1,183	13.47	65	38	0.02	325
Andaman & Nicobar	746	89.99	243	1	4.91	—
Arunachal Pradesh	5,154	61.67	4,354	NA	9.30	—
Mizoram	713	33.81	469	188	NA	—
All India	74,786	22.75	15,995	25,085	0.12	4,100

Source : 'Energy From Forests'—Dr. S. Paul.

NA : Not Available.

Appendix—II

Price Tag for Forests

Effects of Deforestation	*Loss in Rs, Millions*
1	*2*
(a) Loss of 6 million tonnes of soil nutrients swept into sea every year due to floods. (Estimated in 1972 as Rs. 700 crores and now assumed at Rs. 1000 crores).	10,000
(b) Loss of 6000 million tonnes of top soil swept into sea every year. (Assumed at triple the value of nutrients).	30,000
(c) Loss of 8000 hectares of land to ravines at Rs. 25000 of crop value per hectare per year.	200

(Contd.)

1	2
(d) Loss due to flood damages at Rs. 1000 crores per year (1978). (Assumed that 75% is due to deforestation and present damage at Rs. 1200 crores per year).	9,000
(e) Siltation of dams, reservoirs, etc. resulting in the reduction of life by 50% on Rs. 100000 million invested in 30 years. (Requiring additional investment of Rs. 3300 million per year. Trebled to get the current cost).	10,000
(f) Cost of building storage tanks equal to the amount of ground water stored by the forest area lost every year. (Cost of storage tank to hold water equivalent to what is held by 1 million hectare of forest is estimated at Rs. 5300 million.	5,000
(g) Loss by deforestation when there is no contribution to ecology by means of protein conversion only (please see Appendix-IV for details).	10,000
(h) Value of timber and fuelwood lost by deforestation at 1	

million hectare per year and Rs. 5000 per hectare per year without plants to replant the denuded area.	5,000
Total estimated losses per year	Rs. 1,64,200 millions

Price tag for forest at 10 times the losses per year : Rs. 1,640,000 millions*

---

* No price tag has been considered for the whole of wild ife, recreation and tourism.

INSPIRATION : "The Economics of Forestry'—G. S. Ranganathan.

Appendix—III

Service Rendered by Trees

The value of the services rendered by a 50 year old tree is Rs. 15.7 lakhs according to the estimate worked out by the scientists. The contribution of the tree is estimated as follows :

	Rs.
Production of oxygen	250,000
Control of air pollution	500,000
Control of soil erosion and soil fertility	250,000
Recycling of water and control of humidity	300,000
Bird and animal shelter	250,000
Protein conversion	20,000
	1,570,000

Contribution of the tree in terms of prices of timber, fruits and flowers have not been computed in the estimate.

Out of the above factors, let us consider the value of protein conversion only and the loss due to deforestation.

Value of protein conversion =Rs. 20,000 in 50 yrs.
=Rs. 400 per year per tree

Discounting the value by 40% for a tree with a life of 20 yrs. and not 50 years, the value of protein conversion =Rs. 160 per year per tree

Assuming only 1000 trees per hectare,
value of protein conversion =Rs. 160,000 per hectare per year

At a deforestation rate of 1 million hectare per year, loss in value of protein due to deforestation
=Rs. 160,000 million per year

Taking practical value as only 60% of the calculations, loss in protein value due to deforestation
=Rs. 100,000 million per year.

Appendix—IV

Energy Plantations

1		*2*
Energy for lighting and domestic work at 2 KWH/family for 3000 families in 10-15 villages.	:	6000 KWH/day
Energy for water pumps for agriculture and for small scale industries.	:	14000 ,,
Total energy requirement in a group of 10-15 villages.	:	20000 ,,
Calorific value of 1 tonne of bone dry wood (10-15% moisture) at 3700 Kcal./kg.	:	37×10^5Kcal.
At 30% efficiency of conversion of woodfuel thermal generators, available Cal. value of 1 tonne of wood.	:	11.1×10^5Kcal. equal to 1290 KWH

At 85% efficiency of the power plant, 1 tonne of wood will produce.	:	1100 KWH
Therefore, wood requirement for 20000 KWH = 18 tonne/day	:	6570 t/year
Dry wood production/yield per hectare	:	260 tonnes in four years.
Area required for giving an yield of 6750 tonne $=\frac{6750}{250}$	:	27 hectares.
Min. area required to get a continuous yield of 6750 t/year	:	145 ,,
Area occupied by roads and storage facility	:	7.5 ,,
Area utilised for energy plantation	:	137.5 ,, (in 5 blocks of 27.5 hectares).
Species for plantation	:	Casuarina, Sesbania, Eucalyptus, Populus or other fast growing trees depending upon the region.
Planting density	:	15,000 plants per hectare

(*Contd.*)

1		2
Mortality rate	:	33%
Net yield	:	10,000 plants per hectare
Planting period	:	June to September
Method of planting	:	Every year from Ist to 5th year one block of 27.5 hectares will be planted.
Harvesting	:	Will commence from the 5th year.
Energy generation	:	Will commence from the 6th year.

SOURCES : 1. 'Blue Print for Energy Plantations'—K. Gurumurty and P. P. Raturi

2. 'Planting for Energy' —. R. N. Kaul and K. Gurumurty

Appendix V

Summary of Action Plan for Afforestation

Action Plan	*Acreage*	*Trees per hectare*	*Agencies*
1	*2*	*3*	*4*
1. Increase tree coverage in the present 48 mha forests devoid of vegetation.	48 mha	2500	Forest Departments
2. Convert at least 60% of the area degarded and not useful for agricultural purposes (43.43 mha).	12.5 mha	2000	Forest and Revenue Departments
	12.5 mha	10000	Private leases for Energy plantations.

(*Contd.*)

	1	2	3	4
3.	Utilise at least 30% of culturable wastes and fallow lands (40 mha).	12 mha	1000	Private Entrepreneurs, Industrialists, Voluntary Organisations—Rotary, Lions, Giants, Jaycees, etc.
4.	Plant trees on 15% of area on roadsides, railway lines, canal banks, farm boundaries (3.6 mha).	0.5 mha	1000	PWD, Railways, National Highway Dept., Irrigation Dept., Village Panchayats.
.	Woodlots around villages, school yards, public buildings, church yards, cemetries, market squares and houses.			Individual institutions. Aim should be to plant as many trees as possible within the area.
6.	Improve Forest Productivity and yield in the present forest area (83 mha).			From 0.2 cub. mtr./ha. to at least 1 cub. mtr./ha. Forest Depts.
7.	Ban illegal and indiscriminate felling.			All Government agencies.

8.	Energy plantation for rural electrification round villages.	5.5 mha	15000
9.	Avoid wasteful use of fuel.		
	Total area for new plantation	91 mha	
	Total trees required for plantation	36500 Crore trees	

Bibliography

1. *Before the Forests Disappear*—Pravin Kumar—Science Today, Oct. 1981.

2. *The Second Energy Crisis —'Firewood Crops'*—Report of the Board on Science and Technology for International Development, USA.

3. *Planting for Energy*—R. N. Kaul & K. Gurumurty—Science Today, Oct. 1981.

4. *Blue Print for Energy Plantations*—K. Gurumurty & P. P. Raturi—Science Today, Oct. 1981.

5. *Forest Resources in India*—K. Venkatasubramanian & B. Bowonder—Features, August 1980.

6. *A Policy for Land and Water*—B. B. Vohra—Sardar Patel Memorial Lectures, 1980.

7. *A Chapter for the Land*—B. B. Vohra—Eastern Economist, 2nd & 9th Jan. 1981.

8. *Energy Plantations*—N. N. Sachitanand, The Hindu, 13th Feb. 1982.

9. *Environmental and Social Costs*—G. S. Ranganathan—Second Workshop on Environmental Management, March 1981.

10. *The Cost Benefit of Conservation*—G. S. Ranganathan—Seminar on 'Approaches to a Conservation Strategy for Gujarat', Jan. 1981.

11. *The Economist of Forestry*—G. S. Ranganathan—Seminar on 'Nature Protection & Modern Society', Nov. 1980.

12. *Ecological Planning for Prosperity*—G. S. Ranganathan Workshop on Wildlife Resources in Rural Development, July 1980.

13. *Population : The Neglected Factor and Relevant Forestry* G. S. Ranganathan—Vaigyanik,—Jan-June 1981.

14. *Discussions with Mr. K. C. Shroff,* Managing Director Excel Industries Ltd., Bombay.

15. *Fuelwoods : India's Untapped Potential*—S. Paul & Prem Shankar Jha—Financial Express, Oct. 8, 1980.

16. *Need for Planting 190 Crore Trees*—V. P. Agarwala—Times of India, 8th May, 1982.

17. *Development of Waste Land Through Social Forestry*—N. D. Bachketi—Times of India, 8th May, 1982.

18

Forecast of Energy, Energy System of Load, Modelling and Mix Optimization : Application of Operations Research Techniques in Power Company

*A.M. Salsingikar**

Introduction

Based on forecast of energy, peak and load curves, firm commitments for installation of new generating capacities are to be made. These forecasts are made using mathematical model and simulation. The preferred hydro, thermal and nuclear mix is decided using a mix-optimisation model with the objective of cost minimisation, the constraints being various technical considerations. Linear programming technique is used in handling this model.

*Dy. Distribution Engineer, Bombay Suburban Electric Supply Ltd., Bombay
(Paper presented at 24th Annual Convention).

Energy Forecasting

Forecast Based on Past Trends

There are many mathematical models available for forecasting energy requirements based on past trends. These are known to yield realiable results in developed countries like USA and Japan where sectoral growth has stabilised in desirable direction. It should be emphasised that, in a developing country like India, planning aims to correct existing imbalances and affect structural changes to achieve desired pace of growth in various sectors. For example, emphasis on mass public transport system, development of compact cities, containment of urbanisation, promotion of hand spun Khadi, selection of certain types of industries for development, deciding their size and location are policy decisions which will decide the future trends. So when our aim is to reverse existing trends, forecasts of energy based on past trends should not be used as basis for power planning. However, three such trend models are discussed below.

(1) *Trend Model*

This model uses the exponential trend equation given by the following relation.

$$Y = 3411.39 + 8555.05\,[e^{0.0988}]$$

where, Y = Power requirement in million Kilowatt hours.

X = Number of years.

(2) *Regression Models*

These have been developed by studying past relations between power requirements and various indices as given below. In all these cases, Y is power requirement in million tonnes of coal replacement (MTCR)—1 Kg. of coal is equivalent to 1 Qilowatt hour. Table 1 shows some regression equations.

Table 1

Regression Relations

S. No.	*Regression Relation*	*Standard error*	*Remarks*
1.	$Y = -46.3375 + 0.4994X$	0.0233	X is National income in hundred crores of rupees.
2.	$Y = -22.8506 + 2.0579X$	0.1316	X is income from Mining and Manufacturing sector in hundred crores of rupees.
3.	$Y = -16.6603 + 0.3537X$	0.0166	X is index of industrial production.

(3) *Scheer Model*

Scheer, after studying the historical relationship between actual annual per capita generation and annual load growth in 109 countries including India, presented his thesis that for every hundred fold increase in per capita generation, rate of growth will be reduced by half.

It has been suggested that if in Scheer model

$$\text{Log } G = 1.33 + 0.02\,R - 0.15 \log U$$

where G = Annual percentage growth in generation,

U = Annual percapita generation and,

R = Population growth percentage.

value of R is taken as 1.8% per annum (which is the world's average population growth rate) and the estimated power requirement is modified by multiplying it by a correction factor of (1—0.009 N) where N is number of years since 1965-66 (the year from which estimated value exceeded actual value), reliable predictions are possible for Indian conditions.

Method of Norms (*End Use Method*)

To obviate the shortcomings of trend models, "Method of Norms" establishes total energy requirements by summing the individual sectoral requirements to meet the planned sectoral growth targets. This technique is based on certain normative assumptions regarding factors like population growth, national income, rural electrifications, Gross National Product, transmission and distribution losses, plant factors, diversity factors, auxiliary consumption and specific fuel consumption. This method has been extensively used by Fuel Policy Committee.

Mix Optimisation Model

Objective Function

$C = C_F + C_R$ where is C cost per unit, C_F and C_R being its fixed and variable (running cost) components. Irrespective of installed capacity, it is the lead factor of operation which decides percentage of installed capacity contributing to saleable energy. As financial investment is made to facilitate operation of unit, when needed, at its rated capacity, fixed cost component comprising interest and depreciation very inversely with load factor. As investment is made on plant and transmission distribution network, total fixed investment is the sum of these two. $C_y = (C_{FP} + C_{FT})/F$ where C_{FP} and C_{FT} are investments in Plant and Transmission network and F is the load factor.

$$\therefore \quad C = \frac{C_{FT} + C_{PT}}{F} + C_R$$

If K is installed capacity of plant, energy generated over time T equals KFT.

$\therefore$ Total cost of energy generated per unit time

$$= \overline{C} = C . \frac{KFT}{T} = CKF$$

$$\therefore \quad C = \left(\frac{C_{FP} + C_{FT}}{F} + C_R \right) K.F.$$

$$= (C_{FP} + C_{FT} + C_{RF})\, K$$

It is this objective equation which has to be minimised. In this equation, C_{FP} and C_R are readly calculable. C_{FT} is computed indirectly by determining effective distance as weighted average of the distance of the plant from different load centres. The specified demands (loads) from the weightages.

$$\text{Effeetive distanced} = \frac{\sum_{i=I}^{m} Di\, di}{\sum_{i=1}^{m} Di}$$

when Di is demand at load centre i, di is distance of plant from load centre i and m is total number of load centres.

$$\sum_{i=1}^{m} Di = K \text{ where K is known a priori,}$$

$$= K \text{ max if only the bounds of capacity are given.}$$

Modified Objective Function

An year is divided into 5 seasons.

Eij = Energy capacity of 'i' th plant in 'j' th season at 100% load factor. This is a variable in optimisation.

Fij = Load factor of 'i' th plant in 'j' th season

Ki = Capacity of 'i' th plant.

Eij = Ki Fij

$$KiFi = \sum_{j=i}^{4} \frac{Eij}{4}$$

substituting this value in original objective function

$$\overline{Ci} = (C_{FP} + C_{FT})i\ Ki + \frac{CRi}{4} \sum_{j=i}^{4} Eij$$

This modified objective function will be used for mix optimisation. During different seasons, different types of plants will have to be operated at different load factors. In a system there will be nuclear, hydel and thermal generation and each mode of generation will be from many plants, value of 'i' for each mode of generation being different. For the system, total minimum cost is obtained by minimising total cost under different modes of generation over the four seasons, 'j' ranging from 1 to 4 representing seasons and 'i' ranging from 0 to N^1

to N_6 as the case may be, representing total number of nuclear, thermal, run of the river hydel, pumped storage hydel etc.

Constraints-based on Load Factor Capabilities Nuclear Generation

Actual energy generated will be within the energy capability bounds, subscripts U and L denothing upper and lower bounds. The load factor will be between 0.5 and 0.6 during monsoon to optimise hydro generation and during all other periods, load factor will be between 0.75 to 0.9. These are represented by

$$KiI \leqslant Ki \leqslant KiU \text{ for } i = 1 \text{ to } N^1$$

$$0.5\ Ki \leqslant Eij \leqslant 0.6\ Ki \text{ for } i = 1 \text{ to } N_1 \text{ and } j = 1 \text{ (monsoon)}$$

$$0.75\ Ki \leqslant Eij \leqslant 0.9\ Ki \text{ for } i \text{ to } N_1 \text{ and } j = 2,3,4$$

Hydel Generation

These are proposed to be used as peaking plants with storage reservoirs. The load factor at all times will be less than 0.9 and energy generation will be less than or at best equal to its upper bound of energy capability. Also, sum of water resources left unutilised in all four seasons should not exceed maximum storage capacity. These are represented by

$$Eij \leqslant 0.9\ Ki \quad \text{for } i = 1 \text{ to } N_2;\ j = 1 \text{ to } 4$$

$$\sum_{j=1}^{x} Eij \leqslant \sum_{j=1}^{x} EijU \text{ for } i = 1 \text{ to } N_2\ x = 1 \text{ to } 4$$

Where EijU is upper bound of generation of 'i' th plant in 'j' th season.

$$\sum_{j=1}^{x} (EijU - Eij)\ T = Esi \text{ for } i = 1 \text{ to } N_2;\quad x = 1 \text{ to } 4$$

where Esi—Storage capacity of 'i' th plant

Thermal Generation

The load factor during monsoon and winter will not exceed 0.65 to optimise hydel generation and at all other times be between 0.4 and 0.85.

$Kil \leqslant Ki \times KiU$ for $i=1$ to N_6

$Kij \leqslant 0.65\ Ki$ for $i=1$ to N_6 and $j=1,2$ (monsoon and winter

$Eij \leqslant 0.85\ Ki$ for $i=1$ to N_6 and $j=1,2,3,4$

$Eij \geqslant 0.4\ Ki$ for $i=1$ to N_6 and $j=1,2,3,4$

Constraints—Based on Energy and Capacity Balance, Balancing of Energy Requirement

If Dj is total energy requirement in 'j' th season

$$Dj=\sum_{l=1}^{N_2} Eij+\sum_{j=1}^{N_2} Eij+\ldots+\sum_{i=1}^{N_6} Eij$$

for six types of plants discussed above for

j=1, 2, 3, 4.

Balancing of Demand Requirement

If D is the peak demand,

$$D \geqslant \sum_{i=1}^{N_1} Ki+\ldots+\sum_{i=1}^{N_6} Ki \leqslant D'$$

for six types of plant discussed above for the system. D' is introduced to avoid situations where it is technically impossible to simultaneously balance energy and capacity requirements. D' is such that it is adequate to meet maintenance and spinning reserves.

Load Growth Model

The manner in which load is anticipated to grow determines the characteristics and utilisation of proposed new plants and likely adjustment required in the operation of existing plants. The two criteria to be examined before one advanced thermal or nuclear plant or a high load factor unit hydel is proposed to be added will be—

(1) Will the system load model permit high load factor

(2) What will be the impact of such high load factor operation on existing units ?

such a study is facilitated by use of "Plant utilisation diagrams".

Conclusion

It is, therefore, evident that tools like Mathematical Modelling, Simulation and techniques of Operations Research are constantly used—and with advantage in every phase of power planning. It will not be an exaggeration to observe that without these tools, power planning will be in a naive exercise.

19

Procurement of Blast Hole Drill Bits in Open Cast Mechanised Iron Ore Mining Industry

*Major Har Krishnan**

Introduction

The degree of mechanisation plays a very important role in the two broad classifications of metaliferrous mines, viz. open cast and underground. In any open cast mechanised mine the blast hole drilling operations are performed to fragment the rock so that it can be leaded easily by excavating equipments and transported by hauling. The most common drills which are being employed in such operations have tungsten carbide drill bits of sizes 4" and above. These drills bits are also used in water hole drilling operations for irrigation purposes where drilling is carried out under explored rock conditions. In all such operations drilling forms a constliest division in which the major share of running cost is taken up by drill bits. In this article attempt has been made to develop

* Senior Stores Officer, IDPL, Hyderabad.

simplified procedure for the procurement of drill bits in a fully mechanised iron one mine on the basis of consumption patterns which should provide the best operational conditions at minimum inventory holding costs.

Operational Conditions

After fixing the yearly production target the planning cell prepares the excavation schedule in tons which converted into drilling metrage is handed over to production department for carrying out drilling in varying grades of iron ore from very hard steel grey haematite to loose blue dust. Depending on following operational conditions, the average life of drill bit which forms the basis of yearly requirement, is determined in different grades of iron ore.

(a) Type of Rock—Homogeneous or heterogeneous.

(b) Drilling equipment with which it is used.

(c) Pressure—With down the hole hammers optimum pressure is estimated at 100 psi.

(d) Design of down hole tool.

(e) Skill of grinding.

(f) Internal of grinding.

After conducting actual studies and experiments the critical wear limit of bit in metres in different rock conditions is established. The bit under no circumstances should be allowed to drill above its critical wear limit as it may cause a permanent damage to the bit.

Drill Metrage

In order to determine drill metrage required to achieve the excavation target in tons, the depth of hole is measured at the time of blasting to get the Blast metrage. The actual quantity of ore lifted from particular blast is also weight.

$$\frac{\text{Weight}}{\text{Metre}} = \frac{\text{Weight of ore lifted from particular blast}}{\text{Blast metrage or depth of hole in metres}}$$

It varies according to the composition of ore e.g., in one of the soft ore blasting the following readings were obtained.

Blast Metrage	*Ore lifted in tons*	*Weight in tons per Metre of drilling*
292.4	39,014	134
252.6	30,886	122.6
093.3	9,265	99.3
332.7	27,835	83.6
280.7	21,425	76.2
133.4	9,925	74.4

Thus the average tonnage per metre of drilling in soft ore was found to be 98.5.

Life of Bit

It is expressed in drilling metres in particular type of ore at which the bit becomes unserviceable, cannot take any more grinding and hence rejected e.g., in hard ore drilling the following reading were obtained :

Serial Number of bit	*Drill metrage at which bit was rejected*
S	310
S1	290
S2	340
S3	302
S4	315
S5	360

Sl. No.	DESCRIPTION	TYPE OF ORE					
		Very hard ore (VHO)	Hard Ore (HO)	Soft Ore (SO)	Loose Ore (LO)	Waste Ore (W)	Total
1.	Yearly Excavation	0.400	2.00	1.20	0.80	0.80	5.20
	Schedule in Million Tons						
2.	Tonnage/Drilling	60–80	70–90	80–120	100–150	100–240	
	Say in this example	75=X	85=X1	110=X2	140=X3	200=X4	
3.	Drill metrage	$\frac{0.4\times10^6}{X}$	$\frac{2.0\times10^6}{X1}$	$\frac{1.20\times10^6}{X2}$	$\frac{0.80\times10^6}{X3}$	$\frac{0.80\times10^6}{X4}$	
		5333	23530	10909	5714	4000	
		=y	=y1	=y2	=y3	=y4	

4. Life of bit in Metres	120—150	300—350	800—1000	2000—3000	5000—6000	
Say in this example	140=a	300 = al	1000 = a2	2500= a3	5000=a4	
5. No. bits	y/a	y1/al	y2/a2	y3/a3	y4/a4	
	31	79	10	2	1	123+Al-lowance=Z

The average metrage at which the bit got rejected was 319.5 or 320. Hence the average lift of bit in hard ore was found to be 320 metres.

Estimated Demand

Let us take the case of a mechanised open cast iron ore Mine with seven blast hole drill machine using tungsten carbide or T.C. bits of 6" size. If the years production i.e., from April 73 to March 74 is fixed at 5.2 million tons the detail calculations for estimating yearly requirement of bits are given as under.

The allowances are given because of air pressure, the quality of down the hole tool with which bit is attached, composition of rock whether homogeneous or hetrogeneous.

Operational Losses

These losses are because of

(a) Sticking of drill rod in hole causing loss of bit.

(b) Breaking of bit in hole due to manufacturing defect or over grinding.

(c) Breaking of one of the tungsten carbide tip, thus making the bit unsuitable for drilling.

For reasons mentioned above the requirement 'Z' is increased by 10% and for the operational losses another 5 to 10% of 'Z' is added. In practice it is found that increasing the calculated demand 'Z' by 17% gives a fairly accurate estimation of annual demand.

Thus in this example the total annual requirement of bits $+Z+17\%\ Z=Z$

$(1+0.17)=1.17\ Z=1.17\times 124=144.$

If the unit cost of bit be Rs. 6,000 the rupee value of

annual demand comes to be Rs. 8.64 lakhs which makes it a high value inventory item and forms the 'A' category of Selective Inventory Management.

Procurement Policy

Analysis of the last 3 years month-wise figures revealed that the demand followed a poisson distribution. In this case the average monthly demand = 144/12 = 12; standard deviation = 3.46 or 4. Also the demand varies according to excavation schedule which has its peak periods from October to May and lean periods during monsoon season i.e., from June to September. The system designed for procurement should be such that it should give a quick response to increase in demand but should also prevent high inventories during periods of lower demand and result in lower operating costs. The optional replenishment or Maximum Minimum system is best-suited for this purpose. Under this system the quantity in hand and on order should not exceed the maximum level i e. 'S' but should not fall below the minimum level 'S'.

(a) *Shortage Costs and Level of Protection*

Bit is a highly critical item, its out of stock can bring the production to stand still. If the average daily production be 12,000 tonnes and if recovery be 65%, the lump ore production will be 12,000×0.65=7,800 tonnes per day. If the selling price be Rs. 75 the loss sustained for one day out of stock=7,800× 75=Rs. 5.85 lakhs. For such a high shortage cost with poisson distribution of demand the maximum protection against stock out which can be provided will be 98%. The probability of stock out occures when normal demand exeeeds estimated demand or lead time i.e., time elapsed between the raising of demand by user and the materials are finally received in stores. This can occur when we are awaiting supplies from Vendor which depends on the number of order periods. If two orders are placed during year, we can except one stock out in 25 years, for which the level of safety stock can be fixed at 36 Nos., or equivalent for 3 months supply and the stocks must be reviewed 4 times in a year.

(b) *The system*

As per the conditions mentioned above the system will operate as under. Average inventory can be maintained at 6 months supply. The system can be further simplified and stated as "Whenever stock in hand falls below six months supply, an order equal to 72 number of bits can be placed immediately."

(c) *Simulation*

The system will maintain an average inventory of Rs. 4.32 lakhs at unit cost of Rs. 6,000 and will give inventory holding cost of Rs. 86,400 at 20% inventory carrying cost with probability of one stock out in 25 years.

Salvage Value

Both the tungsten carbide and special alloy steel matrix used in bits form high value imported material. By heating the steel matrix with (acetylene flame) the tungsten carbide tips can be separated. The salvage cost of tungsten carbide is Rs. 50 per kg. and special allow steel of matrix is Rs. 5 per kg. It has been found that average weight tungsten carbide recovered from a 6" bit is 3 Kgs. and steel matrix is 5 Kg. Thus the salvage value of a rejected 6" bit is 3 Kgs. and steel matrix is 5 Kg. Thus the salvage value of a rejected 6" bit is Rs. 175. If there are 200 such bits, Rs. 35,000 can be recovered from that.

20

Manpower Planning and Training Needs in Coal Washeries

H.M. Dingolia, R.L. Mittal**, C. Ghosh****

Introduction

The depleting assets of good grade metallurgical coal on the one hand and increased demand with stricter specifications by the growing steel industry on the other hand have brought a revolution in the field of coal washing in India. To cope up with the increased demand a number of new washeries have been planned to be set up in the years to come.

The washeries, being mechanised process industries, are not as labour-intensive as coal mining industries in India. This mechanisation/automation has induced an increase in such category of man requiring skill and knowledge of keeping the machines working effectively for increased productivity of both men and machines. This skill/knowledge may come through

* Dy. Manager (IE).

** Manager (IE).

*** Addl. Chief Engr. (W), Central Washeries Organisation (SAIL) Dhanbad.

right type of training to right type of persons at right time under proper guidance only. While many new washeries have been planned to be set up involving huge investment, an investment towards training of personnel engaged/to be engaged in the field of coal washing is a matter of paramount importance. Without this, investment in other factors of production would not give the desired results.

Manpower

The manpower in washeries has been assessed through rational systems and procedures of modern management aiming at optimum utilisation of all the resources including manpower and machines. An integrated system of men, materials and equipments has been installed at the washeries drawing upon the special knowledge and skill in the field of coal preparation/benefication, materials handling and other branches of management services with an aim to have increased productivity including the labour productivity.

At present there are 15 Washeries operating in India, out of which 9 are prime Coking coal and the remaining are medium coking coal ones. These washeries are all in Public Sector excepting Jamadoba and West Bokaro which are run by Tata Iron & Steel Co. The present total annual capacity and manpower deployment in coal washeries in India approximates to 27.10 M.T. and 8,000 persons respectively including ministerial staff as can be seen from the following table :

Since the washeries are mechanised industries, the deployment in the supervisory and skilled categories of staff is on the higher side, presently being more than 50% of the total manpower deployment. The percentagewise, employeewise deployment in different categories of managerial, supervisory, skilled/semiskilled, unskilled and ministerial staff is appended below :

Employer	*Washery*	*Annual Capacity (M. ton)*	*Manpower Deploymenl*
1	*2*	*3*	*4*
A. **Steel Authority of India Limited (SAIL)**	Dugda-I	2.4	1137
	Dugda-II	2.4	1137
	Bhojudih	2.0	625
	Patherdih	2.0	661
	Durgapur Steel Plant	1.5	450

(*Contd.*)

1	2	3	4
	Chasnala	2.4	344
		12.70	3217
B. **Central Coal Fields Ltd.** (C.C.I.)	Kathara	3.0	950
	Kargali	2.70	1136
	Swang	0.75	306
	Gidi	2.48	520
		9.29	2912
C. **Bharat Coking Coal Ltd.** (BCCL)	Lodna	1.20	324
D. **Tata Iron & Steel Co.**	Jamadoba	1.44	350*

	(TISCO)	West Bokaro	0.70	300*
			2.14	**650**
E.	**Western Coal Fields Ltd. (WCL)**	Nowrojabad	0.50	250
F.	**West Bengal**	Durgapur Project Ltd. (DPL)	1.27	**486**
		W. Total	27.10	7839

*Estimated deployment

(The above does not Include the Manpower Deployment for the Jobs being done on Contract)

Categories	SAIL %	CCL %	WB %	Average %
1. Managerial	3.4	2.6	1.0	2.3
2. Supervisory (Tech.)	6.4	3.0	3.2	4.5
3. Skilled	32.9	33.2	27.7	31.3
4. Semiskilled	10.4	22.5	16.5	16.5
5. Unskilled	38.5	33.2	47.4	39.7
6. Supervisory (Non-tech)	0.5	0.8	1.2	0.5
7. Ministerial	7.9	4.7	3.0	5.2
	100.0	100.0	100.0	100.0

Skilled category of workmen in general are required for the following jobs in washeries :

(a) Operation and maintenance of sophisticated machines/equipments like Heavy Media Bath, Rece-procating screens, thickness, jigs, pumps vibrators and filter, etc.

(b) Use of different instruments like Cavity controller, weigh-bridge. Weightometers, pressure & vaccum guages, etc. for monitoring purposes.

(c) Operation and maintenance of all material handling equipments and allied machineries like scraper/flight conveyors, bucket conveyours belt conveyor skip hoist, etc.

(d) Operation and maintenance of electrical equipments like control panels, feeders, transformers, motors, relays, etc.

(e) Stores-handling, and procurement actions.

(f) Coal sampling and analysis thereof for effective quality control.

(g) Project planning including development of indigenous resources.

The engagement of unskilled workers is normally for jobs like plant cleaning, spillage/slurry reclamation and helping the skilled category of workmen. The increased deployment in this category of workmen may be attributed to : (a) Inadequate attention towards job enrichment. (b) Poor manpower-utilisation and (c) increased work content due to below standard, indigenous substitutions of imported equipments/machines. However, with the introduction of multi-crafts system, improved manpower utilisation and standard indigeneous substitutions the employment in unskilled category may be substantially decreased.

The manpower deployment in supervisory (non-tech.) and ministerial category of staff constitutes nearly 6% of the total manpower deployment. The engagement in this category is in the functional areas, viz. personnel, welfare and finance etc.

Job Enrichment/Multi-Crafts Concept

With the introduction of multi-craft, there will be no room for unskilled or semiskilled labour in the organisation. A small, competent, well trained, better contended and a more flexible workforce is what multicraft promises to give to the industry.

It is widely appreciated now that in the sophisticated process industries much of the work-load being delegated from humans to automation, a different approach to manpower problems, work organisation and trade association would be necessary. The situation calls for a mobile and versatile skills inventory and a wider association of workers with the objectives of a technical enterprises. This, however, in no way attempts to stunt and frustrate the individual worker and make of him an individual non-entity. This basic ideas and thoughts prepared the soil out of which the present multi-craft or polyvalent concept has germinated.

Benefits of Multi-crafts System

(a) Minimum variety of crafts required to complete each task, hence lesser delays and job hold-ups.

(b) Better co-ordination and more efficient manning.

(c) Increased output—by exploring the possibilities of three shift running of the washeries without earmarking one shift for maintenance only.

(d) Increased effective force with education in manpower.

(e) Improved flexibility, better utilisation.

(f) Reduction in systematic overtime hours.

(g) Better labour relations.

(h) Better worker morale—by minimising the problem of "ennui" to the worker and a higher level of added responsibility.

(i) Better labour job security and improved avenues of employment.

Manpower Planning

Planning is one of the most important functions of management of any organisation. Manpower planning has been now recognised as an important part of the overall planning of any organisation. Without the procurement and maintenance of adequate member of personnel, it is not possible to realise the goals of the organisation.

A stream of qualified personnel must be kept flowing into the organisation as the organisation is dynamic, its requirements, keep on changing and many employees leave during a year because of retirements, deaths, resignations and many other reasons which lead to shortage of manpower of right type. Similarly there may be surplus manpower in the organisation because of poor planning. Therefore, there arises the need for manpower planning which acts as a sound basis for administrative action to avoid situations of shortage or surplus of manpower in the organisation.

Manpower planning is the process of developing and determining objectives, policies and programmes that will develop, utilise and distribute manpower so as to achieve the goals of the organisation. It is an important aid to frame the training and development programme for the personnel, because it takes into account the effects of anticipated changes in technology, markets and products on manpower requirement and educational and training programme requirements. Manpower plans may be modified or adjusted according to the changes in circumstances.

Manpower planning may be done at national or organisational level. In the developing countries like India where there is an abundance of manpower, manpower planning assumes a more important role as the pace of economic development must be at a considerably faster rate than in the countries which are already economically well developed.

At the organisational level, there are various levels of manpower planning, but each has its own objectives and techniques. It may be broadly carried out at corporate, divisional and local or plant levels. The purpose of carrying out manpower planning at various levels is the systematic projection of manpower requirements for the future. The manpower planning should begin at the lowest organisational level and be reviewed at successively higher organisational echelons. After the manpower planning has been done at the top level in the organisation, it will be integrated with all other planning in the organisation if it is to make its power planning.

The manpower in any industry is influenced, among other things, by the following factors :

(a) The degree of mechanisation and automation of work.

(b) The skill and gratification of workers.

(c) The intensity of his effort in the process of labour or the intensity of work.

(d) Absenteeism.

(e) Turnover.

(f) Manpower utilisation.

(g) All those factors affecting the work content of any job.

Future Fore-Cast

The major determination of future manpower demand are : Employment trends, replacement needs, productivity changes and growth and expansion.

As per the tentative plan of Coal India, Ltd., another sixteen washeries have been planned to be set up in its different subsidiaries in the next decade with annual capacity of 30.75 million tonnes of raw coal input. These 16 washeries, will be for prime, medium and semi-coking coals as indicated below :

The washing of coal is not a new phenomenon in India, and the basic data for making a manpower for-cast or for that matter any forecast are available. The basic data required for manpower fore-cast may be :

(a) Technological development in the field of coal washing. (b) Future demand of washed coal. (c) Turnover,

*Name of the Subsidiary**	*Prime Coking* (1)	(2)	(3)	*Medium Coking* (1)	(2)	(3)	*Semi Coking* (1)	(2)	(3)
BCCL	6	17.20	3956	3	1.53	351	—	—	—
CCL	—	—	—	3	8.60	1980	—	—	—
ECL	—	—	—	1	0.80	184	1	0.95	219
WCL	—	—	—	1	1.20	276	—	—	—
NEC	—	—	—	—	—	—	1	0.47	108
Total	6	17.20	3956	8	12.13	2791	2	1.42	327

* (1) No. of washeries, (2) Annual rated capacity, (3) Estimated manpower requirement. (Details are at Annexure-II).

i.e. retirement, deaths, resignation, etc. (d) Existing manpower deployment and utilisation thereof. (e) Skill and knowledge required from the manpower. (f) The analysis and job specification etc. and (g) Time estimates for assessment of manpower requirement etc.

The total manpower requirement for the coming washeries is estimated at 7500 persons (details are given at Annexure-II). In other words the deployment is going to be doubled in the next decade. In addition, if other aspects like expected further technological development and turnover etc. are taken into account, more manpower probably with higher skill may be required. This can be achieved only if a concerted and a sincere effort for training of men in this area is made.

In future, care must be taken that all craftsmen constituting the maintenance and operation crew are by the State Authorities before being employed by the Washeries. This would have a significant impact on achieving and maintaining high maintenance standard and technique.

Training—A Need

The standards of management, line supervision and general work performance call for a greater stress on industry training than has been applied in the past. From pre-entry familiarisation through all stages to senior management, the industry will need to set up individual and, in some cases, central training arrangements to ensure that a high standard of training to an acceptable level is available to all those concerned.

Though it has become possible to install new washeries using latest technologies with indigenous technical know-how, it has not been possible to completely do away with imported units/machineries. Even otherwise, the operation and maintenance of a washery is not a simple matter. So far supervisory and other skilled categories of personnel engaged in the field of coal washing had mastered the trade through experience only. In the absence of adequate training facilities there is likely to be a dearth of skilled hands required for the proposed new washeries. Just as the strength of a chain is the strength of its weakest link, the efficiency of any plant is no better than that of the lowest level of operating and maintenance personnel. In order to operate the washeries at its optimum level, generation and accumulation of skilled manpower is as important as efficient production and generation of capital. Regular and systematic method of training are the only tools in the hands of management to attain this objective.

Objective of Training

The following objectives have been set forth for effective utilisation of existing manpower as also with a view to provide maximum job satisfaction and career development opportunities to the workman deployed in coal washing industry.

(a) Ensuring that every single employees is given an exposure to basic training requirement in his present job in a manner additional skilled personnel can be met to maximum possible extent by upgrading skills of existing personnel.

(b) Making available on a continuous basis an inventory of skilled and qualified technical supervisory personnel within the organisation to meet the additional requirement of supervisory personnel in the context of modernisation, i.e. implying new technological developments in the field of coal beneficiation.

(c) To provide maximum opportunity for self development towards acquiring highly professional qualifications and competence.

(d) Training of fresh graduates, technicians and trade apprentices—a statutory requirement.

(e) Containment of surplus manpower, if any, by imparting training for their gainful utilisation.

System of Training

The training, both theoritical and practical, may be imparted to different categories of washery personnel in the manner given below.

Theoretical Training

Theoretical training to Engineers and Supervisors on the fundamentals of coal preparation/beneficiation and uses thereof, fundamentals and general principles, equipment/machineries and instruments used in the washeries glossary of terms relating to coal and its preparation may be imparted in the institutes like Indian School of Mines, Dhanbad and Central Fuel Research Institute, Dhanbad. Such trained Engineers and Supervisors would in turn train the lower categories of workmen in the local training centres operating at washeries.

Practical Training

(*a*) *On the Job Training*. To give opportunity to acquire technical know-how in a relatively shorter period and in a proper manner under the guidance of efficient operators and supervisors.

(*b*) *Training During Installation*. To assign operators and maintenance personel full time during the period of installation and creation and of a new equipment right from the beginning. This would help them greatly when the equipment's come in regular.

(*c*) *Training for Maintenance*. The maintenance personnel must be specially trained beyond the level of ordinary craftsmen, as the washeries are process industries. Even for a small breakdown in any equipment the whole plant may have to be stopped. Specially trained maintenance personnel are a must for keeping the downtime to an irreducible minimum.

Management Development

Training to executives may be imparted in the general management principles and other established branches of modern management for developing them for making timely and correct operational, tactical and strategic decisions. This may be done by sending them to established management institutes in India. This will go a long way to boost up their morale, increase their professional skill resulting into increased productivity of the washery.

Gains of Training

The major gains of training, expected to be derived may be summarised as : (a) Reduced learning time. (b) Better performance. (c) Reduced Supervision. (d) Standardisation. (e) Economy. (f) Heightened morale. (g) Fill manpower needs. (h) Better management. (i) Organisational stability and flexibility.

The multi-craft system can be introduced in washeries through training, re-training and job rotation of the workers which would call for readiness on the part of all concerned to train and be trained. Introduction of such system would result in increased manpower utilisation and the possibilities of three shift running in place of existing system of two shifts running of washeries may also be explored.

The fruits of the productivity are to be shared both by the employer and the employee; in the later case by recognising his contribution by improving his status, earnings and employment conditions.

Training Facilities

At present there are local training centres operating at washeries catering to the needs of imparting training for day-to-day operation, maintenance and personnel matters. The centres are, however, inadequately equipped. At times workers are required to be sent to other training institutes/schools for long-term training too. It is proposed, that, a full fledged training centre be set up at Dhanbad for advanced training in different disciplines catering to the specific needs of coal washeries. If need arises, the operators/maintenance technicians may also be sent to manufacturers works to acquire a thorough knowledge of the equipments installed/to be installed in the washeries.

Curricula for Training

Last but not the least is the development of proper theoretical and practical curricula for training in various basic crafts. Based on the requirement of the crafts, the courses are to be developed. The mannuals setting texts for training in coal preparation/beneficiation operation/maintenance are not available in this country. A syllabus for imparting theoretical and practical training to the technicians has been prepared, based upon the actual experience gained in operation and maintenance of coal washeries, which may be seen at Annexure-III.

Conclusion

Formulation of policies on Manpower planning and training needs of the washeries would thus facilitate the organisation to project plans on the future manpower needs in respect of skills, job specification and the training needs to obtain the desired objectives of the organisation. This would facilitate optimal manpower assessment, improved manpower utilisation, job enrichment and reduced cost of production, thereby resulting in increased overall productivity of the organisation including the labour productivity.

Annexure I

Manpower Deployment in Existing Washeries in India

Name of the Employer/ Washery	*Executive*	*Supervisory*		*Skilled*	*Minis-terial*	*Semi-skilled*	*Unskilled*	*Total*
		Tech.	*Non-tech.*					
1	*2*	*3*	*4*	*5*	*6*	*7*	*8*	*9*
A. Steel Authority of India Ltd.								
Dugda-I, II	40	79	8	391	97	130	392	1137
Bhojudih	23	34	3	391	54	56	251	625

(Contd.)

1	2	3	4	5	6	7	8	9
Patherdih	23	36	3	187	54	66	292	661
Chasnala	6	24	—	111	9	32	112	294
Total	92	173	14	893	214	284	1047	2717
% of total	3.4	6.4	0.5	32.0	7.9	10.4	38.5	100.0
B. Central Coal Field Ltd.								
Kathara	28	19	7	378	42	206	270	950
Kargali	21	28	6	335	52	259	135	1136
Swang	11	14	5	99	26	71	80	306
Gidi	15	27	5	156	18	118	181	520
Total	75	88	23	968	138	654	966	2912

% of total	2.6	3.0	0.8	33.2	4.7	22.5	33 2	100.0
C. Bharat Coking Coal Ltd.								
Lodna	1	11	—	22	3	37	250	324
% of total	0.3	3.4	—	6.8	0.9	11.4	77.2	100.0
D. West Bengal								
Durgapur Project	5	20	1	135	15	80	230	486
% of total	1.0	4.2	0.2	27.7	3.0	11.5	47.4	100.0

Details of DSP, Jamadoba, West Bokaro and Nowrozabad, have not been indicated.

Annexure II

Estimated Manpower Requirement in the Forthcoming Washeries in India

Name of the Employer	Washery	Capacity in MT (R/C input)	Estimated Manpower Requirement
A. Bharat Coking Coal Ltd.	Sudamdih	2.00	460
	Munidih	2.00	460
	Bhalgora	4.20	966
	Pootkee Bullihari	3.60	828
	Barora	1.80	414
	Dharmaband	3.60	828
	Barora I	0.48	110
	'hunkumdar	0.42	97

	Mohuda	0.63	144
		18.73	4307
B. Central Coal Field Ltd.	1. Ramgarh	3.00	690
	2. Kedla	2.60	600
	3. Parej	3.00	960
		8.60	1980
C. Eastern Coal Field Ltd.	1. Sampore	0.80	184
	2. Sodepur	0.95	219
		1.75	403
D. Western Coal Field	1. Nandan	1.20	276
E. North Eastern Coal Field	1. Tipong	0.47	108
	G. Total	30.75	7074

Annexure-III

Syllabus of Training Courses in Coal Preparation Practices Operation & Maintenance of Washeries.

1.0 PARTICIPANTS : Supervisors (E & M) & Technicians.

2.0 COURSE CONTENT :

2.1 *Coal Preparation Fundamentals* :

2.1.1 Origin and nature of coal with its physical & chemical properties, purpose of coal washing and uses thereof, general principles of washing of coal. Glossary of terms relating to coal and its preparations.

2.1.2 Description of the plant and schematic flow-sheet method of working of the plant.

2.1.3 Coal sampling and analysis thereof for carrying out the washability characteristic determination and presentation of results. Use of laboratory analysis data for control of plant operating conditions and quality control.

2.1.4 Different operations and methods of sizing, screening, crushing, picking, conveying, stocking, blending, loading and despatch of washed products.

2.1.5 Cleaning, dry cleaning, jigging, dense Media Bath cleaning, H.M. cyclone cleaning Froth Flotation and other cleaning equipments.

2.1.6 Dewatering, clarification, thickening, filtering, drying. dedusting and polution control.

2.2 Elementary knowledge and different measuring and

weighing instruments different type of bearing, ability to read simple drawings and knowledge of bench work in workshop practice etc.

2.2.1 Functions of and familiarity with different measuring and weighing instruments and ability to read the same, i.e. scale, vernier, calliper, screw guage, Right angle (try square) Micrometer, Depth Guage, tachometer, etc.

2.2.2 Use of guages, i.e. pressure guage, vaccum guage, snap guage, filter guage, dial guage etc.

2.2.3 Knowledge of different type of bearings and their utility at different places.

2.2.4 Knowledge of bench work, e.g. drilling, tapping, threading, chipping, filling etc.

2.2.5 Ability to read simple drawings.

3.0 Types functions operating & maintenance procedures, knowledge of spare parts/components and functions thereof in respect of the following machines/equipments. Feeders, Trippers Reclaiming machines, crushers/rotary breakers, tramp Iron magnet/manetite pulleys, vibrating screens, Sievebends/cross flow screens, cyclones megnetite separators vaccum pumps, compressors/blowers, scales, mixers, samples, etc.

3.1 *Vibrating centrifuges* :

3.1.1 Location, functions, general description and design feature of different types of vibrating centrifuges with its salient features, i.e. (a) Uniformity of feeds; (b) Liquid solid ratio; (c) rate of feed and feed free of foreign material; (d) smooth flow of feed, effluent and product discharge; (e) Operational cycle and special care etc.

3.1.2 Maintenance of centrifuges (routine and preventive), checking of oilcircuit, oil pump limit switches, basket, adjustment of 'V' belts, greasing of bearings, starting of machines on no load and observance of any unusual vibration sound, need for dynamically balancing, plate checking of rubber buffers, function of distribution cone, feeding and discharging clutches.

3.2 *Thickeners* :

3.2.1 General description and constructional features of thickeners and its functions overload indication system and alarm, causes of thickener overloading and overload correction.

3.2.2 Thickener drive machine, major parts and their functions, different types of rake lifting mechanisms, routine checking of machines for (a) Lubrication, (b) Drive, (c) Feeding launder.

3.2.3 Periodical checking of rakes, i.e. chaining of thickener cleaning and checking of rake, overhauling of driving machanism, checking of feed well balancing of rakearms and adjustment of scrapers.

3.2.4 Flocculation and its purpose in process control, nature and use of flocculating agents machanism and theories of flocculation.

3.3 *Discfilter* :

3.3.1 Location, functions and types of vacuum filters, uniformity of slurry consistency in smooth filter operation, function of agitators, vaccums, blowing and scrapers, etc. effect of discs feed on performance of the filter starting and stopping of filter.

3.3.2 Cleaning of disc, after operation, checking of disc and replacement of filter cloth/bags, adjustment of automatic valves, changing and adjustment of filter scrapers, replacement of worn out agitator blades, sealing of agitator glands to avoid leakages of slurry, checking of barrels for any inter-connection, and leakage, checking and maintenance of lubrication system and pipe lines, trough and maintenance of drives.

4.0 *Electrical and Instrumentation* :

4.1 General electrical concepts, general description of sub-station and distribution system, protection system, control system, L.T. distribution net work, various electrical equipments installed in the plant and their function (HT/LT) gears, electrical motors and their controls, etc.), interlocking system, general precaution for operation of electrical units.

4.2 *Instrumentation* :

4.3 Purpose and function of instruments, different types of instruments used in the coal preparation plants for level and gravity controls, Bin level indicatots, prematically operated gates, solenoid valves, gates, despatcher and communication system, principles of operations and controls and instruments major components, their functions and maintenance.

5.0 *Lubrication* :

5.1 Knowlebge of different grade of the lubricants (oils and grease, etc.) and its proper uses in different units, frequency of replacement of lubricants with its running duration, viscosity and colour, etc., charts, of lubrication recommending different grades of lubricants to be used in different machine and units.

5.2 Checking, cleaning of bearings for lubrication, checking of oilseal and its function, couplings for proper lubrication.

5.3 Checking of oil levels and oil conditions in gear boxes and screens, oil filtration and reclamation.

6.0 *Safety and House Keeping* : *2 Sessions*

6.1 Importance of safe working conditions to the persons of the technician and their families. Knowledge of safety provisions and gudgets provided in the plant, safety appliances and safety apparatus used in the plant, discussions of some practical cases in leave session, effect of unsafe practices on production and equipments.

6.2 Importance of house keeping for better maintenance and production, provision and methods of house keeping, systematic stacking of materials within the working area and plant premises.

7.0 *Practical Training* :

7.1 The technicians of various categories and supervisors, after having received theoretical training, will undergo, on the job practical training in the plant. The group of technicians and supervisors will be allocated to a supervising officers/Engineers who will be responsible for ensuring effective practical training and exploitation of the scheme. The technicians and supervisors trainees will be divided into small batches and assigned to chargeman/fitters of the concerned section for maintenance training of different equipments and machine

7.2 *Practical Training in Plant Operation* :

After completing training in maintenance, the technicians and supervisors will be assigned to the concerned engineers/chargeman of the production shifts for on the job training in the plant operation techniques, preparation of coal, working of circuits, rectification of breakdowns and operational difficulties and maintenance of operation and production log books and records.

21

A Physiognomical Approach to Human Engineering

*R. N. Bhattacharya**

Introduction

While assessing an individual for the purpose of selection, placement, training, development, or promotion, a manager is faced with the problem of quantification and evaluation of the following three basic parameters :

(a) The 'Knowledge' possessed by the individual, (b) The 'Skill' possessed by the individual and (c) The 'X-factor'. With the aid of the various available managerial techniques, the first two parameters can be assessed to a fair degree of accuracy. However, inspite of the best efforts by some of the pioneers in human engineering and considerable amount of research work the third parameter, the 'X-factor' still remains elusive. What is this X-factor and why is it so elusive ?

* Industrial Engineer, East India Pharmaceutical Works, Ltd., Calcutta.

The 'X-Factor'

The 'X-factor' may be defined as : "An individual's potentiality to perform well in a given job." A close scrutiny of this definition would reveal that it does not merely confine itself to the motivational aspects alone. The word 'potentiality' in the definition encompasses and individual's entire personality and behaviour pattern in general.

It is worthwhile initiating a brief discussion regarding the need for such a generalized definition of the 'X-factor', for, herein lies buried perhaps one of the major causes of the elusiveness of this parameter.

Ever since the pioneering work of Elton Mayo, and infact even before that the main attention of almost all human relations theories has been focussed on the isolation and quantification of the motivational factors of human behaviour. Maslow, Adler, Goldstein, McClelland and many other pioneers have tried to analyze the dynamics of motivation. Two things appear to be common in almost all theories. The motivational factors appear to have been studied in isolation, and almost all theories tend to determine a 'common denominator'. For example, Maslow's hierarohy of needs appears to be a rigid framework within which almost every individual is expected to fit in. A number of other theorists, such as Adler, Goldstein, etc., seem to emphasize on a single motive common to all human beings (the 'power motive' of Adler, the 'achievement motive' of McClelland, the motive for 'self actualization' of Goldstein, etc.). However, the fact is that there is no single motive that determines how all the individuals will react to all jobs, and hence it is not possible to formulate any single strategy to keep moral and productivity high for everyone everywhere. To quote Saul W. Gellerman :

> "The first and most important thing to be said about motive is that everybody has a lot of them and that nobody has quite the same mixture as anyone else."

Since nobody has quite the same mixture of motives, the

search for the 'X-factor' must necessarily be made on a much broader scale encompassing an individual's entire behaviour pattern and recognizing individual differences in personalities. It must be remembered that the human organism is a single unit. What happens in a part affects the whole, and the whole, in turn, affects the part. Motivational aspect is only a part of an individual's over-all personality pattern, and hence can not be viewed in isolation.

From the above discussion we may conclude that the elusive nature of the 'X-factor' stems from two basic reasons :

(i) Most of the theories have tried to determine a common denominator, tending to disregard individual differences. However, the fact is that no two individuals make exactly the same adjustments to their environment, and thus no two individuals have the same personality. In the words of Gordon Allport, the eminent scholar and editor of the influential 'Journal of Abdominal and Social Psychology' :

> "Personality is the dynamic organization within the individual of those psychophysical systems that determine his unique adjustments to his environment."

(ii) Most of the theories on human relations have attempted to study motivational factors in isolation, while the 'X-factor' is actually an integrated personality pattern. One must evaluate the entire personality pattern for an assessment of the 'X-factor'.

Thus, in order to properly evaluate the 'X-factor' one must :

(a) Recognize the important role played by individual differences.

(b) Consider the entire personality patrern of the individual.

The Boundary Conditions

We are now in a position to define the boundary conditions within which any model for the evaluation of the 'X-factor' must operate. These are :

(a) The model should be an integrated approach towards the determination of an individual's entire personality pattern.

(b) The model must recognize individual differences in personalities and should be able to evaluate each case individually.

(c) The model must be simple to understand and operate.

It is the purpose of this paper to introduce '*Physiognomy*' as a workable model which operates within these boundary conditions and can be mastered without much effort even by a layman. The principles of physiognomy are simple to comprehend and, when applied judiciously, lead to a comprehensive understanding of human personality.

It is not possible to enter into a detailed discussion on the various principles of physiognomy within such a short space. Our discussion will therefore be necessarily brief and confined to the following topics :

(a) Justification of using physiognomy as a model.

(b) The basic hypothesis and definitions.

(c) A brief outline of the historical development of physiognomy as a science.

(d) The scientific validity of the principles of physiognomy.

(e) A very brief discussion on the physiognomical principles.

Physiognomy as a Model

Goldstein, attempting to solve the problem of how to determine an individual's potentialities, says :

> "...this can best be done by finding out what the person prefers and what he does best. His preferences correspond to his potentialities."

This means that if we are to evaluate the 'X-factor' of an individual we must familiarize ourselves with what he likes to do and what he has a gift for doing. But how does a manager familiarize himself with an unknown stranger, whom he meets, possibly for the first time, across the interview table ?

The answer may lie in the application of various quantitative and qualitative psychological tests and techniques. However, the difficulties in their application in a business organization are quite obvious. Firstly, their application demands a comprehensive knowledge of psychology and also a specialized know how in the application of these techniques. Only a trained psychologist is competent enough to administer these tests and interpret the results correctly. Another major difficulty lies in the fact that the application of these psychological tests is usually cumbersome, time consuming and expensive.

Is there an easier, quicker and less expensive way of determining an individual, potentialities ? Is there a technique that can be learnt and applied by an average manager ? The answer is—YES. Physiognomy is one such technique. Even though it has a firm scientific and psychological basis, as will be evident from the discussion that follows, its application does not require a thorough training in psychology, and when mastered, yields results very quickly.

What is Physiognomy ?

The Random House Dictionary describes physiognomy as : 'The art of determining character or personal characterstics from the form or features of the body, especially of the face.' Chamber's Dictionary describes it as : 'The art of judging character from appearance, especially from the face.'

Although these descriptions give the general idea of what physiognomy is, for the purpose of the present paper a more rigorous definition is called for. Hence, in the context of the present paper physiognomy is defined as :

> "The science of determining an individual's personality (behaviour) on the basis of observable aspects of his constitution."

It may be noted that the terms behaviour and personality are considered to be synonymous for the purpose of the present definition. Another point to be noted it that physiognomy has been called a science and not an art in the above definition. The reason this will become obvious during the course of our discussion. At this stage it only needs to be mentioned that : "Science is any skill that reflects a precise application of facts or principles."

A word of explanation is needed about the term 'constitution' used in this definition. We shall consider 'constitution' as defined by M.H. Sheldon :

> "...Constitution refers to those aspects of the individual which are relatively more fixed and unchanging—morphology, physiology, endocrine functions, etc.—and may be contrasted with those aspects which are relatively more liable and susceptible to modification by environmental pressures, i.e. habits, social attitudes, education, etc."

Thus we begin with the basic hypothesis that : *Behaviour is Related in Important Respects to Observable aspects of the*

Individual's Constitution and proceed to examine the scientific validity of this hypothesis after a brief review of the historical outline.

Historical Outline

Theories suggesting a relation between physique and behaviour antedate by many centuries the birth of Christ. In India the ancient texts speak of a specialized branch of knowledge known as 'Samudrik Shastra' which deals with the delineation of character through observation of anatomical and physiological signs. Astrologers, palmists, philosophers, poets and even charlatans all over the world have been using such theories through ages. We find references of such theories in the works of Shakespeare, in the great epics of Ramayana and Mahabharata and even in the works of the celebrated philosopher Aristotle.

The man who is generally credited with having begun a systematic study in this area is no less than Hippocrates, the 'Father of Medicine' (C 460—C 360 B.C.). It is interesting to note that his suggestions are highly congruent with the current emphasis upon the importance of endocrine secretions as determinants of behaviour, which have been studied by R.G. Hoskins.

Many of the early investigators tried to compile dictionaries of such diagnostic statements as "fat men are jolly", "lean men are shy and morose", "short and thick men are prone to apoplexy", etc. We have the work of J.C. Lavater, who, as early as 1804, published 'Essays on physiognomy : for the promotion of the knowledge and the love of mankind.' A similar work was published in 1809 by J.F. Gall and J.G. Spurzheim in France.

An important contribution was made by L. Rostan, a French investigator. In 1824 he published a four-fold classification of physiques. These were called the digestive, muscular, cerebral, and respiratory types. In 1909 G. Viola, an Italian anthropologist, simplified Rostan's classification in terms of three types. Other scholars like C. Sigaud, S. Naccarati and E. Kretschmer have investigated the relationship between behaviour and constitution and have frequently tried to introduce empirical control into the demonstration of such relations.

The work of Ernst Kretschmer deserves special attention because it was with him that physiognomy was converted to a formal discipline of 'Constitutional Psychology, and it embarked on its modern course. It may be mentioned here that a constitutional psychologist is one "who looks to the biological substream of the individual for factors that are important to the explanation of human behaviour."

Perhaps the most important contribution to the scientific study of physiognomy has been made by the famous constitutional psychologist W.H. Sheldon. We shall now discuss briefly some of his experiments and findings in order to understand the scientific validity of these principles.

Sheldon's Experiments

The work of William H. Sheldon, Director of the Constitution Laboratory, College of Physicians And Surgeons, Columbia University, stands as unique contribution to the development of 'Constitutional Psychology'. In Sheldon's Theory we find a clear exposition of the crucial importance of the physical structure of the body as a primary determination of behaviour. His techniques for assessing the structural characteristics of the body involve the use of standard photographs and a much more carefully specified and reproducible procedure than that of his predecessors. Sheldon believes that the riddle of the human behaviour will be unravelled only with the help of incraesed understanding of the biological-hereditary factors. In his work 'Varieties of delinquent youth : an introduction to constitutional psychiatry' published in 1949, Sheldon wrote : "...It has been growing increasingly plain that the situation calls for a biologically oriented psychology......This is perhaps tantamount to saying that psychology requires a physical anthropology for its immediate foundation support.

After an elaborate experiment involving four thousand standard photographs of male college students, Sheldon arrived at the conclusion that there were only three principle variables that from the basis of physique variation. These were called : Endomorphy, Mesomorphy, and Ectomorphy. Briefly, a physique heavily developed in mesomorphy is hard and rectangular with a predominance of bone and muscle. On the other hand, an ectomorphic individual is usually thin and lightly muscled. He also has the largest brain and central nervous system in proportion to his size. An individul who is high in endomorphy is characterized by softness and spherical appearance. There is an underdevelopment of bone and muscle and the digestive viscera are highly developed in this physique.

Having identified the three primary components of physique, Sheldon recognized that most of the individuals are a mixture of these three components and that within any single combination there is still room for tremendous variation. He therefore also introduced a series of secondary components.

The next step in Sheldon's experiments was to determine and classify the primary components of human temperament. Here also he conducted elaborate experiments using statistical techniques to finally identify three primary components, each consisting of twenty definite traits. These three components, were called Viscerotronia, Somatotonia, and cerebrotonia. Briefly, viscerotonic individual loves comfort, is sociable and affectionate. Somatotonic temperament is characterized by love of physical adventure and a strong need for vigorous physical activity. A high score on cerebrotonia implies restraint, inhibition and desire for concealment.

Finally Sheldon attempted to find out the correlation between physique and temperament. He carried out a study on two hundred male subjects and computed correlation coefficients for various combinations of physique and temperament. The results were unambiguous in suggesting that :

"...there is a close correspondence between temperament as measured by observer ratings and physique as derived from somatotype photographs..."

The following simplified table gives the values of the correlation coefficients of Sheldon's experiment.

Correlation Between Physique Components and Temperament Components

	Viscerotonia	*Somatotonia*	*Cerebrotonia*
Endomorphy	+0.79	−0.29	−0.32
Mesomorphy	−0.23	+0.82	−0.58
Ectomorphy	−0.40	−0.53	+0.83

Sheldon's emperical research stimulated numerous leading scholars to conduct research work of their own in the field of constitutional psychology. Prominent amongst them are H.C. Smith, C.C. Seltzer, I.Z. Janoff, W.W. Howells, I.L. Child, etc. A careful examination of these studies furnishes us with enough evidence in favour of the scientific validity of the hypothesis that :

'Behaviour is related in important respects to observable aspects of the individual's constitution.'

A number of theoretical models have been suggested for explaining the physique-temperament association. The 'Theory of selective experience' suggests that given a particular physique and a normal environment, the individual finds that certain kinds of responses are rewarded and eertain other kinds of responses are punished. For example, an individual with a frail body cannot successfully adopt a domineering manner in relation to most people. Thus, the person develops patterns of behaviour according to his physique. The 'Cultural determination theory' suggests that a persons with a particular physique "occupies a social role which includes a set of behavioural specifications and in the normal course of events the person will conform to these specification." A third theory suggests that both physique and behaviour are the outcome of environmental factors, while yet another theory stresses the influence of genetic factors.

It is important to realize that the principles of physiognomy are more inductive and less of a theory than many other brands of human relations theories. Although classical texts on physiognomy discuss in detail the philosophical implications of these principles and the existence of a 'Cosmic Order', for our purposes we may consider the principles to be merely statistically validated emperical observations.

Keeping this fact in mind, let us briefly examine some of the basic principles of physiognomy.

The Principles of Physiognomy

Before entering into a discussion on the principles of physiognomy, it is necessary to emphasize that an elaborate exposition of these principles is beyond the scope of the present paper. In fact, such an exposition may run into several hundreds of pages. We shall therefore merely discuss the outline of the general plan of physiognomical classification and see how these principles work. The present discussion is intended to furnish a generalized idea about the science of physiognomy and the task that lies ahead for an executive who decides to take up the subject more seriously.

One more point needs to be mentioned at this stage. As has been discussed earlier, different scholars have attempted to classify physique and temperament differently, based on their own experimental findings. For the purpose of the present paper, however, we shall follow the classical scheme of sevenfold classification. The reason for this is that this classification is more detailed and exhaustive as well as gives more scope for the accomodation of individual differences than the four-fold or the three-fold classifications. In fact, by a proper hybridization of these seven basic types, it is possible to analyze each individual case separately.

The seven-fold classification scheme assumes that human constitution and temperament can be classified in terms of seven broad categories. In the classical theory, each category has been associated with one of the seven celestial bodies of our solar system and is named after them. Thus we have such names as Jupiterian, Mercurian, etc., each relating to one particular category. We need not be unduly disturbed by these names, because, for our present purpose, we shall re-label them with more appropriate titles.

The seven broad categories constitute the seven 'Basic Types' of physiognomy. However, it must be remembered that it is extremely rare to find a person who belongs purely to one of these basic types. More after than not we find persons who are a hybrid of as many as three basic types. Hence, a careful observation and evaluation of the individual's constitution is neccessary to determine :

(i) The basic types which constitute his personality.

(ii) The weightages to be given to each of these types while synthesizing the personality pattern from analytical data.

Following is a brief desciption of the seven basic types.

Type I : The 'Brilliant' Type

(a) Physical Characteristics

Handsome and manly, shapely, well built, and muscular body; fine and firm skin; straight and finely shaped nose; large and intelligent eyes having a frank and honest expression; broad and full forehead; full and expansive chest. On the whole, there is a picture of healthy conditions, beautiful proportions, and symmetry of body.

(*b*) *Temperament*

Versatile, intutive, brilliant, frank, ambitious, honest, and adaptive. A very important temperamental characteristic of this type of person is that he is always the centre of attraction in whaever company he may be found and will adjust himself very easily to circumstances and people.

In the classical nomenclature, this type is called *The Appolonian.*

Type II : The 'Changeable' Type

(*a*) *Physical Characteristics*

Soft and spongy skin; round head; round face; round bulging and watery eyes; large and bulging abdomen; thin and high pitched voice; short, upturned, and small nose. In general, there is a soft flabby and spongy appearance.

(*b*) *Temperament*

Extremely lazy, fickle, restless, changeable, sensitive, and imaginative. Lacks energy, perseverance, and self confidence. Classically, they are called *The Lunarians.*

Type III : The 'Athletic' Type

(*a*) *Physical Characteristics*

Very strong and muscular body; bullet shaped head, thick and strong skin; short, stiff and sometimes curly hair; large, bold, and often reddish eyes; big and strong bones. On the whole, the appearance is one of a strong, robust and aggressive person.

(*b*) *Temperament*

Brave, energetic, aggressive, generous, determined, and domineering. This type is called *The Martian* type in the classical texts.

Type IV : The 'Diplomatic' Type

(*a*) *Physical Characteristics*

Very short height, oval face, sharp and penetrating eyes, thin and evenly set lips, unusually large chest, graceful and agile limbs. Altogether, the picture is that of a well knit, agile, strong, and intelligent man.

(*b*) *Temperament*

Intelligent, quick witted, crafty, atlkative, tactful, versatile, studious, and diplomatic. Classically, this type is known as the *Mercurian type*.

Type V : The 'Generous' Type

(*a*) *Physical Characteristics*

Largeness is the key word of this type. Large, strongly built, fleshy body; large and expressive eyes; large mouth with full and red lips; Roman nose, rich and musical voice; dignified walk.

(*b*) *Temperament*

Warm hearted, generous, good leadership qualities, conservative, peace loving with a strong sense of justice. In the classical nomenclature, they are called *Jupiterians*.

Type VI : The 'Beautiful' Type

(*a*) *Physical Characteristics*

Beauty is the key word of this type. Shapely and beautiful

body : soft and velvety skin; long, silky, and wavy hair; beautifully curved and well marked eyebrows; high and round hips; long and shapely neck.

(*b*) *Temperament*

Gay, joyful, unselfish, honest, sympathetic. There is a great love for music, fine arts, and in general all beautiful things.

They are called *Venusians* by the classical texts.

Type VII : The 'Cautious' Type

(*a*) *Physical Characteristics*

Tall, thin and pale; harsh hair; thin face; deep set eyes; thin and barrel shaped chest; stopping shoulders.

(*b*) *Temperament*

Cautious, cynical, prudent, conservative, tenacious and serious. Such persons are known as *Saturnians.*

From the above discussion it is evident that once the temperamental prerequisites for any given job are known, it is not difficult to determine the physiognomical type or types that must be looked for in an individual to ensure proper selection. For example, for the job of a 'Training Manager', one must select a person who is a balanced mixture of the diplomatic type (for oratory power, intelligence, and judgement of human nature), the cautious type (for tenacity, depth of knowledge, and seriousness of purpose), and the generous type (for justice, warm heartedness, and acceptance). Similarly, for a job involving hard physical labour, friendliness, and talkativeness, such as the job of a salesman, the person selected should be a mixture of the athletic type and the diplomatic type. Conversely, given the man, one can analyze his X-factor by observing his physiognomy and thus decide his training needs, his suitability for promotion, etc.

Concluding Remarks

It has been the purpose of this paper to examine the

elusive aspects of human engineering problems from a radically different point of view in order to formulate a workable model within stipulated boundary conditions. Considerable amount of systematic research work has been carried out by constitutional psychologists and its scientific validity is established beyond any doubt. The time has come to recognise the importance of this discipline and apply its principles for the benefit of business and industry. The main advantage of the physiognomical approach lies in its simplicity. No special training or Know-How is required and an average manager can learn and apply it easily.

Finally, a word of caution is needed for the rational and pragmatic managers. The classical physiognomy is unfortunately contained in so-called 'occult' books on astrology, palmistry, etc., which also include many other obviously controversial matters. It is therefore necessary, while studying these texts, to behave like the mythological swan, who is said to be capable of separating milk from water, drinking the milk and leaving the water behind.

Bibliography

1. Elton Mayo, 'The social problems of an Industrial Civilization', Harvard Business School, Boston, Masachusetts, 1945.

2. David C. McClelland and others, 'The achievement motive', Appleton-Century Crafts Inc., New York, 1953.

3. A.H. Maslow, 'Motivation and Personality', Harper, New York, 1954.

4. Alfred Adler, Individual Psychology. In C. Murchison (Ed.) (Psychologies of 1930). Clark Univ. Press, Worcester, 1930.

5. K. Goldstein, 'The Organism', American Book Co., New York, 1939.

6. K. Goldstein, 'Human nature in the light of psychopathology', Havard Univ. Press, Cambridge, 1940.

7. G.W. Allport, 'Personality : a psychological interpretation', Holt, New York, 1937.

8. R.G. Hoskins, 'Endocrinology : the glands and their functions', Norton, New York, 1941.

9. J.C. Lavater, 'Essays on physiognomy : for the promotion of the knowledge and the love of mankind', Whittingham, London, 1804.

10. E. Kretschmer, 'Physique and character', Harcourt, New York, 1925.

11. S. Naccarati, 'The morphologic aspect of intelligence', Arch. Psychol. 1921, No. 45.

12. L.L. Thurstone, 'Factor analysis and types', Psychometrika, 1946, 11, 15-21.

13. W.H. Sheldon and others, 'Varieties of delinquent youth : an introduction to constitutional psychiatry', Harper, New York, 1949.

14. W.H. Sheldon and others, 'The varieties of temperament : a psychology of constitutional differences', Harper, N.Y., 1942.

15. W.H. Sheldon and others, 'The varieties of human physique : an introduction to constitutional psychology', Harper, N.Y., 1940.

16. W.W. Howells, 'A factorial study of constitutional type', Amer. J. Phys. Anthrop., 1952, 10, 91-118.

17. Alan Leo, 'The art of synthesis', Indian Edition, Sagar Publications, New Delhi, 1970.

18. W.G. Benham, 'The laws of scientific hand reading', Indian Edition, D.B. Taraporevala Sons, Bombay, 1962.

7. G.W. Allport, Personality : a psychological interpretation, Holt, New York, 1937.

8. R.G. Hoskins, Endocrinology : the glands and their functions, Norton, New York, 1941.

9. J.C. Lavater, Essays on physiognomy : for the promotion of the knowledge and the love of mankind, Whittingham, London, 1804.

10. E. Kretschmer, Physique and character, Harcourt, New York, 1925.

11. G. Naccarati, The morphologic aspect of intelligence, Arch. Psychol., 1921, No. 45.

12. L.L. Thurstone, Factor analysis and types, Psychometrika, 1946, 11, 15-21.

13. W.H. Sheldon and others, Varieties of delinquent youth : an introduction to constitutional psychiatry, Harper, New York, 1949.

14. W.H. Sheldon and others, The varieties of temperament : a psychology of constitutional differences, Harper, N.Y., 1942.

15. W.H. Sheldon and others, The varieties of human physique : an introduction to constitutional psychology, Harper, N.Y., 1940.

16. W.W. Howells, A factorial study of constitutional type, Amer. J. Phys. Anthrop., 1952, 10, 91-118.

17. Alan Leo, The art of synthesis, Indian Edition, Sagar Publications, New Delhi, 1970.

18. W.G. Benham, The laws of scientific hand reading, Indian edition, D.B. Taraporevala Sons, Bombay, 19[illegible].

22

Application of Group Technology in a Multi-Product Switchgear Factory

P. Haridas S. Sahu***

Introduction

Group technology, which is now being considered as a new integrated manufacturing philosophy in small and medium batch production, has been successfully implemented in many engineering industries. Central Machine Tool Institute (CMTI), Bangalore is propagating, the concepts and principles of Group technology (GT) among the Indian Engineering Industries for the last 10-12 years. In the beginning major work was done to increase the machine tool utilisation by forming component families and group tooling thereby reducing the setup time. In many cases the reduction was reported to be 60-80%. The CMTI-GT team has implemented a number of projects and

* Dept. of Mechanical Engg., College of Engineering, Trivandrum.

** Dept. of Industrial Engineering and Management. I. I. T., Kharagpur.

good results are reported by the firms after the implementation of this philosophy.

Case Study

This case study was conducted in the press shop of a multi-product switchgear factory. The company manufactures a complete range of low tension electrical switch gears, contractors, thermal overload relays, motor starters, etc. Different products in the company are made in different assembly lines. Quality control personnel will check the assembly at frequent intervals so that the high quality of their products are maintained.

In the press shop of this company 497 different components for different products are manufactured. The machine shop is arranged on a functional basis. The shop has altogether 52 machines with 105 operators, including helpers and setters. There are 5 setters, and on an average nearly 20 set-ups are done per day, each set-up requiring time varying from 15 minutes to 2 hours. The batch quantity in the present system varies from 2000 to 100,000, depending upon the component variety. The waiting, time, transit time, set-up and change-over time, all constitute a major portion of the component through-put time. No planned loading sequence is adopted. The machine types in the shop include presses of various capacities, drilling machines, tapping machines CO_2 welding machines, brazing machines, spot welders, etc.

The company works for six days a week and 306 days per year. No individual or group incentive system is introduced in the press and assembly shops. Some of the parts are vendored or off-loaded due to technical or economic reasons. Manufacturing lead time varies from 6 days to 30 days, depending upon the nature and complexity of the component and their quantity requirements in the main assembly line. Labour performance indices (PI) calculated machine group-wise were found to vary from 63% to 73%.

The company wants to double its production by the year

1985-86 since the products are fast moving ones. Because of space contraints imposed by the Government, the company cannot expand the existing plant. Moreover, the rent in this area is very high. Hence, it was found necessary to assess the feasibility of introducing a GT-based production system in the shop in the context of the existing problems and entanglements of the manufacturing areas. Some of the basic information collected from various departments justified the need for a GT-based production system in the existing shop. The main observations are as follows :

(a) Throughput time varies from 6 days to 25 days.

(b) Investment in work-in-process inventory (WIPI) varies from Rs. 18.46 lakhs to 21.5 lakhs (on monthly basis).

(c) Existing layout is based on process layout.

(d) Set-up time varies from 15 minutes to 2 hrs.

(e) Stock/sales ratio varies from 14.45% to 17.99%.

(f) Batch quantity varies from 200 to 100,000.

(g) More area is occupied by WIPI.

(h) Labour absenteeism is 12% on an average.

Discussions with the shop personnel showed that there was a high level of WIPI, long throughput times, poor work-flow between various production facilities and overloading on certain critical machines. Data were collected regarding the components, list of machine tools, annual demand of products and components, availability of manhour, existing layouts, etc. The process sheets of the various components gave the operation number and the machines to which it was being allotted. Elemental time for each operation was collected from the Master File which gave the time in milli-hours/100 components which helped to calculate the load corresponding to annual demand.

The reorganisation of the workshop had been attempted by two methods, (a) Production Flow Analysis (PFA), (b) Component Flow Analysis (CFA).

Production Flow Analysis (PFA)

Burbridge's manual method of PFA has been effectively used for the GT cell formation [3]. This is mainly concerned with group analysis. Many process layouts include operations on machines which are undesirable to consider when forming groups. These are called 'immaterial machines', numbering eighteen for this case study. Since these are mainly low cost machines, these can be allocated to any group which will required them and they should not be considered when forming groups. Thus, the analysis was carried out for 34 machines.

15 machine usage sheets were prepared for the 11 types of machines. Nucleus selection sheets, which aid in forming groups, were also prepared. Module specification sheets were also prepared for the 11 machine types, and 29 sheets were thus prepared. Finally, with the help of modular synthesis sheet the required number of groups were prepared. In this case it was decided to go for 5 groups, because various studies have shown that 6-12 operators are desirable for good supervision, management and ideal working. When combining modules to form groups, one of the objectives is to have as many machine types as possible, each existing in one group only.

Analysing the process layouts of all 497 components, it was seen that 332 components were using the shearing machine which was the only one available in the shop. So it was decided to put this machine as a centralised facility. Depending upon the load coming on each cell, adequate machines were allotted. Total available hours/machine/year were calculated on 2 shift basis with 306 working days per year; the first shift was for 7.85 hrs and the second shift was for 7.5 hrs excluding lunch and tea break. So available machine hours/machine/year $=[7.85+7.5]\ 306 \times 0.88=4133.5$ which takes into consideration

12% labour absenteeism. Similarly, for calculating the time required by each component on various machines, labour PI and machine utilisation factor of 90% were taken into account. With the above informations the machine load chart was prepared which helped in finding the overload or the excess capacity available in each group on each machine type. Based on these calculations the available machines were judiciously allocated to the cells.

Once the allotment of machines in the cells was over, we had to go in for the layout within the cell. In the layout the machine which was used for the maximum number of times in the first operation was put first, next maximum to the second position, next maximum to the third position......etc. This arrangement of the production facilities within the cell simplified material flow system within the cell. This was done with the help of the machine/operation number frequency chart. While preparing the layout, enough space was provided for keeping the WIPI and other accessories. In this case five time the machine area was allocated for this purpose.

The various GT cells within the available space were arranged according to the cascading Principle. Similarly, indices between various cells were calculated in order to determine the exact positioning of the cells in the shop floor. The value varied from 0.14 to 0.6. The layout which looked ideal may become obsolete with passage of time. Therefore it is highly essential that the plant layout specialist should periodically keep track of the need for alternations and modifications that are to be incorporated in this shop layout from time to time.

Given below is the distribution of the total operations in the whole production system—

GT cell 1	168 Operations
GT cell 2	244 Operations
GT cell 3	302 Operations

GT cell 4 126 Operations

GT cell 5 270 Operations

The planning period is proportional to the through-put time, which in turn is proportional to the number of moves in the production system. Before the cell formation the number of moves were calculated as 514, excluding the movement of material from raw material stores and to finished goods stores. The movement from the centralised shearing machine is also not taken into account. Since each cell is a compact 'Product shop' which is self-contained and self-regulated, the movement within the cell can be assumed to be small. The total number of moves after the cell formation in this methodology was found to be 136. Analysis of these moves showed that most of them are due to the immaterial machines allotted to the various cells. Duplication of some of the immaterial machines can reduce the moves, but it will require additional space and money.

Reduction in move is estimated to be 73.5%, which will cause a corresponding reduction in the WIPI also, and the reduction is estimated as Rs. 14.85 lakhs.

Component Flow Analysis (CFA)

This is another methodology for cell formation. All the data collected for PFA, is made use of here also. After collecting the process layouts of all the 497 components the sequences were thoroughly checked. The different machine types and their combinations to make the different components were identified. The next step is to list the components for each combination. Altogether 55 machine types and combinations were found which varied from 1 component to 117 components. These combinations of components were made to form sub-groups. Then the machines used in each group were noted and load imposed on them by each of these were determined. Depending on the load pattern, machines were allocated. Care had been taken to load the machines in each machine type almost equally. Where the machine was overloaded, some components were shifted from one cell to another. While doing this care had been taken to see that the intercell movement was avoided as far as possible. It was found that the total number of moves reduced from 514 to 118.

The number of components allotted varied from 25 to 116. In some cases changes in the process layouts were also suggested. The manning of the machines was recommended as in the existing system and no change was suggested.

In this case also line analysis was done as in the case of PFA. A machine/operation number frequency chart was prepared for each of the GT cells. The distribution of operations in the various cells is given below :

GT cell 1	325 Operations
GT cell 2	254 Operations
GT cell 3	318 Operations
GT cell 4	134 Operations
GT cell 5	79 Operations

Similarity, coefficient index was also calculated between various cells and it varied from 0.14 to 0.6. Based on line analysis a GT based cellular layout was proposed and it was arranged according to the cascading principle, so as to result in a 'Flexible Manufacturing System'. Sometimes the space constraints may not permit to adhere to all the similarity coefficients. So a compromise best layout is done taking into consideration all the constraints. This requires some logical reasonings to position the cells in the optimal layout design.

Results of the Study and Estimation of Benefits

The following details indicate the estimates of benefits expected after applying GT.

Item	*Figure*
1	*2*
Total components	497
Normal batch quantity (NBQ)	200 to 100000
Setup time before GT	15 mts to 2 hrs.
Throughput time before GT	6—25 days
Total machines	52
Total number of operators	105
Total number of operations	1110
No. of shifts per day	3
Investment in WIPI before GT	Rs. 20.196 lakhs
Stocks/sales ratio before GT	16%
Total GT cells	5
No. of components/cell	25—166 in CFA 37—101 in PFA
No. of machines/cell	5— 8 in CFA 3— 10 in PFA
No. of production operations in cells	79—325 in CFA 126—302 in PFA
No. of operators/cell	1—14

(*Contd.*)

1	*2*
Estimated % reduction in WIPI and throughput times	77% in CFA 73% in PFA
Estimated savings in cost as a result of reduction in WIPI	Rs. 15.55 lakhs in CFA Rs. 14.85 lakhs in PFA
Estimated savings in space	230 sq. m.
Present worth of space saved at 10% discount rate	Rs. 7.84 lakhs
Estimated throughput time after GT	2—6 days in CFA 2—7 days in PFA

If 'tooling analysis' is carried out and a planned job loading sequence is implemented, considerable reduction in set-up and change-over times could be achieved which in turn would result in greater cost savings than estimated.

Suggestions and Conclusions

The analysis was done on 2 shift basis. In the case of overload in certain types of machines, it was recommended to go in for 3rd shift or for overtime or for both. Some changes in the process layouts were also suggested to keep the intercell movement minimum and to avoid overload in other cells. This study showed that drilling and tappling machines were under-loaded and most of the presses except 100 T and 63 T were overloaded. One tapping machine was found to be in excess. In the immaterial machine side, one conveyor brazing and two heat treatment furnaces could be shifted from the floor. On a study of the HT furnaces it was seen that % utilisation was only 25% with the existing three furnances. For convenience two furnaces were put side by side.

However, in case the transfer is not feasible, technically or for any other reasons, any one of the following alternatives could be attempted :

(i) procure one or more machines of the same type,

(ii) increase the machine utilisation,

(iii) subcontract the additional load,

(iv) tighten the time standards by conducting new time study.

23

Extract of Mr. Talavalikar's Lecture at College of Engineering, Poona

I have spent more than 20 years of my career in trying to work with one company or the other and in such diversified fields like textile and forgings and now in cutting tools. I have used these years to learn many things and particularly in the field of management. I would therefore like to share with you some thoughts on my experiences. I do hope that this may give you some insight in what is expected of a good manager and possibly therefore could save some of your time in finding it out. While I firmly believe that "experience" is one thing which cannot be purchased or bought, but is required to be acquired through hard way, one can always learn from other's experiences to possibly avoid pit-falls.

While there are a number of good books on the subject of, "management", and indeed possibly this is the subject on which anyone can write or talk including novice like me. There are no set norms by which whatever is written or talked can be judged for its correctness. It is a science, but it is equally an art, and, therefore, while through scientific methods you could try to set norms for the managerial behaviour, it is substantially influenced by the way in which you practise it. It is also influenced heavily by your own temperament, as well as by the temperament, of the people with whom you work. To my mind, therefore, managment is more an art than science.

The word "Manager" has been generally defined as one who manages people and certain areas of business or business in its totality. I believe that this is not entirely true, as in these democratic days people who work with you are aware and conscious of their rights and privileges, though not necessarily of their responsibilites. The job of a manager is not to 'manage' these people, but to get along with them in such a manner as to make best use of these people to satisfy the objectives of the business in the best possible manner. Every person has good points as well as bad points, and the job of the manager, in my view, is to make full use of the good points and not to expose the bad points to cover the bad points with his own ability, so that the business earns maximum benefits. I can compare this to Lord Shiva who, in the Hindu mythology, is said to have accepted poison and turned it into Amrut. When you qualify yourself through this Institute and join the industry whether in the private sector or public secter or even your own, and at whatever level, you will have some people working for you, with you and you would be also in turn working for someone. At all levels people you meet will have their own eccentricities as well as good points, and your success will depend on how best you are able to extract from these people their good points and cover up their deficiencies. The same rule will apply with other people when they deal with you. It is interaction between the people in your working life. Your success is not merely dependent on the good virtues that you have, but on your ability of making use of the good points others have.

Arnold Bennet has described "marriage" as marriage of differences, and for a successful life—whether business or personal—one is required to reconcile with various positions. This does not mean that you give up your own values of life but the measure of success lies in properly managing these opposing positions.

The second thing that I have learnt is willingness to accept your own faults howsoever trifle or serious they may be. To say to others that you never make mistakes is untruthful, and no one will belive it. To err is human, and, there fore, if you have made a mistakes, be bold and large-hearted enough to accept it, and you will find others responding to it. You will not be hanged for making mistakes, but people will certainly take you amiss if you try to cover them. So long as majorityof your decisions are right and there are no mala-fides for wrong decisions. You need not worry. Mistakes should be honest. That is important. I have yet to meet a person who has been successful in his life but who is not bold enough to accept his mistakes. Indeed, a coward cannot really become great because he does not have the mettle to be so.

Thirdly, while you may have contributed totally to the success of the project or a company or whatever job that you may be doing, please do not, even in your dreams, think that it is entirely due to your efforts. In the present business set-up it ts impossible for any one person to contribute to its successingly. It is always a co-operative effort, may be shares of co-partners will be uneven. The success that you have achieved is in no small measure therefore due to the people who are around you, and in the long run you will always find it to your advantage to say that success is due to them in large measure and you are only a minor contributory to it. Not only will everyone appreciate your large-heartedness, but, infact, you will also be more truthful to the situation, as it is really a joint and co-operative effort in which you may merely be an instrument. It is, therefore, wrong for anyone to claim credit for the good things and put the blame on others when in misfires. The garden rule which I have learnt is precisely to the contrary. If things have gone wrong be honest enough and say that you are entirely responsible for it. If things go well, give the credit for it totally to other and claim no share for you. In this process, you will achieve more than what you set out to achieve for yourself.

I will like to draw your attention to one more point and this relates to Dignity of Labour. From my experience I have found that a lot of people get sensitive of their positions in the organisations and treat work below their level with scant respect. Sometimes it goes to such a ridiculous levels, that for carrying a file to the senior officer for discussions they insist that it is carried by a peon. Every job, at whatever level, is important and should be respected. This does not mean that you should do all the time a peon's job, but if on occasion it is necessay to do so, you should not be ashamed of it.

Arising from the above, there is one more aspect I would like to draw your attention to, and this concerns the habit of accepting help from others without we helping them. We want our Government to do various things for us. We want college and institutional authorities to do various things for us, and this applies to practically all aspects of our lives.

I would like to add one more point. One of the keys to success is to never refuse any job or work that comes your way. You may be asked to undertake certain work which is totally out of your line, accept it. This will help in two ways, it will give an opportunity to learn something new and secondly the management will have good opinion of your willingness to get into wider fields as well as sincerity to the company.

Common Weaknesses of Managers

They often tend to be work and effort focussed rather than the contribution and result focussed. Therefore, quite often activity is mistaken for accomplishment. If you ask them "What do you do that explains your being on the payroll ?" You would not believe how rarely one gets an answer. One fellow says that he has 50 Accountants working for him. Another says he does quality control. Rarely do you get a man who says it is his job to see through the decisions our management will have to make in the next year and make sure that it gets the information. That is what we have those Accountants for. Rarely do you get a man who says it is his job to know what our customers are paying us for and to be sure that it is in the product. That is quality control. You have to be result and contribution oriented and not work or effort oriented. That counts.

A common failing is the failure of managers to concentrate their efforts on key areas. "The need to concentrate to set priorities is something managers do not like". The reason simply is that like all human beings they resist abandoing yesterday and abandoing failures. They put their best people on to keeping a corpse from beginning to stink which is a very difficult undertaking but not very productive.

Failing number 3 concerns the assessment of people. There is always a talk of people who are good and those who are not so good——but good for what ? All good managers spend a good deal of thought on what X is really good at. Where does he properly belong, may be, elsewhere ? The replacement possibility which I consider they key to management of people is simply not being discharged.

Finally, many managers make the wrong demands on people. If you ask people from which of their bosses they have learnt anything, they will always come up with the boss who is the opposite of the human relationship stereotype. Instead of a pleasant, able and courteous boss, he was rather tough, usually aloof and made fabulous demands not only on you but on himself.

As Engineer, you will easily appreciate the important of productivity——rather the management of productivity instead. Of all the factors of production in industry, namely the machine, the man, the materials and the money, what is, however, talked of is the productivity of either the man, machine or the material, neglecting the productivity of money, i.e. capital. It is now realised that it takes much more for capable management to deal with productivity of capital. Our goal, in my view, should be to get twice as much work out of money as we get out today. In other words, we must work smarter rather than harder, and that is where we must set a target for doubling the productivity of capital in times to come. The point I wish to emphasis is that, of the resources you have, money is the most expensive. It is frightfully expensive. Yet money is the only resources that does not charge overtime, that does not get tired. It is the only resource one exploits and really sweats. It is worth managing well. I find that few businesses really know the cost of ideal capital and equipment or pay enough attention to money management. You need more than a strong Financial Director. You need to have someone who is conscious of productivity.

As you enter Industry, you will be somewhat like a new animal in a zoo. Ambitious but perplexed, self-conscious but lacking self-confidence. People around are bound to watch you with the same curiosity as they watch a new animal in a Zoo. No wonder you will stumble on the steps of the ladder. I have found it very useful, based on my experience, to recapitulate the natural growth of skill which one has to have in a clearly distinct function as one grows. To begin with, you have to have technical skills. Later on, there will be a demand and on your relationship skills and finally on conceptual skills. At this stage, you must develop an ability to unlearn or subject specialisation and get into a perspective.

24

Capacity Balancing for Expansion Simulation Approach

M. Satyanarayana

The Associated Cement Cos. Ltd. Bombay

Introduction

The paper is an account of how a Chemical Company determined the size of the balancing equipment and storage to be provided under its expansion programme in the face of fluctuating availability of Railway wagons and trucks for despatches of its product and other variations in production and packing facilities. It is a case of calculated risk in long term committed of company's resources. It is a case of applying simulation.

For reasons of anonymity the name of the company and products are disguised and the data altered to the scale.

PART—A

The Company and its Operations

The Nirvana Fertilizers Pvt. Ltd. was founded in 1961.

The company has grown over the years as a producer of a fertilizer mix. Its present capacity is 54,000 tonnes per annum. The company is embarking upon an expansion programme to raise the annual capacity to 64,000 tonnes.

The manufacturing process of Nirvana is quite simple. The raw materials are proportioned and mixed in a panamixer and the finished product is stored in silos of 150 tonnes capacity each. In the packing stage, material is extracted from the bottom of the silos and packed into 50 kg. bags by means of semi-automatic packers. There are two modes of despatch, Rail and Road.

The existing capacities of mixing, storage and packing are as per the table 1.

Table 1

	No. of Units	*Effective Capacity per Unit***	*Total Capacity*
Mixing	7	1.35 tonnes/hr.	9.45 Tonnes/hr.
Storage	6	120 Tonnes	720 Tonnes
Packing—Rail	3	60 Tonnes/day	180 Tonnes/day
—Road	1	40 Tonnes/day*	40 Tonnes/day

** These capacities are based on levels actually obtaining now and are below the rated capacity.

* The packer meant for despatches by road cannot be used for despatches by rail, whereas despatches by trucks can be effected using the packers meant for despatches by rail. Thus, there is ample flexibility in the packing capacity for road despatches.

The question before the Management now is to decide upon the additional capacities to be provided at each stage of process. The issue is rather complicated by the following uncertainties inherent in the system.

(*a*) *Mixers*

Although the effective capacity has been estimated on the basis of the performance in the recent past, the number of hours for which the mixers are operated governs the daily output. This in turn has day-to-day fluctuations depending upon the maintenance requirements and power availability. The operation of mixers is also affected by the fact that the mixers cannot be operated if the storage silos are full.

(*b*) *Despatches*

The despatches are primarily dependent upon the availability of wagons supplied by the railways against the company's indent. It has been the experience of the company that despite careful planning of the requirement of wagons, many a time the actual supply made by the railways is far below the requirement, mainly because of the shortage of wagons, priority given to movement of foodgrains and congestion in movement by rail.

The shortfall in despatches due to inadequate wagon supply is partly made up by augmenting road despatches. However, here again there are certain limitations. Despatches by road have never exceeded 120 tonnes in a day. The truck contractors have to cater to the needs of nearby collieries and are not prepared to increase their fleet size in the absence of an assured regular demand. From the company's point of view, preference is always given to despatch by rail as it costs less on freight.

Thus, there are several interacting factors which have a bearing on the total despatches that can be achieved by the company in a year : (i) daily output of mixer (ii) availability of wagons and trucks and (iii) capacities for storage and packing.

Approach

The company has a good system of maintaining records, and data relating to the past can be useful in projecting the company's scale of operation for the future. The interaction of several variables can be brought into play by developing a simulation model. The company considers the following alternatives feasible and thereby narrows down its choice.

Mixing

— Improve the hourly output through technological changes after a through industrial engineering study. A 5% increase is considered feasible.

— provide one additional mixer

— provide two additional mixers

Storage

— Provide no additional storage

— Provide 120 tonnes of additional capacity (one silos).

Packing

— Provide no additional capacity

— Provide 60 tonnes of additional capacity (1 packer)

— Provide 120 tonnes of additional capacity (2 packers)

Several combinations of the alternatives under each stage of the process are possible. Simulation is carried out using nine of the combinations to assess the performance of the company under different conditions. The details are given in Part B.

Conclusion

(i) *Storage*

Adequate number of wagons being available for loading,

the despatches are not sensitive to the storage capacity. Therefore it is not advisable to invest on additional storage facilities.

(ii) *Packing*

With the existing storage capacity at Nirvana, the expected despatches would be as per table 2.

Table 2

Despatches in Tonnes Per Annum

PACKING CAPACITY	*MIXING* *One additional mixer with 5% extra output from each mixer*	*CAPACITY* *Two additional mixers with Present rate of output from each mixer*
One additional Packer	62,400 (97.5%)	62,950 (98.4%)
Two additional Packers	63,100 (98.6%)	64,150 (100.2%)

With one additional packer, the plant will be able to achieve despatches to the tune of 98.4% of the expanded capacity. If 100% capacity is to be reached, two additional packers would be required (besides providing two additional mixers for mixing). In view of the uncertainty involved in the availability of wagons from the railways, initially only one packer may be added. Installation of the second packer may be considered, say, after one year of operation with expanded capicty, depending upon the trends of improvements in wagon supplies.

(iii) *Despatches*

According to the simulation model, by providing one

additional mixer about 97.5% of rated capacity of despatches can be achieved, provided the output from all the mixers can be improved by 5% from the existing level. This improvement may be in terms of running hours per annum, or the rate of output or both.

(iv) *Demurrage*

The % No. of wagons carried over to the next day (Annexure VI) are indicators having a bearing on the final decision.

PART—B

Objective

To assess the additional requirement of mixing, storing and packing capacities for the company's expanded operations of 64,000 tonnes per annum.

Basis

A simulation model based on analysis of past data on the daily running hours of mixing units and the pattern of daily receipt of wagons from the railways.

Data and Assumptions

(*i*) *Running Hours of Mixers*

(a) Running hours are analysed for a period of one year omitting the days on which the running was affected for want of adequate storage capacity. The frequency distribution and the range of random numbers are shown in Annexure I.

(b) The average output of mixers was 1.35 tonnes per hour during the "dry" months and 1.25 tonnes per hour during the monsoon months (July-September).

(*ii*) *Pattern of Receipt of Wagons*

(a) The daily receipt of wagons during the reference

period is expressed in terms of equivalent tonnage and taken as the available capacity for rail loading.

(b) As the despatches by road cannot be increased beyond the present level, the despatches by rail have perforce to be raised by 10,000 tonnes per annum. In view of this, the pattern of receipt of wagons after expansion is obtained by prorating the receipts during the reference period correspondingly.

(c) Any number of wagons which could not be loaded either for want of product stocks or for want of packicg capacity are to be carried over to the next day for loading :

— If the balance carried over on a day is less than 50 tonnes, no action is taken on the indent for wagons on the next day.

- If the carry over persists for 2 consecutive days, the indent for the third day is cancelled.

— If the carry over is over 50 tonnes or more on a day, the indent for the next day ltself is cancelled.

Although such an action is not specifically revealed by the daily reports, in practice certain adjustments on the indents are necessary if the incidence of demurrage has to be controlled.

(iii) *Pattern of Despatches by Road*

(a) The despatches by road are assumed to follow the same pattern and to be at the same level as during the reference period even after expansion.

(b) The pattern of despatches by road in the past during the monsoon months was different from that during other months. However average daily despatches during the monsoon months were found to be 25% less. Hence, no separate pattern of despaches for monsoon months is considered and a derating factor of 0.75 is used to represent the conditions of the monsoon months.

(c) Although the despatches by rail gain priority over those by road, whenever the product stocks are inadequate to meet both the rail and road despatches in full, a minimum of 15 tonnes is assumed to be despatches by road. The maximum road despatches are limited to 120 tonnes.

(*iv*) *Packing Capacity*

The Plant at present has 4 packers of type I for despatches by rail/road and one of type II exclusively for road despatches. The possible output from the machine are :

Type I packer—60 tonnes per day.
Type II packer—40 tonnes per day.

Out of the 4 packers of type I, one is to be kept as standby. Therefore, the present packing capacity works out to 180 tonnes per day by rail and a total of 220 tonnes per day (by rail and road).

(*v*) *Storage Capicity*

The present storage capacity (effective) is considered to be 720 tonnes, i.e. 80% of the rated capacity. The silos to be provided under expansion are taken to be of the same size as those in use at present, i.e. 120 tonnes capacity.

Simulation

The decision tables shown in Annexure IV incorporate the various assumptions and the logic for simulation of despatches with different combinations of facilities.

In each case the simulation covers a period of 340 days—the normal days of operation in a year.

Simulation is carried out for 9 such combinations of facilities with the aid of a computer. The format of the output (in part) is shown in Annexure V. The results are summarised in Annexure VI.

Annexure—I

Pattern of Mixing Operations

S. No.	*Running hrs. Class (interval)*	*Equiva-lent output Midpoint of existing units (tonnes)*		*Frequency*	*Cumu-lative frequency*	*Range of random Numbers*
1	*2*	*3*	*4*	*5*	*6*	*7*
1	75— 80	77.5	105	2	2	00—01
2	80— 85	82.5	111	3	5	02—04
3	85— 90	87.5	118	1	6	04—05
4	90— 95	92.5	125	4	10	06—09
5	95—100	97.5	132	2	12	10—11

(*Contd.*)

1	2	3	4	5	6	7
6	100—105	102.5	138	7	19	12—18
7	105—110	107.5	145	7	26	19—25
8	110—115	112.5	152	9	35	26—34
9	115—120	117.5	159	10	45	35—44
10	120—125	122.5	165	6	51	45—50
11	125—130	127.5	172	12	63	51—62
12	130—135	132.5	179	11	74	63—73
13	135—140	137.5	186	12	86	74—85
14	140—145	142.5	192	5	91	86—90
15	145—150	147.5	199	5	96	91—95
16	150—155	152.5	206	3	99	96—98
17	155—160	157.5	213	1	100	99

Annexure—II

Pattern of Availability of Wagons for Despatch

S. No.	*Equivalent No. of wagons (class interval)*	*Midpoint*	*Equivalent tonnage for increased capacity*	*Frequency*	*Cumulative frequency*	*Range of Random Nos.*
1	2	3	4	5	6	7
1	0— 1.0	0.50	14	16	16	00—15
2	1.0— 2.0	1.50	42	13	29	16—28

(Contd.)

1	2	3	4	5	6	7
3	2.0— 3.0	2.50	70	17	46	29—45
4	3.0— 4.0	3.50	98	11	57	46—56
5	4.0— 5.0	4.50	126	12	69	57—68
6	5.0— 6.0	5.50	154	13	82	69—81
7	6.0— 7.0	6.50	182	6	88	82—87
8	7.0— 8.0	7.50	210	6	94	88—93
9	8.0— 9.0	8.50	238	3	97	94—96
10	9.0—10.0	9.50	266	3	100	97—99

Annexure —III

Pattern of Road Despatches

S. No.	*Tonnage (Class interval)*	*Midpoint (Tonnes)*	*Frequency*	*Cumulative Frequency*	*Range of Random Nos*
1	15— 25	20.0	4	4	00—03
2	25— 35	30.0	5	9	04—08
3	35— 45	40.0	6	15	09—14
4	45— 55	50.0	20	35	15—34
5	55— 65	60.0	24	59	35—58
6	65— 75	70.0	20	79	59—78
7	75— 85	80.0	11	90	79—89
8	85— 95	90.0	7	97	90—96
9	95—105	100.0	1	98	97
10	105—115	110.0	1	99	98
11	115—125	120.0	1	100	99

Annexure—IV A

Steps for Simulation

1. Select random number, corresponding to mixing capacity and determine day's mixing output.

2. Find total stock=Opening stock+Mixing Output for the day.

3. Select random number corresponding to wagon capacity and determine day's rail despatches as well as tonnage carried over to the next day.

4. Select random corresponding to road capacity and determine day's road despatches.

5. Compute total despatches=Rail despatches+Road despatches.

6. Compute closing stock=Total stock−Total despatches.

7. Opening stock for the ith day=closing stock of the (i−1)th day.

8. Repeat steps 1 to 7 for i=340 days.

Annexure—IV B

Decision Tables

The decision tables enumerate the various possible conditions which can occur when the mixing capacity, wagon capacity and the road capacity arc set on the basis of the respective random number selected. The mixing output, rail despatches and road despatches are dependent upon factors, like adequate availability of product and packing capacity.

The table are self-explanatory. Select the column corresponding to the applicable conditions occuring and read against the column the decision to be taken as indicated by 'X'.

Decision Table—1
Mixing Output
S=Storage Capacity

Conditions occuring	1.	Mixing Capacity > (S−Opening Stock)	x	
	2.	Mixing Capacity ⩽ (S−Opening Stock)		x
Decision	A	Mixing Output =(S−Opening Stock)	x	
	B	Mixing Output =Mixing Capacity		x

Decision Table—2
Indent for Wagons

Conditions Occurring	1.	Carry Over ⩾ 50	x		
	2.	Carry Over For One Day < 50		x	
	3.	Carry Over For Two Consecutive Days > 0			x
Decision	A	Wagon Indent For Next Day=0	x		x
	B	Wagon Indent For Next Day =Wagon Capacity		x	

Decision Table—3

Despatch by Rail

P=Packing Capacity by Rail

Conditions Occuring	1.	Wagon Capacity > (Total Stock—15	x	x		
	2.	Wagon Capacity ⩽ (Total Stock—15)			x	x
	3.	Wagon Capacity > P			x	
	4.	Wagon Capacity ⩽ P				x
	5.	(Total Stock—15) > P		x		
	6.	(Total Stock—15) ⩽ P	x			
Decision	A	Rail despatch= (Total Stock—15)	x			
	B	Rail Despatch=P		x		x
	C	Rail Despatch= Wagon Capacity				x

Annexure—V

Simulation Model for Expansion—Typical Computer Output (Partial)

Mixing 0% Additional Mixer 0—Add Packing—180—220 Storage 720—Add Wag—1.

Day	*Opening Stock*	*Random No.*	*Mix Cap.*	*Day's Output*	*Product Avail*	*Random No.*	*Wagon Capacity*	*Dispatch by Wagon*	*Bal. of Wagon*	*Random No.*	*Road Capacity*	*Despatch by Road*	*Total Despatch*	*Closing Stock*
1	*2*	*3*	*4*	*5*	*6*	*7*	*8*	*9*	*10*	*11*	*12*	*13*	*14*	*15*
1	500	83	186	186	686	82	182	180	2	67	70	40	220	466
2	466	24	145	145	611	29	70	72	0	19	50	50	122	489
3	489	65	179	179	668	58	126	126	0	11	40	40	166	502
4	502	30	152	152	654	19	42	42	0	10	30	30	72	582

Annexure VI

Nirvana Fertilizers Private Limited

Summary of Results

Alternatives	*1*	*2*	*3*	*4*	*5*	*6*	*7*	*8*	*9*
Mixing	0	+5%	+5%	+5%	+5%	0	0	0	0
No. of additional Mixing Units	0	1	1	1	1	2	2	2	2
Packing Capacity	180/220	240/280	240/280	300/340	300/340	240/280	240/280	300/340	300/340
Effective Storage Capacity	720	720	840	720	840	720	840	720	840
Wagon Supply pattern	Normal	Prorated	Prorated	Prorated	Prorated	Prorated	Prorated	Prorated	Prorated
% No. of days wagons carried over to the next day for want of packing	10.58	16.77	16.77	10.88	10.58	16.47	16.17	7.90	7.64

% No. of days wagons carried over to the next day for want of product	0.59	3.53	3.23	6.17	5.29	1.18	0.29	2.35	2.06
No. of days stock was Nil	0	5	4	9	8	2	0	5	3
Total Mixing Capacity	55,300	66,400	66,400	66,400	66,400	71,150	71,150	71,150	71,150
Total Mixing loss due to limited Silos	5,850	4,100	3,800	3,450	3,050	8,250	8,000	7,150	6,850
Total grinding done	49,450	62,300	62,600	62,950	63,350	62,900	63,150	64,000	64,300
Total wagon capacity available	30,400	45,600	45,600	45,600	45,600	45,600	45,600	45,600	45,600
Total loss due to limited packing capacity	150	1,700	1,700	900	800	1,450	1,450	550	550
Total despatches by Rail	30,250	43,800	43,800	44,650	44,750	44,050	44,050	45,000	45,000
Road Despatches	19,200	18,600	18,700	18,450	18,600	18,900	19,000	19,150	19,300
Total Despatches	49,450	62,400	62,500	63,100	63,350	62,950	63,050	64,150	64,300

25

Plant Layout through Group Technology A Systematic Approach

K. Bhargava

Final year PGP student, NITIE, Bombay.

Introduction

The main aim of group technology (GT) is to solve sum of the basic economic and management problems concerned with small batch production. GT is the technique of forming families or groups of components having similarities in production procedure. A group of machines or production cell consists of the workers and machines required to produce certain items from raw materials state to finished goods state. In other words GT aims at processing or manufacture of a particular item completely within a cell.

According to Soloja, "Group Technology is the realisation that many problems are similar and that, by grouping similar problems, a single solution can be found to a set of problems, thus saving time and effort".

GT is a manufacturing concept which affords an opportunity to drive benefits of mass production while going for batch production.

A few advantages are :

(a) Reduction in work-in-process inventory (WIP), throughout time and set up time.

(b) Improved costing, quality and work system.
(c) Enhanced productivity, ability to maintain delivery dates, co-ordination and control.

Literature survey reveals that in production shops where GT has been introduced, satisfactory production management has resulted. For example, in some cases paperwork, throughout time and WIP were reduced by as much 80, 75 and 70 percent respectively. Also, the introduction of GT builds up a perfect scenario for introduction of management by objectives.

At this stage a natural question arises, "why is it then that GT does not find much favour with the layout planner ?" Infact, due to absence of good methods required for family formation, planners find it is very difficult even to start. According to C. C. Gallagher and W. A. Knight, "the crux of the problem in GT is the identification from a large variety and total number of components of the families requiring similar manufacturing operations and tools."

Many methods of family formation have been advocated from time to time. The explanations are normally fuzzy and highly situational. In this paper an efforts has been made to suggust a simple, quick and systematic method of family formation. To have an easy understanding and ready comparison with other existing procedures of family formation, the new systematic procedure is explained through the production situation taken from a report by J. L. Burbidge.

Technique of Family Formation

Production Flow Analysis (*PFA*)

PFA was introduced by J. L. Burbidge as a step towards family formation. In PFA the machines and components are represented by rows and columns respectively.

Similarly Co-Efficient (SIMCOF)

The SIMCOF between two machines attempts to describes how alike the two machines are in terms of number of parts which visit both the machines and number of parts visiting each machine.

	m/c J +	
+ m/c K	NJK	NJK
—	NJK	NJK

where NJK=No. of parts visiting both the machines

NJK=No. of parts visiting machine K but not J

NJK=No. of parts visiting machine J but not K

NJK=No. of parts not visiting either of the machine

Then SIMCOF between two machines is

$$\text{SIMCOF} \quad JK = \frac{NJK}{NJK + NJK\ NJK}$$

Thus, SIMCOF is measure of interdepency between machines J and K.

Though the PFA matrix under consideration is very small SIMCOF computation can be done manually; however with a view to giving a universality to computation, a computer programme was written.

Cluster Analysis (CA)

Cluster Analysis is the term used to describe a variety of procedures for grouping items with similar characteristics. There are many techniques of CA, but none of them leads to an optimum grouping. The SIMCOF gives inter-dependency index. CA searches for hidden similarities among production facilities that are not immediately obvious. It is similar to descriminant analysis (DA), with one basic differences. In DA the problem is how best to discriminate between given populations that are assumed to be seperable in ambiguous manner by some externas criteria. In DA, task is one of finding partitions or boundaries that separate individual items in an optimal manner according to a discriminant function.

In CA, on the other hand, the problem is one of finding groupings whose population are not known in advance, i.e. the objection is to discover "Natural Cluster of the families based upon the internal criterion."

How Efficient is Layout Senerated by GT

Various minimum average index values, say 0.2, 0.15, or 0.1 will generate different groups. Before a final decision for implementation is taken, it will be desirable to take decision quantitatively. The two parameters which help in decision making are :

1) GT layout efficiency

2) Alternative choice cofficient

GT layout efficiency is defined as the ratio of number of

parts which can be wholly manufactured in any one of the groups formed to the total number of parts analysed.

$$\text{GT layout efficiency } n_{GT} = \frac{N-n}{N}$$

where N = Total number of parts analysed

n = Number of parts that visit more than one group,

$$\text{Alternative choice coefficient} = \frac{\sum_{i=1}^{m} i X_i}{n \times m}$$

$$\text{Where } X_m = \sum_{i=1}^{n} X_i$$

X_i = No. of parts that can be manufactured in number of groups

m = Number of groups formed.

Different values of minimum average dependency will give different values of n_{GT}, m, X_1, X_2......X_m hence ACCOF.

All these parameters will help in decision making as to which GT layout will be preferable.

Cell Design

Once the group are decided, a computer programme can be run to find out as to which parts can be manufactured in which group; some of the parts may require manufacturing facilities of more than one group. Thus, we can have a PFA matrix for each group by considering those parts which can be fully and partly manufactured in that group. The sequence of machines entering the cluster and knowledge of natural logical flow will help in placement of machines within the cell.

Is this Group Formation Approach Pragmatic ?

The group formation approach described above was

applied for replant layout of a workshop engaged in manufacturing a large variety of inspection gauges. Apart from this, it under takes manufacture of equipments required for proof of weapons. There were 180 machines, which could be categorised in 28 different manufacturing facilities. To cover all the production activities, as many as 640 different parts were considered for PFA.

The 28×640 PFA matrix was too big for mannual SIMCOF computation. A computer programme in FORTRAN IV programming language was written to generate the output directly in the triangular matrix from. The minimum average index value of 0.1 resulted in 4 clusters. The layout efficiency was 93.3%, as compared to acceptable 75%. The value of ACCOF was 0.52. Since both the parameters were favourable, the layout was acceptable to management. Based on type and number of machines, the area requirement of each cell was computed. The type and requirement of ancillary department were decided in consultation with management. Activity relationship charts (ARC) were prepared and preferred, aisle and gangways were ear-marked. The area requirement table, ARC was fed into the computer and 'Automated Layout Design Programme (ALDEP) was run. The ALDEP generated many alternative layouts, and the one choosen finally was recommended.

Future of Suggested Procedure

The procedure for systematic GT plant layout can either be performed manually or partly computerised, depending upon availability of resources. However, an effort is being made at National Institute for Training in Industrial Engineering (NITIE) to computerised the whole system. The input will be in the form of PFA and output as different plant layouts. New methods of cluster analysis are being explored to over come the computation. NITIE is optimistic that fully computerised system for a plant layout through GT will be eventually possible.

26

Waste Control in Spinning Mills

*K. Lakshmanan**

Synopsis

More than 65% of the total cost if yarn produced in a spinning mill is their raw material cost only. The raw material especially in cotton mills are wasted even upto 30% during preparatory operations such as beating, cleaning, carding, combing, and drawing. The waste at comber—one of the preparatory machines alone is 5 to 26%. This paper is therefore aimed controlling the waste at comber by scientific approach. The at net saving of waste will be realized upto 1000 kgs/day (equivalent to Rs. 15,000 day) for a spinning mill of 25,000 spindles working 3 shifts in a day.

Introduction

In the manufacture of cotton yarn, combing is not a necessary or inevitable preparatory operation like carding. If combing is done properly, it will facilitate further operations such as drafting and spinning and thereby adds more strength

* Dy. Manager, IE, Steel Industrial Kerala Ltd., Calicut.

to the yarn; gives better appearance and maintain a high degree of uniformity. But the above benefits are reaped only in a limited range. If combing is over-done, instead of improving the quality of the yarn, it will deteriorate by reducing the strength and producing more NEPS—an objectionable fault in the yarn. Above all, it generates more waste. This waste is known as *Noils*. Therefore, the necessity and degree of combing must be thoroughly studied to reduce the *Noils*.

Combing as known in the Textile Industry

Depending upon the variety of cotton fibres and the final yarn Number or Count, the mill management draws a policy of *Noils Extraction* by Weight basis. It will be expressed generally as a percentage and is about 15% on an average. This policy when deciphered by the production & maintenance people they set the comber heads by trial & error methods for the given percentage of *Noils* extraction.

Those who are quality conscious, may try to ensure that the percentage is maintained within tolerable limits; head to head and comber to comber variations in the percentage are within the tolerable limits by repeated checks and corrections. In other words, they ensure systematic generation of waste.

Combing—Its Real Meaning

As the fibre is a natural product, due to various reasons such as soil, climate, quality of seeds and the like, the cotton is bound to exhibit a lot of variation in all its physical properties such as staple length, strength uniformity, maturity, fineness, etc. With a view to producing a uniform yarn of good strength, the fibres should be above certain length depending upon the count.

This calls for removal of short fibre. Combing therefore serves this purpose of removing short fibres below a pre-set length of fibre. In almost all types of combers the fibres are fed intermittantly in a sliver form. A comb will so be actuated that it will remove the floating fibres from the tuft of fibres held between the nipper and the detaching roller. This removal is effected in 2 ways :

(i) By forward feeding, and

(ii) By backward feeding.

Necessary or not Necessary ?

Combing being, a harmful and luxury operation, need be avoided wherever possible. "Is combing really a must for our final product from the point of its end use ?" Is the first question everybody should ask. In fact many end-uses such as warp yarn & weft yarn of many loom woven fabrics are not combed. In some cases the hosiery market also does not ask for combed yarn for their outer garments. Low priced under garments too sometime are not made out of combed yarns.

The required strength for the yarn need not be achieved by combing which is likely to produce more neps & noils. Instead, a better draft plan and twist plan will give the strength. 90% of the carded yarns are comparable with the combed yarn in reality in all aspects.

Therefore, combing—a harmful and luxury operation need be resorted to only when the market demands.

Assessment

When the market demands combed yarn, the next question arises as "How much combing is really necessary to satisfy the customer ?" Because, overdoing, the combing operation creates more neps & noils.

To answer the second question, we require some more basic information such as :

(i) Minimum strength of the yarn required.

(ii) Minimum mean length of cotton fibres to get the above minimum strength at the appropriate twist and draft.

These information are not readily available in any text book. Therefore, a statistical approach was taken to form an empirical relationship between the strength; count; mean length and the end uses. Strength in absolute terms is not popular in textile industry. Instead, strength is measured as CSP—i.e., Count (Ne) strength (pounds) product. The following 3 formulae were derived empirically by fitting the data to a linear equation. However, the assumption of linearity holds good enough without much loss of accuracy for the Quality & Production purposes.

$$\text{Basic CSP} = 1700 + \text{Count (Ne)} \times 1.05 \quad \ldots(1)$$

$$\text{Minimum CSP} = X + \text{Basic CSP} \times K_1 \times K_2 \times K_3 \quad \ldots(2)$$

Minimum mean length of fibres in mm=

$$\frac{\text{Minimum CSP} + 18.27\ \text{Ne} + 70.3}{115.263} \quad \ldots(3)$$

where, CSP = Count strength product

Ne = Count number in English system

x = 0 for industrial average

x = 150 for the best mills average

K_1 = 1 for weft yarn & K_1

= 1.15 for warp yarn

K_2 = 1 for loom weaving & K_2

= 1.06 for other weaving or knitting or so

K_3 = 1 for carded yarn & K_3

= 1.115 for combed yarn

Using the above 3 empirical formulae the mean length of fibres required at the minimum for the required end use and/or market demand may be calculated. Fibres below this length need be removed. Short fibres are removed in the Blow Room & Carding machine regardless of comber. Therefore, the sliver combing out of the carding machine need be analysed with the help of a fibrograph.

Extraction of NOILS

Having analysed the silver of the carding machine, we will get a diagram of fibres which should be used for setting the comber. Combers can be operated as said earlier with both forward and backward feeding.

In case of forward feeding the maximum length of fibres removed will be equal to A—B/2 and in the case of backward feeding it will be equal to A+B/2.

where, A—is the distance between the detaching roller and the nipper

$$B\text{—is the feed amount} = \frac{\text{circumference}}{\text{no. of teeth of feeder}}$$

B will be normally 0.3 to 0.5 mm per nip. When the fibre diagram shows a high degree of uniformity i.e., almost 80% of the fibres are of the same length, forward feeding is suggested. Otherwise, backward feeding is good. However, it is subjected to the limits of A & B available in each comber. Equate the minimum mean length of fibres calculated to A+/−B/2 and fix the values of A & B subject to the available ranges of A & B.

Precaution

Depending upon the machine condition, maintenance and the like factors, the combing effectiveness will vary to a large extent. For instance if "L" is equated "A+/−B/2" & comber is set for a "A & B" we cannot be 100% sure of the extraction. Some fibres longer than "L" may be removed and fibres shorter than "L" may not be removed. Normally for a good comber this will be +/−5%. However, for each machine this tolerance has to be identified exactly by trials. Then a corrective factor has to be used for the "L" before equating to "A+/−B/2" depending upon the company's policy on the quality of product.

Some academically interested people will approximate the fibre diagram to a triangle and find out the percentage of waste. But it is an unnecessary exercise and also is not going to give the correct picture because of the approximation. Moreover the above approach is again based on the weight of waste and not on the length. It is therefore recommended to attack the problem of combing directly on the basis of length.

Economical Purchase of Raw Materials

Naturally anyone in the industry will be now interested to know the economical purchase of raw materials for the purpose of cost reduction. A simple procedure therefore is suggested to work out the economy hereunder :

Step No.

(1) For the given count, find out the minimum mean length required using the empirical formulae—suggested earlier.

(2) Calculate the landed cost of every cotton fibre available in the market.

(3) Find out the processing cost of the fibre through your Blow Room machineries, carding machine and combers—This cost is made up of machine hours; labour hour and the services such as power, compressed air and the like cost.

(4) Calculate the total cost per MT or kg of card silver to be processed in the comber.

(5) Find out the percentage of useful fibres from the fibre diagram with the help of a graph sheet. In the absence of fibrograph, find out the useful fibres by

trials. Let this useful fibre be expressed in decimal as x for each fibre separately as well as blend proportion wise.

(6) Collect the selling price of Noils per kg or MT Ex/mill price say P.

(7) Calculate

$$\frac{\text{Total cost/MT or kg}-(1-x)\text{ Rs P}}{x}=Z$$

Let this value be "Z" for each set of calculation. This is nothing but the cost of combed fibre/MT or kg of each fibre as well as blend. Choose the lowest Z and hence its raw materials which is economical.

Note : If necessary there are other sophisticated techniques such as linear programming, non-linear programming and the like for the above purpose. In addition to the minimum length, these techniques will enable us to optimize all the physical properties such as maturity, fineness, strength, smoothness ratio, etc. of the cotton fibre/blend for a given end use count of the yarns.

Conclusion

When combing is demanded the degree if combing operation has to be assessed on Length basis instead of conventional Weight basis.

It is to be noted that an average mill of 25,000 spindle capacity producing on an average 40 Ne Yarn, will be able to same minimum 1 MT=1000 kg of raw materials of waste every day by this scientific approach. Saving is therefore equal to Rs. 15,000 day. In addition, the production capacity can be better utilized by gaining more machine hours from the comber which is the critical machine in a few south Indian spinning mills. Above all, the mill can assure its customers a better quality than ever before by this approach of assessing the combing requirement on Length basis.

terials. Let this useful fibre be expressed in the mill as x for each fibre separately as well as blend proportion wise.

(6) Collect the selling price of Neps per kg or MT i.e. mill price say P.

(7) Calculate

$$\frac{\text{Total cost/MT or Kg } (Y \times 100) \text{ Rs P}}{X}$$

Let this value be "Z" for each set of calculation. This is nothing but the cost of combed fibre/MT or kg of each fibre as well as Blend. Choose the lowest Z and hence its raw materials which is economical.

If necessary there are other sophisticated techniques such as linear programming, non-linear programming and the like for the above purpose. In addition to the minimum length, these techniques will enable to optimise all the physical properties such as maturity, fineness, strength, smoothness, [illegible] etc. of the cotton fibre/blend for a given end use/count of the yarns.

Conclusion

When combing is demanded the degree of combing operation has to be assessed on Length basis instead of conventional Weight basis.

It is to be noted that an average mill of 25,000 spindle capacity producing on an average 40 Ne Yarn, will be able to save minimum 1 MT = 1000 kg of raw materials of waste every day by this scientific approach. Saving is therefore equal to Rs. 15,000/day. In addition, the production capacity can be better utilized by gaining more machine hours from the comber which is the critical machine in a few South Indian Spinning mills. Above all the intelligent wastage ensures a better quality than ever before by this approach of assessing the combing requirement on Length basis.

27

Computerized Production and Manning Record System A Case Study

*S.B. Vagal**

Introduction

Initial thrust of computer applications in most of the Indian companies had been limited to traditional areas, like Finance and Sales—Distribution. However, realising its true potential in tackling complexities and utilization of resources, more and more organizations have already started venturing into new but more paying areas of operations. Importance of effective Information Systems in areas, like Materials Management, Production Planning and Control, Machine Scheduling, Productivity Evaluation for improving decision making and control has also been now well recognized. In fact, with ever increasing competition in market place and prevailing economic environment in the country, computerization of various operational systems has become imperative for all progressive

*Manager, IE. Goodlass Nerolac Paints Ltd. Bombay.

companies. Advent of micro computers in the country has, in addition, made change-over to computerization more acceptable economically, even to small scale organizations.

The author had an opportunity of working on development of such information system connected with day-to-day shop-floor operations in a company from light Engineering—Printing/Packaging industry. Unit had some manual system operating to provide data on machine and labour productivity levels, machine utilizations, downtime details, etc. In order to make it a worthwhile component of an overall integrated information system under company-wide computerization plans, system was taken up for modifications. Manually operated system had its limitations namely : (a) Machine Make Ready/Downtime reports used to be available only at the end of the month making it impossible to take corrective action at a point during the month. (b) Instant comparison of utilization/downtime data in various critical equipments with immediate past, was not available. (c) Information history on production/manning/machine utilization/productivity levels could not be efficiently retraced. (d) The existing format for recording production and manning returns had been found to be inadequate to improve upon above shortcomings. (e) The format also did not have sufficient controls to ensure quality of reporting in terms of discipline and timeliness.

Improved System

To gear it up as a part of total integrated system, the computerized system labelled as 'Production and Manning System' was to have : (a) Weekly reports in place of Monthly reports giving machine/work-centre/factory utilization latest by third working day of the following week. (b) More exhaustive reports in the areas of Make ready/Downtime on a weekly basis. Individual operator performance figures in critical areas, were also to be highlighted through separate report. (c) Information history on Production/Manning/Machine Utilization/Productivity levels stored for a maximum period of three years and the information was to be available for reference at any time. (d) Weekly Downtime/Make ready/Machine Utilization figures presented alongwith comparative figures from past four weeks. (e) System was also to be extended at a later stage for evaluation of labour productivity levels as well as bonus amounts earned by different individuals in connection with Productivity Bonus Scheme that was in operation. This was expected to help in comparative assessment of current productivity levels with that in past for individuals or group of individuals. (f) System was to take up detailed machine/equipment break down or filure Analysis, highlighting trends and more susceptable areas on critical equipments. This was in turn thought to be essential for building up data base for regular updating of Preventive Maintenance programmes.

Salient Features of the Computerized System

As an initial requirement, the existing form was thoroughly modified taking into account objectives of the new system. Inspite of initial resistance from shop-floor management staff, it was insisted that all important data be filled in by operators on the job themselves. Filling of forms was accordingly made very simple and easy to understand. Major input features of new system could be stated as follows : (a) The same form was to be used for all work centres. Previously there were four different forms available to different group of work-centres. (b) Work-centres/machine were appropriately classified and codified. These codes were to be filled in the form for identification. (c) Standard Machine speeds pertaining to different product specifications were codified to ensure computation of Utilization indices. (d) Each product was to be identified by an eight digit product code. Exhaustive finished product coding was already available and the same was to be used for storing product-wise information history.

Some of the output formats which were recommended as part of the system are as follows :

Weekly report highlighting Utilization/Downtime/Make ready indices for different work-centres in the factory where

'Utilization' also essentially meant effective utilization of a work centre or its operational efficiency level. Exceptions over and above specified range of norms (indices) were to be indicated by asterisk. The different fields in the report could be explained as follows :

(*i*) *No. of Machine Shifts*. This is total number of machine shifts run or actually plained in the work centre over a week.

(*ii*) *Downtime* %. Ratio of total downtime in hours on all machines in the work centre and total machine hours available in the work centre (multiplied by 100). Available time per machine was 8 hours in 1st and 2nd shifts and 6.5 hours in 3rd shifts.

(*iii*) *Make Ready* %. Ratio of total Make Ready time reported on all machines in the work centre and total machine hours available in the work centre (multiplied by 100).

(*iv*) *Utilization Index*. $\frac{100-(\text{D.T.}\%+\text{M.R.}\%)}{100}$

(*v*) *Work Centre Effective Utilization Index* (*WEUI*). Ratios of total production quantity in terms of 'Standard Machine Hours' from all machines (based on standard production norms developed) in the work centre and total machine hours available (Multiplied by 100). This concept was introduced for the first time in the organization. Philosophy behind it was that, once any investment is made and a machine or equipment made available, it is applicable for any organization to earn revenue for all 24 hours. Also the company will recover its money and earn profits only if production of acceptable quality is actually achieved, is a common experience to find machine efficiencies made to look higher, allowing expensively for unavoidable downtime, set up times and other beyond-the-control situations. Concept of Effective Utilization Index is designed to take into consideration combined efficiencies of various interrelated functions and would fall if, say, Production Operators do not run machines efficiently or Maintenance Mechanics do not maintain at peak performance, Production planning man does not schedule them in optimum fashion or if Marketing man does not fetch longer run orders or enough orders. Given this background it would be very clear that achieving 100% figure for such an Index would have been highly unrealistic. However, achieving a figure near about 100, it was thought; could still prove to be the one ensuring highest possible utilization in every sense from any equipment Break-up of the difference between 100 and the index figure actually achieved was also to indicate further improvements possible in labour efficiencies and machine scheduling and also the spare capacities available.

(*vi*) *Overall Factory Effective Utilization Index.* To be computed on similar lines.

Weekly report highlighting details of utilization/downtime/make ready/excess manning indices for all machines in a work centre. Exceptions over and above specified range of norms were similarly to be indicated by esterisk. The different fields in the report were :

(*i*) *No. of Machine Shifts.* Total no. of machine shifts run or actually planned for a machine over a week.

(*ii*) *Downtime % (Total).* Ratio of total Downtime reported on a machine over a week and total machine time available (Multiplied by 100).

—Downtime % for specific reasons would also be computed on the same basis, denominator remaining same in each case.

(*iii*) *Make Ready % (Total).* Ratio of total Make Ready

time reported on a machine over a week and total machine time available (multiplied by 100)

—Make ready % for specific reasons would also be computed on the same basis.

(*iv*) *Utilization Index.* $\dfrac{100-(\text{D.T. }\%+\text{M.R. }\%)}{100}$

(*v*) *Machine Effective Utilization Index* (*MEUL*). Ratio of total production quantity in terms of Standard Machine Hours' obtained from a machine over a week and total machine hours available (multiplied by 100).

(*vi*) *Excess Manning.* Cumulative difference between actual and standard manning, expressed in terms of 'Man-shifts' over a week for a machine. It is common experience to see many a machines manned with excessive manning even after setting standard manning for these machines, on one pretext, or the other. Some action would be initiated, it was thought, if some cumulative figure on such misuse of manpower is made available to persons asking questions.

A weekly report highlighting individual performance of operators from critical areas in term of total quantity produced and average production quantity per 8 hours shifts. The different fields in this report are explained as follows :

(*i*) *Sheets/Cartons Produced.* Total no. of sheets, Cartons produced over a week by individual operator.

(*ii*) *Sheets/Cartons for 8 Hours Shift.* Ratio of total no. of sheets/Cartons produced by one operator and total no. of hours he was present during a week, multiplied by 8.

—Operator performance ratios were recommended in two most critical areas where their performance would have immediate and substantial impact on overall output level achieved at the unit. Inspite of differences in Production norms of different product categories these performance ratios in absolute quantities were found to give some idea about productivity levels of individuals, over a span of one week. This was expected to be of some help for the shop-floor supervisor while manning critical jobs.

This salient information from daily production and manning record sheets (input formats) reproduced on a weekly basis. Input formats in the old system used to be preserved for a period of at least one year to enable answering queries that may arise during this period. Besides occupying large storage space, retrieval of information also was very tedious. Computerized print-out, occupying only one line for each format filled, was expected to provide efficient ways for storage and retrievel.

would have immediate and substantial impact on overall output level achieved at the mill. Insight into differences in production norms of different product categories, their performance ratings and absolute quantities were found to give some idea about productivity levels of individuals over a span of one week. This was expected to be of some help in the shop-floor survey of what manpower critical jobs.

Thus, salient information from daily production and manning record sheets (input formats) reproduced on a weekly basis, in input formats in the old system used to be preserved for a period of at least one year to enable answering queries that may arise during this period. Besides occupying large storage space, retrieval of information also was very tedious. Computerized printout, occupying only one line for each format filed, was expected to provide efficient way for storage and retrieval.

28

Computerised System of Establishing Time Standards

D.S. Kulkarni, V.J. Nagar & D.N. Dharbale***

Introduction

Hindustan Aeronautics Limited, Nasik Division is presently engaged in manufacturing of aircraft to cater to Indian Air Force needs. This is a front line tactical interceptor/fighter aircraft powered by a single turbojet engine. The factory was established in 1966 and has well laid out plant having manufacturing shops, assembly shops, process shops, flight hangar and aerodrome. The manufacturing shops are equipped with modern machinery and equipment to facilitate fabrication of large variety of components. The assembly shops have equipment for progressive assembly from details and sub-assemblies and testing of aircraft systems.

In the manufacture of aircraft, complexity of components

* Dy Manager (Computer).
** Industrial Engineer, Hindustan Aeronautics Limited Nasik Division.

requires use of wide range of technology, such as precision machining, metal forming, welding bonding, rubber and plastic forming, etc. These consequently necessitate the use of complex tooling to meet production requirements. The manufacture of this aircraft requires that each of the components and assembly, numbering more than 22,000 are produced within a specified tolerance to ensure that components do not have any mismatch during various stages of progressive assembly operations and also to maintain the requirement of interchangeability. Different ferrous and non-ferrous material, such as structural steel, various alloy steel, aluminium and magnesium alloy, etc. in the form of bars, sheets plates, rods, castings and forgings are used in manufacture of aircraft.

The machining of the above materials has necessitated the use of variety of conventional machines as well as special purpose machines, like copy milling, copy turning, 3D milling, etc. The factory has over 1100 machine tools of which turning and milling machine alone account for about 45% of the total machine tools. Besides conventional machine tools, numerically controlled machines and certain precision machines are also being used in this factory. These include light and heavy duty CNC lathes, CNC skin and profle mills, CNC plano mills, CNC machining centre, CNS vertical mills, jig boring, jig grinding machines, etc. Over 2500 standard and production (special) cutting tools of high speed steel, super HSS, carbide tips, coated carbides, cubic boron nitride inserts, etc. are being used in machining of components.

Need for Work Measurement

In an aircraft factory, establishment of time standard for carrying out different operations involved in fabrication/ assembly is of prime importance. This data is of multifarious use especially in the following areas : Manpower planning for multi-trade requirements; Facility planning and plant balancing; Shop scheduling and monitoring of shops performance; Preparation of cost quotation for selling of aircraft as well as spares to Air Force; Operating productivity linked incentive scheme.

Need for Synthetic Data

The establishment of time standards is a very voluminous task as it involves assessing the work content for each of about 4 lakh operations carried out on a variety of raw materials at different work centres using a wide range of tooling. In the light of above facts it is not practicable to conduct time studies for establishing the time standards. In view of this, the factory has developed synthetic data for development of time standards on an elaborate basis to cover entire range of machining/manual operations.

Synthetic data basically comprises of two parts : Manual elemental data; Machining parameters; The first part of synthetic data gives different manual elements involved in the different work centres and their detailed descriptions, clearly mentioning start and end point of each element. It also gives the time values for each element in normal man-minutes (NMM) which is time taken by a qualified worker to do that element once. Generally, necessary compensatory relaxation allowance is also added to each elemental value and the time is then given in standard man minutes (SMM).

The second part of synthetic data gives information regarding machining parameters, like cutting speed, feed, depth of cut, etc. for different types of operations for materials, tools and machine class combinations. It also gives the extent to which the machining parameters required to be modified under various constraints, such as slenderness ratio, tool radius, tolerance, etc.

Development of Synthetic Data

The factory has developed a synthetic data by conducting extensive time studies on different work centres involved in fabricating aircraft components. While developing it, care has been taken to see that time studies are conducted on entire range of operations, components, machine tools, materials and tooling. The statistical tests were applied to the data compiled from time studies to ensure that the elemental time values derived from above are applicable to total population with the desired accuracy. As the task was of large magnitude, it took the factory more than two years to develop synthetic data by deploying a team of experienced Industrial Engineers.

Use of Synthetic Data in Rate Fixing

Normally for assessing the standard time, i.e. rate fixing for each of the operations of a component, Industrial Engineer uses following set of documents :

Component Drawing. It provides information like material, geometrical configuration of component, various dimensions with finish tolerances to be obtained on component and the stock supplied for fabrication.

Technology. It provides information, like machine tool, holding devices and cutting tool to be used for different operations; process details for carrying out the operation; tolerance to be maintained during intermediate operations, etc.

Synthetic Standard. It is a catalogue of elemental time values for different job handling, machine manipulation elements and the various metal cutting parameters.

Procedure of Rate Fixing Component

Rate fixing involves the study of component drawing, technology and breaking down of operation into different elements, mainly into machining and manual elements. Time required for machining elements is decided by referring different cutting speed, feed, depth of cut and RPM tables and by taking into account effect of various machining constraints, like slenderness ratio, tool radius, rigidity of holding, etc. Time for manual elements is arrived by identifying various manual elements involved in job and by selecting the appropriate elemental time values from synthetic standard. Finally, time required is computed by adding time for manual and machining elements with necessary allowances.

Problems and Constraints in Manual Rate Fixing

Aircraft manufacturing involves a large number of components of varying complexity where manual rate fixing requires considerable cycle time and deployment of quite a few number of experienced Industrial Engineers. There is a dearth of experienced Industrial Engineers which makes rate fixing a bottleneck in the pre-manufacturing activities. There is every chance of varying interpretation of synthetic data by different Industrial Engineers which may affect consistency, accuracy and finally quality of rate fixing.

Computerisation of Rate Fixing

The study of the methodology of the manual rate fixing and problem experienced in it bring out the following points : Frequent reference of the synthetic data catalogue by Industrial Engineer for selection of appropriate elemental time values and machining parameters; Monotonous/cumbersome calculations for computing machining time taking into consideration the different constraints involved; Errors in rate fixing due to wrong interpretation of synthetic data.

If synthetic data catalogue containing the elemental time value and the various machining parameters could be stored in computer memory in the form of master fines and a suitable logic is developed to select the various machining parameters and elemental time values, the manual effort involved in referring the synthetic data, carrying cumbersome calculations on the part of Industrial Engineer could be eliminated.

Computerisation Facilities at Nasik Division

The factory has a 4th generation UNIVAC 1100/60 On line computer with following configuration : Gentral Processing Unit, 524 K words (2MB) memory; 2 disk drives of 600 MB capacity each; 3 magnetic tapes; Line printer (900 lines per minutes); 12 CRT Terminals (4 with hard copy); Graphic Terminal; Plotter; Paper tape reader/punch; Communication system.

During the last couple of years, significant progress has been made in computerisation of Production, Planning & Control System, Materials Management. Accounting and other applications. In all the areas instead of adopting any standard software package from the market, the factory has developed its own in-house system to meet the specific requirements of aircraft production. The factory has a pool of experienced System Analysis and Programmers to undertake programming work. The system would be utilised to update files on-line from various user locations and give on-line query response at the point of use.

In-house Development of System for Computerised Rate Fixing

The factory has drawn plans for changing over to a new sophisticated product during the next couple of years. As discussed in foregoing paragraphs, taking up of new product would involve a major task of rate fixing for Industrial Engineering Department. Establishing the standard times for new product will require the services of a large number of experienced Industrial Engineers for a period of more than two years. With manual rate fixing, it will not be possible to undertake this task within the stipulated time frame even after augmenting the IED staff.

Considering the limitations of conventional way of rate fixing to cope with the forthcoming task of the new product, a need was felt about exploring the possibility of computerisation of rate fixing. Since no software package for such purpose was readily available in the country or abroad to suit our requirements, it was considered necessary to develop an in-house system with a team of experienced staff from Industrial Engineering and Computer Services Departments. In order to make the Industrial Engineers familiar with programming concepts, an appreciation on FORTRAN Programming was organised.

As the major portion of machining is being carried out on different types of lathes, the system development was first taken up on operations carried out on Turning machines.

Rate Fixing Through Computer

System Design and Computer Programming

After careful analysis of the problem of rate fixing, a comprehensive system design for the problem was thought of, taking also into consideration the facilities that are available on the new UNIVAC 1100/60 computer.

Inputs

(A) Master File

This file contained the permanent and basic information which will be used in the calculations. The file consisted of about 1500 master records. In order to facilitate proper updating as well as maintaining the file sequential file organisation was planned.

The master records was classified into different types of records. These were broadly as follows : Cutting speed table for different materials, machine tools, cutting tools, etc.; Feed tables and Depth of cut tables for different materials, equipments, nature of operations, etc.; Tolerance charts and finish cut charts—RPM tables for different machine tools—Charts for job handling and machine manipulation elements.

(B) Detail Data File

This file consisted of the records containing the detail data which had to be supplied by the Industrial Engineer for each of the machining operation to be rate fixed. As shown in the example given below, each of the operation consisted of sub operations which were carried out in one setting, such as facing, turning, grooving, drilling etc. the input data is categorised in two parts.

Main Operation Data. This contained Job material; Work Centre; Holding device; Number of parts machined at a time.

Sub-Operation Data. This contained Type of sub-operation; Initial diameter; Final diameter; Length of cut; Feed mode whether Auto or Hand; Type of cutting tool used (HSS/CT/SHSS); Tool radius; Tolerance to be maintained on the component.

Operation No. 40 *Work Centre No. 114*
(Centre—Lathe)

(a) Tern dia 18.3 with R_1 on L=142.5

(b) Turn dia $16L_4$ on L=15.0

(c) Turn groove width B=4

(d) Turn chamfer

(e) Cut thread M16×1.5 Class-2.

Processing

After feeding the input as given above, the selection of cutting speed, feed and depth of cut was done by programme by retrieving various master files needed for reference. The RPM and number of cuts required were calculated. The calculated RPM was compared with the available RPM on the machine and appropriate RPM was selected. Finally, machining time required for each sub-operation was calculated. On the basis of the output generated during the computation of machining time, lie RPM, feed, number of cuts the manual time was computed by referring the synthetic time value tables for different manual elements involved. The selection of the manual elements and the frequency of their occurance was decided by the programme. A sample flow chart for one of the sub-operations (that of turning) for machining time computation is given for reference at Appendix-A.

Output

This gives the total time required for an operation. A comprehensive record is printed for each sub-operation, containing all the fields of input, like initial dia, final dia, tool radius, tolerance to be maintained etc. and the critical output elements like RPM value selected, feed value selected, number

Input Data

Main Operation Data

Opn. No.	*Material*	*Work Centre*	*Holding Method*	*Holding dia.*	*No. of Parts**	*No. of Tools*
40	STR	114	Between-Centre-1	24.0	1	3

*No. of parts to be machined at a time.

Sub-Operation Data :

Opn. Desc.	*Initial Dia.*	*Final Dia./Pitch*	*Length of cut*	*Feed Mode*	*Type of Tool*	*Tool Radius/ Cl. of thread*	*Tolerance*
TURN	27.70	18.3	142.5	AUTO	CT	1.0	—
TURN	18.30	16.0	15.0	HAND	CT	1.0	L_4
GROOVE	16.00	13.8	—	—	HSS	4.0	EXT
CHAMFER	16.00	—	—	—	—	—	—
THREAD	16.00	1.5	11.0	AUTO	S-PT	2.0	EXT

of cuts required, unit time and description of all the manual elements and their frequency of occurance. A sample output report is given at Appendix-B.

Advantages of Computerised System

Computerised system of rate fixing has the following distinct advantages over conventional system : Significant reduction in the time required for rate fixing. Rate fixing is simplified and hence can be done by relatively less experienced or fresh Industrial Engineers. This would enable better utilisation of experienced Industrial Engineers; Increased consistency and accuracy in rate fixing; Increased flexibility to incorporate refinements, additions, modifications in the synthetic data as the system is modular in nature; Improved documentation which enables easy understanding of the derivation of standard time.

Conclusion

The rate fixing, using synthetic data, envisages considerable familiarity of the subject by Industrial Engineer. It would be necessary to visualise the various machining operations and select the appropriate parameters under given conditions. Therefore, the scope and extent of computerisation and its feasibility was not fully clear in the beginning when assignment was taken up. A detail study of the assignment by a team of experienced Industrial Engineers and System Analyst has made it possible to develop a suitable computerised system of rate fixing. It is gratifying to note that the system could be successfully developed in this factory and meets the main objective of simplifying and expediting the rate fixing procedure, making it more consistent and accurate as well as flexible enough to incorporate any further additions, refinements, etc. to the synthetic data. Successful implementation of this project brings out the vast potential available in this field to Industrial Engineers to increase their effectiveness and further enhance their capabilities.

[illegible] various reports [illegible] the

on all required [illegible] time and description of all the standard elements and their frequency of occurrence. A sample output report is given at appendix-II.

Advantages of Computerised Systems

Computerised system of rate fixing has the following distinct advantages over conventional system: A significant reduction in the time required for rate fixing. Rate fixing is simplified and hence can be done by relatively less experienced staff in the Industrial Engineering. This would enable better utilisation of experienced Industrial Engineers; increased consistency and accuracy in rate fixing; increased flexibility to incorporate amendments, additions, modifications in the synthetic data as the system is modular in nature; improved documentation which enables easy understanding of the derivation of standards.

Conclusion

The rate-fixing using synthetic data has many advantages [illegible] in a [illegible] should be [illegible] the various machines, operations and [illegible] the appropriate parameters under each [illegible]. Therefore the [illegible] extent of computerisation and its [illegible] was not fully clear in the beginning when [illegible] was taken [illegible] study of the [illegible] of [illegible] Industrial Engineering and System Analysis has made it possible to develop a [illegible] computerised system [illegible] to work out the system could be [illegible] developed in this factory and [illegible] the [illegible] consistent and accurate as well as flexible enough to incorporate any further additions, refinements, etc. in the synthetic data. Successful implementation of this project throws out the vast potential available in the field to Industrial Engineers to increase their effectiveness and further enhance their capabilities.

29

How to Increase the Engineer's Individual Productivity

*Roger L. Kirkham**

Summary

The bottom line for management is getting the expected results. How hard one has worked, how busy he has been is incidental to getting the job done. The most important resource in getting results is people. Therefore improving the productivity of this most important resource should be of vital concern to management.

The engineer's personal productivity can be improved by :

1. Effective use of the time he spends on the job.

2. Focusing his creative and innovative abilities on expected results.

---

* President, American Training Alliance.

* Reprinted with courtesy A.I.I.E.

3. Structuring the job environment to avoid job dissatisfaction.

4. Recognizing individual accomplishments and providing opportunity for advancement and increase responsibility.

5. Basing performance standards on the achievement of realistic, measurable objectives stated in terms of expected results.

Efficient Use of an Engineers Input

All engineers bring with them to the job as input the time they will spend on the job, and their creative and innovative abilities. As additional input, the company structures the environment in which the engineer works. There are several steps which can improve the individual engineer's productivity by ensuring efficient use of each of these inputs.

Time, The Most Valuable Individual Resource

Why are some engineers more effective than others? Even though backgrounds may be similar, education the same, experience comparable and job assignments related some seem to achieve more, accomplish more, get more out of life than others. Part of the answer lies in their use of their common, personal resource, time. The use of time is the result of hundreds of thousands of big and little choices made each year, month, week, day and minute.

If were not entirely satisfied with the pay off from those decisions, that is if we feel its possible to achieve more and accomplish more, then more conscious control is required. Control starts with planning. Planning is bringing the future into the present so we can do something about it now.

Selective choices of effort are more important in improving individual productivity than simply increased effort. We are paid for getting results not putting in time. Therefore effective time planning should focus in getting results.

Some goals to include in effective time planning are :

1. Prioritize an action list for each day.

2. Stick to your priorities as you are the best judge of your time.

3. Separate the vital few from the trivial many.

4. Do the most important thing first.

5. Schedule regular private time when you are to be undisturbed to allow focussed concentration.

6. Schedule interruption by reserving time each day when you are available for discussion and questions.

7. Select the best time of day for the type of work required.

8. Set deadlines for yourself and others.

9. Handle each piece of paper only once.

10. Identify the expected results before taking action.

Creativity is the Means, not the end

Creativity and innovation are the means by which results can be achieved. The activities of creativity and innovation should lead to the accomplishment of stated objectives. Dictatorial management can stifle creativity. However, emphasizing free rein on innovation can substitute activity for objectives and being busy for getting results. More and more the necessity is realized to establish a balance between the need for individual creative freedom and organizational objectives. This balance, can help optimize a company's most valuable innovative resource : the individual engineer.

Objectives need *not* be dictated from management to engineers in order to achieve desired results. In a study of more than a thousand scientists and engineers in eleven research organisations, (1) Donald C. Pelz and Frank M. Andrews found that performance of engineers and Ph.D.'s in development labs was highest when the technical goals were decided by "his chief and himself". This was compared with the situations where technical goals were set by "mainly chief", or "chief and executives", or "mainly executives". Performance was measured in terms of scientific contribution, paper-published, parents and unpublished reports. This study indicates the need for objectives to be set jointly by management (to provide necessary constraints in light of project and corporate goals) and the engineer (to allow the objective to be realistic in light of limitations management may not be aware of, and to allow maximum creativity and innovation within the bounds which have been set). This allows objectives to be set by those accountable for results, while focusing creativity, on achieving the desired end-results.

Job Environment Determines Job Dissatisfaction

The job environment consists of the conditions and treatment surrounding the work. This environment determines how an engineer feels he's being treated. How he feels he's being treated creates or eliminates job dissatisfaction. Even if an engineer loves his work and gets a great deal of satisfaction from what he does on the job, yet if he's dissatisfied with his environment, his output will go down and results will be decreased.

The job environment (2) is made up of :

1. The *Company Policy and Administration* whioh surrounds the job (including fringe benefits).
2. The competency of Supervision which is given on the job.

3. The *Relationship with the Superviser* while at the job.

4. The *Working Conditions* on the job.

5. The *Salary* received as compensation for the job.

6. The amount of *Status* received in the job.

These factors making up the job environment are the sources of dissatisfaction on the job. The opposite the job dissatisfaction is no job dissatisfaction. That is, just because one is not dissatisfied with how he's being treated, doesn't necessarily mean he gets a sense of satisfaction and achievement from what he's actually doing. Interesting work and a feeling of personal and professional growth are that principal sources of job satisfaction for engineers. (3) The less challenged he is by his work, the more interested he becomes in sources of job dissatisfaction like policies, administrative procedures, status symbols, etc.

The factors making up the job environment represent an expense to the company. It costs money to provide a good job environment, to treat people well.

The problem with these job environment factors is that their positive effect returns to zero. Take Salary as an example.

The company hires a bright prospect at a somewhat inflated starting salary and by the end of the first year (or sooner) he's looking for a raise. In fact if he doesn't get a raise he'll be so *dissatisfied* that his output will probably be affected. The positive effect of his initial salary returned to zero.

In addition the zero point goes up. If this year I get a $1000 raise, next year I'm likely to be looking for a $2000 raise. My zero point escalates. In fact if I receive only a $500 raise after the previous year receiving a $1000 raise, psychologically I've taken $500 cut. If salary is used as some sort of incentive to increase the engineer's productivity, the company is likely to be caught in a trap of escalating zero points.

Effective salary administration doesn't use salary as a carrot on a stick, but rather as compensation for results achieved.

Salary represents the value an organization puts on an engineer's abilities and efforts. When he demands a certain rate of pay, he is demanding the recognition to which he feels his qualifications, performance; and professional contributions entitle him.

Much of the emphasis engineers put on salary and other material benefits stems from an unfulfilled need for personal recognition and stature in the company (3).

Effective Management of an Engineer's Output

Effective management of the engineer's output directly affects achievement of organization objectives. Achieving objectives and getting expected results are the primary concerns of any organization. There are several principles and techniques a minager can use to enhance and increase his professional subordinates' output.

Job Satisfaction Determines Motivation

Motivation is internal to the individual. A person is not motivated by what people think he ought to have, but rather by what he himself wants.

One way to increase the efficiency of an engineering department is to concentrate on improving its effectiveness. This requires making the best use of creative abilities of engineering personnel.

The greatest motivational potential of engineers can be

generated through the task itself where work must be considered as the prime challenge to the individual, and thus worthy of their effort (4).

Interesting work and a feeling of personnel and professional growth are the principal motivators for engineers.

If he is involved in projects that are satisfying to him and are considered worthwhile additions to the state-of-the-art, he gains recognition from his colleagues. This recognition fortifies his feelings of self-worth, demonstrates his abilities to his peers and superiors, and justifies his choice of a techical career as his life's work.

Advancement and increasing responsibility also mean increased income, but their primary value lies in reinforcing the engineer's feelings of self-worth and professional growth.

The opportunities for advancement and increasing responsibility must come from management. The recognition received for results achieved must come from management. If management fails to provide this reinforcement of job satisfaction, then output and productivity is adversely affected.

Getting Results Through Objectives

Objectives are statements of expected results. They should be defined before inputs such as materials, equipment, facilities and personnel are released. They determine which activity to us and what inputs are required. They are the criteria by which the final outcome should be measured.

Standards for professionals should be based on results, not effort. Rules, regulations and evaluation procedures which emphasize being on time, taking early, etc. substitute activity for accomplishment. Looking busy becomes more important than getting results.

The ingredients of any good objective (5) are as follows :

1. *It is stated in terms of expected results.* The statement of the objective establishes a criteria against which results can be measured.

2. *A time period for completion of the objective is stated.* This provides milestones by which progress can be measured and forces emphasis on results rather than activity.

3. *It is stated in terms that are measurable.* The objective should be stated in terms of what the data is expected to be. Statistical measures indicating the desired accuracy, precision, confidence intervals, risk, etc. should also be included in the statement of the objectives to provide evaluation criteria of the data to be collected.

4. *It can realistically be accomplished.* The most difficult of these four is to make the objectives realistic, because what may be realistic in management's eyes may be unrealistic for the individual engineer who will be held accountable for results. Too often this kind of Managing By Objectives becomes Coercion By Objectives where objectives are "handed down from on High" and the engineer is made to feel he'd better perform or else ! This results in "game" playing like "Minimize Losses" and "Protecting Posterior", whereas the goal should be to Maximize Gain.

Setting unrealistically high objectives for engineers in order to "challenge" them and make them "stretch" is poor management. An engineer cannot be held accountable for achieving unrealistic results. Where there is little accountability there is little control. How busy he has been trying to achieve the unrealistic goal is about all he can be held accountable for. Thus activity trapes are created where being busy becomes the focus rather than achieving results.

To ensure accomplishment of established objectives, to avoid being side tracked by unexpected occurances, and to hold accountable those responsible for obtaining the goals, all results after analysis should be justified in light of a present criteria for success, which in turn should be indicated in the statement of the objectives.

This process of justification involves the following steps :

1. Determine if the objective for each analysis, test, experiment, design, etc. was accomplished. If it wasn't, why not.

2. Determine the contribution to objectives and what was learned from the parameters measured and the data collected.

3. Account for all positive results and/or negative results caused by accidents and/or unexpected developments.

4. Account for all descrepancies in the data.

5. Indicate the level of confidence of the results.

6. If the objectives were only partially or were not achieved, make recommendations for future work in terms of measureable objectives.

7. Recommend specific action to be taken based on all positive results and negative results.

8. Designate those individuals responsible for carrying out recommended action.

Gene Cook of General Electric described the use of an appraisal staff (6) in their research and development center to assist R & D managers. The staff essentially focused on the objectives of the research programs. "In retrospect the questions at issue always turned out to be the same fundamental four : The key is *why* was the goal set in the first place !

What is our specific research goal in this program ?

How large a gap exists between our present situation and the specific goal ?

If we reach our goal—at this or that particular point in time—what significance will it have then and what will its implications be then ?

Is the research program consistent with the specific goal ? The following were listed as some of the benefits from their ten-year experiment with this goal-oriented programme :

1. Elimination of a great deal of "frictional" effort.

2. Shortened cycle time.

3. Simulating the generation of new leads.

4. Improved selectivity, effectiveness and productivity of R & D expenditures.

This same outcome can be experienced by any organization which effectively focuses on results through objectives.

A constant challenge for engineering managers is how to increase the individual productivity of his professional personnel. All productivity is a function of Output/Input. Through the efficient use of the input which an engineer brings to the job and effective management of the engineer's output, the engineer's personal productivity can be improved.

30

Simplified Method of Time Standard Development in A Tool Room

*C. P. Shantharam**

Tools Room and its Importance in an Industry

Adaptation of western technology to our environment and building up of indigenous technology stand foremest in our efforts in industrialisation of the country. Ability to manufacture reliable sophisticated tooling required for production of variety of components is one of the basic requirements in building up of self reliant technological base. Tooling up for manufacture of a large number of intricate components with stringents specifications forms the prime activity in an industry. The quality, reliability and performance standards of the product also largely depend on the quality of tools used in the manufacture of components.

Piece or individual production is characterised by the

* Deputy Manager, Corporate Office Steel Industrials Kerala Limited, Cherooty Road, Calicut-673001.

machining of a single part or small lots which are not likely to be produced again. Such a phenomena can be noticed in Tool Room. Typical features of this type of production are : (i) General purpose manufacturing equipment is used. (ii) Most of the jobs will be of one time nature. (iii) Special tools and fixtures are used only in case when work cannot be performed with standard items. (iv) Machine tools are not set up to definite dimensions. (v) Highly qualified workmen are employed.

Tool Room forms one of the major activity centers in an industry manufacturing variety of jigs, fixtures, dies, gauges, templates, cutting tools etc. As each item of tooling will be different from the other, the activity of Tool Room will be similar to any jobbing shop. Preparation of process sheet or technology detailing the manufacturing process of the tool and estimation of standard time forms the main preparatory activity of the Tool Room.

Time Standards and their Importance

Time standards are extensively used for planning, costing and for assessment of productivity. Quality of time standards has got a vital role to play in production planning and control and also in administration of productivity linked incentive schemes.

Time Standards in a Mass Production Machine Shop

Rate fixing with the help of elemental standards is one of the methods of time standard development. In mass production, jobs will be of repetitive nature. But standard development for this kind is a one time job. So it is worthwhile to prepare a foolproff process sheet and develop precise time standard because of the long span of its application. When the standards are ready it is easy to go in for a productivity linked incentive scheme in a mass production machine shop.

Time Standards in a Tool Room

Productivity linked incentives scheme may be one of the

solutions to improve productivity in a Tool Room also. Situation may warrant an incentive scheme in Tool Room as an extension after the introduction of incentive scheme in mass production machine shop in an industry. For starting an individual productivity linked incentive scheme in a Tool Room, it is required to arrive at the standard time for each of the operation carried out for manufacturing of varies sizes/varieties/categories of tooling items and this standard time has to be posted on the job cards prior to their loading to Tool Room for taking up the job by the workers. It is not economical to rate fix one time jobs, such as jigs, fixures, cutting tools etc. by using the elemental standards in the conventional way as it is done for mass production machine shop lines, because of the tedious and time consuming nature of the rate fixing procedure.

Industrial Engineers Dilemma in Tool Room for Standard Development

Following problems will be faced by the Industrial Engineer in a Tool Room :

(a) Development of operationwise time standards.

(b) Clear cut routing of jobs has to be prepared either by separate planning department or by himself.

(c) It is necessary to strike a balance between the accuracy of time standard and the time to be spent for standards development.

(d) Consistency in time standards is also an important feature required for the success of incentives if time standards are used for incentives.

(e) Time standards are to be released quickly in order to cope with the heavy rate fixing load.

(f) There will be many urgent jobs in Tool Room because of the production hold-ups in the mass production machine shop lines for want of tooling items.

Simplified Method of Time Standard Development in a Tool Room

How long will it take—to turn a component—to mill a component—to grind a component in a Tool Room? An accurate estimate of time can be made in a matter of a few minutes while the component is still fresh off the design table and before it has been release for production. All that's needed, in addition to the component drawing, is some knowledge of process planning and ready reckoners/matrics for time estimation as envisaged in this article. A small oversight or two won't impair the accuracy of the calculation and the burden of estimation can be safely handed over to an assistant.

The method of estimating time for non-repetitive jobs using matrix method has been successfully used for a number of tools made in a large Tool Room of a public sector undertaking where productivity linked incentives scheme was in vogue. The reliability of the model has been verified time and again by conducting necessary studies.

Methodology of Matrix Development

To illustrate the principle, face turning operation model is considered and explained. Other operations, such as external turning, drilling, boring, threading, knurling, parting-off, miling, grinding etc. can also be modelled on the same lines and seperate matrices can be developed.

In a matrix, time values depending upon the different technical parameters are arranged in a tabular form, so that the ready made time values can be selected without any elaborate calculations. The steps adopted for the development of matrices are as follows :

(i) Compile all technical data like speed, feed and depth

of cut according to different type of materials used in a tool room.

(ii) Study the practical limitations.

(iii) Compile machine elements both variable as well as constant element and conduct studies to develop elemental time standards.

(iv) Prepare matrices similar to face tnrning matrix.

Practical Limitations

It may be noted that right from the selection of cutting, speed, feed and depth of cut averaging approach is used for the preparation of matrics. Even average machining time also is taken in many causes. Hence, while selling the standard it should be clearly mentioned that the cumulative effect on standards is only to be viewed instead of each operational standards in isolation.

When time standards are used for operation of incentive scheme, it is required to see that consistency is built in the time standards i. e. variation in time standards are required to be within certain limits and variation in time standards from job to job should be commensurate with the work content. Otherwise, comparision of time standards between job to job will arise in shop floor and may give rise to a number of disputes and hamper the success of incentive scheme. So, considerable care has to be taken in the development of matrices required for time standard estimation.

It may not be feasible to prepare a matrix which will suit all technical conditions stipulated in the drawing. Only a general matrix suit in majorty of technical conditions is to be prepared initially and when typical cases whenever arise, these matrix values are to modified with correction factors depending upon the technical conditions. But all the probable complexity correction factors are to be spelt out clearly so that consistency among the rate fixers may be achieved.

Face Turning Matrix Development Basic Approach

Various materials used in a Tool Room have been grouped into 5 categories as per their average cutting speed characteristics. Average cutting speed for each of the above 5 categories is expressed in terms of a material factor with reference to the cutting speed of mild steel. This has been illustrated in the following table, captioned "Face Turning Operation Matrix."

Next step is to estimate the machining time for mild steel for different diameters. In order to arrive at the machining time for a given category of material of a particular diameter, the time given for mild steel for the diameter is to be selected and multiplied with the corresponding material factor. To these time values handling time and policy/relaxation allowance are be added to get the actual work content.

It is noticed that difference of time values between conventional rate fixing and the new method of matrix oriented rate fixing is less than 80%. It is once again stressed that while selling time standards it should be clearly mentioned that cumulative effect on standards is only to be viewed instead of each operation standards in isolation.

Conclusion

The development of Matrix thus simplifies the job of an Industrial Engineer. It also leads to other benefits especially the ones outlined below :

(a) Improved reliability of time standards.

(b) Less tediousness in rate fixing.

(c) No elaborate training for estimators.

(d) Functions of technology preparation and standards assessment can be combined.

(e) Make or buy decisions can be taken expeditiously.

(f) Encourages application of work measurement in Small Scale Industries and helps the application of modern techniques like production planning and scheduling, pricing of products, administration of simple incentive schemes etc. It can be introduced with the help of a small nucleus team.

(g) Comparative statement showing the Time Saving benefit of Conventional Vs. Matrix oriented rate fiixing.

Item	*Average Number of pieces can be rate fixed by Conventional method (In 8 hour shift/rate fixer)*	*Average Number of pieces can be rate fixed by Matrix Oriented method (In 8 hour shift/rate fixer)*
Simple jigs/fixtures	10 details	30 details
Medium jigs/fixtures	8 ,,	24 ,,
Complex jigs/fixtures	6 ,,	18 ,,
Milling cutters	8 cutters	30 cutters
Single point tools	8 tools	30 tools
Broaches	2 tools	6 tools
Reamers/counter bores	8 tools	30 tools

Face Turning Operation Matrix

Machine—Medium Duty Centre Lathe
Cutting Tool—Carbide Tipped

	Mild Steel Category	*Non-ferrous materials*	*Synthetic materials*	*High Carbon & alloy steels*	*Nimonic Category*
Average cutting speed in meters/minute	70	150	85	50	30
Material factor of mild steel with reference to other materials	70/70	75/150	70/85	70/50	70/30
MATERIAL FACTOR	1	0.46	0.82	1.40≠	2.30

Diameter of job in millimeter	*Machining*	*Time Values*	*In Normal*	*Man MInutes*	*Per Cut*
Upto dia 40	0.17	0.08	0.14	0.24	0.40
41 to „ 60	0.49	0.27	0.40	0.68	1.11
61 „ 100	1.20	0.55	0.98	1.68	2.74
101 „ 140	2.64	1.21	2.18	3.71	6.08
141 „ 180	3.75	1.72	3.06	5.33	8.61
181 „ 220	5.93	2.74	4.87	8.31	13.64
221 „ 250	8.50@	3.90	6.96	11.90**	19.51

For machining time values of mild steel category please refer the following para.
Machining time per cut=Machining time for mild steel×Material factor
=8.50@ ×1.40≠=11.90**NMM

Mild Steel Category Face Turning Estimation

Cutting tool	—Carbide tipped
Average cutting speed	—70 meters/minute
Cutting speed	—$\frac{TTDN}{1000}$ where 'D' is the diameter of job in milli meter
Required surface finish	—Medium
Machining time	$= \frac{\text{Length of cut in milli meters} + \text{Approach} + \text{Over run}}{\text{Revolutions per minute} \times \text{feed rate in milli meter/revolution}}$

Example :

Diameter of job in millimeter	Machining time for 50 & 60 millimeter diameter of job	Average machining time in normal man minutes
50	$\frac{25+3+2}{500\times0.15}=0.40$	0.49 N.M.M.
60	$\frac{30+3+2}{400\times0.15}=0.59$	

Handling Time Estimation for Medium Duty Centre Lathe

Elemental Description	*Time Values in Normal Man Minuits*				
	One Cut	*Two Cuts*	*Three Cuts*	*Four Cuts*	*Five Cuts*
Approach cut (Bring carriage, adjust depth of cut engage into feed)	0.26	0.26	0.26	0.26	0.26
Withdraw cut (Disengage auto feed, bring aside carriage)	0.13	0.13	0.13	0.13	0.13

(*Contd.*)

Subsequent cut (Adjust depth of cut, engage auto feed) (Number of cuts—1)	—	0.14	0.28	0.42	0.56
Vernier gauging (0 to 250 milli meter, Elemental value= 0.15 Nmm)	0.30	0.45	0.60	0.60	0.60
Time Value in Normal Man Minutes	0.69	0.98	1.27	1.41	1.55

Note : (*i*) Whenever necessary additional values for loading and unloading of jobs as per technical conditions are to be added.

(*ii*) Elemental standards are taken from direct time study.

Comparison of Rate Fixing Methods

Conventional vs Matrix Oriented

Example :

Conventional Rate Fixing

Material to be turned	—Mild steel
Diameter of job	—6o milli meter, say.
Cutting tool	—Carbide tipped
Material to be removed	—5 mili meter on radius
Surface finish required	—V 5 (medium)
Number of cuts	—2 cuts, say
Standard cutting speed	—70 meters/minute
Feed rate	—0.15 milli meter/revolution
Length of cut	— $\frac{\text{Job diameter}}{2}$ = 30 milli meter
RPM to be selected	—400

(Cutting speed × 1000) / (3.14 × diameter of job)	
Machining time per cut	$= \dfrac{\text{Length of cut} + \text{Approach} + \text{Overrun}}{\text{RPM} \times \text{Feed rate}}$
	$\dfrac{30+3+2}{400 \times 0.15}$
	=0.59 Normal man minute
Machining time for two cuts	—1.18
Approach cut	—0.26
Withdraw cut	—0.13
Subsequent cut	—0.14
Vernier gauging (3 times) (0.15×3)	—0.45
Loading and unloading of job in 3 jaw chuck	—0.49

(*Contd.*)

(as per technical condition)

	2.65 Normal man minutes

Example :

Matrix Oriented Rate Fixing

Machining time (0.49×2 cuts) Refer 3.3.2	=0.98 (Mild steel dia=60 mm)
Handling time for 2 cuts Refer 3.3.4	=0.98
Loading and unloading of job in 3 jaw chuck (as per technical conditions)	=0.49
	2.45 Normal man minutes

31

Inventory Models for Deteriorating Items

A.K. Srivastava, U.S. Rao***

Abstract

This paper extends the model developed by Ghare and Schrader to consider the pack size. Two models are developed; one for a single decay rate and the other for double decay rate. Double decay is characterized by two different rates of deterioration, one before opening the pack and the other after opening the pack. A heuristic solution procedures for this case is also developed.

Introduction

One very common assumption encountered in inventory models is that inventory is depleted only by demand or sales. This assumption is valid if items considered are steel, glassware, etc. In these cases the rate of deterioration is very low

* PGP Student, NITIE, Bombay.

** Professor, NITIE, Bombay.

and hence its effect can be neglected. However, for items like food grains, bakery items, blood, vegetables, medicines, alcohol, turpentine oil, photographic films this factor becomes very significant.

An item is said to have deteriorated if it cannot be used for its original purpose. Inventory models developed taking this factor into account fall in two categories, viz. Models which consider a fixed shelf life for an item and models which consider a gradual loss in utility value or quantity of an item over time. Blood and medicines are examples of items for which former type of models are applicable and turpentine oil, alcohol, photographic films, etc. are examples of items for which latter type of models are applicable. This paper concentrates on the models of the latter type.

Literature Survey

Earliest work in this direction was done by Ghare and Schrader (1963). They considered exponential decay of an item overtime. Assumptions in the model were :

(i) Decay rate is constant over time.

(ii) Item decays exponentially.

(iii) $\frac{1}{\theta} >> T \therefore 1 >> \theta$ where T is time period for one inventory cycle.

(iv) Demand D (x) is a function of time.

Based on these assumptions they derived the expression for inventory level at any time t. Then a recursive formula for obtaining Economic Order Quantity (EOQ) is derived. Various assumptions under which formula is derived are : (a) Demand is known and is constant. (b) Supply is instantaneous and arrives when needed. (c) Shortages are not allowed. (d) No repair or replacement of deteriorated items takes place during a given inventory cycle. (e) Ordering cost is proportional to number of orders. (f) Holding cost is constant over time. (g) Unit cost of an item is constant.

However, this model cannot be used to find out EOQ for day batteries and ethical drugs. Leakage failure of dry batteries and life expectancy of ethical drugs can be expressed in terms of weibull distribution. In both the cases the rate of deterioration increases with the age, or longer the items remain unused the higher the rate at which they fail. At some point in time, all units that had not been used will fail while in inventory. Covert and Philip (1973) developed a model for such items. The deterioration is assumed to follow a 2-parameter Weibull distribution.

Weibull density fn., $f(x)=\alpha\beta^{-1}(\exp-\alpha\times\beta)$ where,

α= the scale parameter $\alpha > 0$

β= the shape parameter $\beta > 0$

x= time to deterioration $x > 0$

Solving this differential equation we get,

$$Ix=\frac{\int_0^x(-R)\exp(\alpha t\beta)\,dt+K}{\exp(\alpha\times\beta)}$$

From this cost fn. is derived and expression for minimum cost obtained. For solution, correction method of Newton is used, because straightforward solution cannot be obtained due to unseparableness of the variables involved.

An improvement of this model was done by Philip (1974). He argued that 2-parameter Weibull distribution can be used for an item with decreasing rate of deterioration if the initial rate is extremely high. Similarly, this distribution can be used for an item with increasing rate of deterioration only if initial rate is approximately zero. To overcome this limitation he suggested the use of 3-parameter Weibull distribution, the third parameter γ, being the location parameter. Therefore, Density fn. $f(x)=\alpha\beta\ (t-\gamma)\ \beta^{-1} \exp[-\alpha(t-\gamma)\ \beta]$

where γ = location parameter; $t \geq \gamma$

In this case,

$$Z(t)=\frac{f(t)}{1-F(t)}$$

$$=\frac{f(t)}{1-\exp[-\alpha(t-\gamma)\ \beta]}$$

$$=\alpha\beta(t-\gamma)\ \beta^{-1}$$

All other assumptions and parameters remain same as in the last model. In this case,

$$-dI_t=f_t\ [\alpha\beta(t-\gamma)\beta^{-1}]\ d_t+Rf_t$$

Solving it weget

$$T_t=\frac{\int_{\gamma'}^{t}(-R)\exp[\alpha(X-Y)\beta]\ dx+K}{\exp[\alpha(t-\gamma)\beta]}$$

where $\gamma'=\gamma$ for $\gamma \geqslant 0$

$\gamma'=0$ for $\gamma \leqslant 0$

Solution in this case is also obtained by correction method of Newton.

Y.K. Shah and M.C. Jaiswal (1977) have extended Ghare and Schrader's (1963) work by considering the demand as random variable which follows a uniform pattern during an inventory cycle. They have considered quantity to be ordered as variable so that hand inventory at the beginning of the period is always constant.

Mossin (1966) has maximised present value of profits for a fixed amount of stock subject to linear demand and exponential deterioration of the stock. He has also assumed rate of sales per unit time and prevailing price, P, to be linear and subject to a constant rate of shifting through time, i.e.,

$$P = a - bse^{-gt}$$

where g is the rate at which quantity demanded would grow at any time.

Nahmias and Wang (1979) have considered effect of deterministic lead time. They have also relaxed the assumption of 'no shortages'. Demand during lead time is assumed to be random variable with a continuous density function f(x). For solving the equations involved simulation technique is employed.

Problem Formulation

Pack Size Consideration

Some items, e.g. turpentine oil may be available in packages of different sizes. Some economy in packaging cost is achieved due to which per unit cost of the item is less for a bigger pack. It may be worthwhile to buy a bigger pack even though loss due to deterioration will be more. Ghare and Schrader (1963) model has been extended to take this situation into account.

Pack Size with Double Decay

Most manufacturer's of deteriorating goods take care to pack their products carefully so that the deterioration is minimised. But still there is some deterioration. On opening the pack the rate of deterioration increases. A generalised model is developed which takes into consideration two decay rates, viz. one before opening the pack and the other after opening the pack, and various pack sizes. It gives a method to find out 'how many' packs to buy and of 'what size' to minimize the total cost.

Model Development

Model for Pack Size Consideration

Following assumptions have been made while developing the model : (i) At one time only one pack of any size is bought. (ii) Demand for the item is a constant, D. (iii) Item decays or deteriorates exponentially. (iv) Rate of deterioration 'θ' remains constant overtime.

Expanding $e-\theta dt$ and neglecting higher terms

$$dI=-I\theta\, dt-D(t)\, dt$$

or

$$\frac{dI}{dt}+I\,\theta=-D(t)$$

The solution for this equation is as given by Ghare and Schrader (1963).

$$I_t=Pe^{-\theta t}-e^{-t\theta}\int_0^k D(t)\,e^{\theta t}\,dt \quad \text{...(1)}$$

In this case,

$$D(t)=D=\text{constant}$$

And at $t=T$, $I_T=0$

Therefore,

$$0=Pe^{-\theta T}-e^{-\theta T}\int_0^T De^{\theta t}\,dt$$

$$=Pe^{-\theta T} - e^{-\theta T}\frac{D}{\theta}\left(e^{\theta t}\right)_0^T$$

$$=Pe^{-\theta T} - e^{-\theta T}\frac{D}{\theta}\left(e^{\theta T}-1\right)$$

$$=Pe^{-\theta T} - \frac{D}{\theta} + \frac{D}{\theta}e^{-\theta T}$$

or $$\frac{D/\theta}{(F+D/\theta)} = e^{-\theta T}$$

or $$-\theta T = \text{In}\left(\frac{D}{P\theta+D}\right)$$

$$T = \frac{\left(\frac{P\theta+D}{D}\right)}{\theta} \quad \text{...(2)}$$

Let us assume that the price per unit is C for a pack. Then total cost per unit time will be,

$$\text{TC/unit time} = p \times \frac{1}{T} \times C$$

Such calculation can be made for each pack and the pack which has got lowest total cost can be purchased.

Illustrative Example

Thinner is available in three packs.

Pack Size	*Price of Pack*	*Price/lt.*
1 lt. Pack	Rs. 10	Rs. 10
5 lt. Pack	Rs. 45	Rs. 9
10 lt. Pack	Rs. 85	Rs. 8.50

let Demand D=4 lt./day.

Rate of deterioration θ=0.1 lt./lt./day.

Applying the above model.

Pack Size	*Total cost/day*	*Total cost/day*
1 lt. Pack	Rs. 40.49	Rs. 40
5 lt. Pack	Rs. 38.20	Rs. 36
10 lt. Pack	Rs. 38.09	Rs. 34

If we change θ=0.2 lt./lt./day then.

Pack Size	*Total cost/day*
1 lt. Pack	Rs. 40.99
5 lt. Pack	Rs. 40.33
10 lt. Pack	Rs. 41.92

Thus, if θ is more or demand is less, it may offset the savings obtained from buying a larger pack.

Model for Pack Size with Double Decay

Following assumptions are made while developing the Model : (i) A new pack is opened as soon as the last pack finishes and the first pack of each lot is opened straight away. (ii) Supply is instantaneous. (iii) Demand is a constant D over time. (iv) Holding cost i, is charged as % of unit cost per unit time and remains constant over time. (v) Ordering Cost per cycle is Rs. A per order. (vi) θ's remain constant over time and θ_1=Rate of deterioration before opening the pack. θ_2=Rate of deterioration after opening the pack. (vii) Deterioration follows an exponential distribution. (viii) No shortages are allowed. (ix) No replacement of deteriorated quantity is performed during a cycle.

Quantity Lost due to Deterioration in Closed Packs will be

$$(P-L_1)+(P-L_2)+\ldots\ldots+(P-Ln)$$

As $L_1=P$ we get

$$\text{Qty. lost}=(n-1)\ P-(L_2+L_3+\ldots\ldots\ldots\ldots Ln)$$

$$=(n-1)P-[P\exp(-\theta_1 t_1+\ldots\ldots\ldots +P\exp(-\theta_1\ tn-1)]$$

$$=P\ [(n-1)-\{\exp(-\theta_1 t_1)+\exp(-\theta_1 t_2) +\ldots\ldots\ldots\ldots+\exp(-\theta_1\ tn-1)\}]$$

Expanding $\exp(-\theta_1 ti)$ and neglecting higher order terms as 0_1 is very small, we get

$$\text{Qty lost}=P\ [(n-1)-\{(1-\theta_1 t_1)+(1\ \theta_1 t_2)+\ .\ +(1-\theta_1\ tn-1)\}]$$

$$=P\ [(n-1)-\{(n-1)-\theta_1 \sum_{i=1}^{n-1} ti\}]$$

$$=P\theta_1 \sum_{i=1}^{n-1} ti$$

Quantity Lost Due to Deterioration in Opened Packs will be

$$It=e-\theta\ t\ (P-\int_0^t D(t)\ e\ \theta\ x\ dx) \qquad \ldots\text{Ref. (1)}$$

Substituting $D(t)=D$ & putting $It=O_1$ we get

$$O=e-\theta\ t\ (P-\int_0^t D\ e\ \theta_2\ x\ dx)$$

$$\text{or,}\quad P=\int_0^t D\, e\, \theta_2\, x\, dx$$

$$\text{or,}\quad P=\frac{D}{\theta_2}(e\ \theta\ 2t-1)$$

$$=\frac{D}{\theta_2}(1+\theta_2 t+\frac{\theta^2{}_2\, t^2}{2}-1)$$

$$=\phi Dt+\frac{D\theta_2\, t^2}{2}$$

$\frac{D\theta_2 t^2}{2}$ is the term which has come because of decay.

Thus, quantity lost will be

$$\frac{D\ \theta_2 t^2}{2}+\frac{D\ \theta_2 t^2}{2}+\ldots\ldots\ldots\ldots+\frac{D\ \theta_2 t^2 n}{2}$$

$$=\frac{D\theta_2}{2}\sum_{i=1}^{n} ti^2$$

Calculation of Cycle Time T

$$\text{Total quantity lost}=P\theta_1\sum_{i=1}^{n-1} ti+\frac{D\theta_2}{2}\sum_{i=1}^{n} ti^2$$

$$\text{Total consumption during a cycle}=D\sum_{i=1}^{n} ti=DT$$

$$\text{Initial Invetory}=nP=D\sum_{i=1}^{n} ti+P\theta_1\sum_{i=1}^{n-1} ti+\frac{D\theta_2}{2}\sum_{i=1}^{n} ti^2$$

$$\text{Cost/Cycle}=\left(D\sum_{i=1}^{n} ti+F\theta_1\sum_{i=1}^{n-1} ti+\frac{D\theta_2}{2}\sum_{i=1}^{n} ti^2\right)\times C$$

$$+A+\left(D \sum_{i=1}^{n} ti+P\theta_1 \sum_{i=1}^{n-1} ti+\frac{D\theta_2}{2} \sum_{i=1}^{n} ti^2 \right)\times\frac{iCT}{2}$$

$$\text{Cost/Unit time}=\left(DT+P\theta_1(T-tn)+\frac{D\theta_2}{2} \sum_{i=1}^{n} ti^2 \right)\times\frac{C}{T}$$

$$+\frac{A}{T}*+\frac{iCT}{T}\left[DT+P\theta_1(T-tn)+\frac{D\theta^2}{2} \sum_{i=1}^{n} ti^2 \right]$$

As θ_1 is very small we can say that

$$t_1=t_2=t_3=\ldots\ldots.=tn=\frac{T}{n} \quad \therefore tn=\frac{T}{\eta}$$

Also,

$$t^2{}_1+t^2{}_2+\ldots\ldots.tn^2=\frac{T^2}{n^2}\times n=\frac{T^2}{n^2}$$

or, $$\sum_{i=1}^{n} ti^2=\frac{T^2}{n}$$

Substituting these in the above equation we get

U=Cost/unit time=

$$\left[\frac{C}{T} DT+P\theta_1 (T-\frac{T}{n})+\frac{D\theta_2}{2} (\frac{T^2}{n})\right]$$

$$+\frac{A}{T}+iC\left[DT+P\theta_1 (T-\frac{T}{n})+\frac{D\theta_2}{2} (\frac{T^2}{n})\right]$$

$$U=CD+CP_1 (1-\frac{1}{n})+\frac{D\theta_2 T}{2n}+\frac{A}{T}+iCDT$$

$$+iCP\theta_1 (T-\frac{T}{n})+\frac{iCD\theta_2 T^2}{2n}$$

Differentiating with respect to 8 and putting it equal to zero we get,

$$\frac{d\theta}{dT} = 0 = \frac{D\theta_2}{2n} - \frac{A_2}{T} + iCD + iCP\theta_1\left(1 - \frac{1}{n}\right) + \frac{iCD\theta_2 T}{n}$$

$$\text{or, } T = \sqrt{\frac{A}{\frac{D\theta_2 C}{2n} + iCD + iCP\theta_1\left(1 - \frac{1}{n}\right) + \frac{iCD\theta_2 T}{n}}}$$

This equation cannot be solved by normal procedure as T occurs on both sides of the equation. Also 'n' is not known. A heuristic procedure is developed to find out optimum value of 'n'.

Heuristic Procedure for Solution

Step 1. Choose a 'n'. Initial guideline for choosing 'n' is,

$$n = \frac{\text{Demand/Unit time} \times T}{\text{Pack size, P}}$$

where,
$$T = \sqrt{\frac{A}{iCP}}$$

Step 2. For this value of 'n' calculate

$$T_1 = \sqrt{\frac{A}{\frac{D\theta_2 C}{2n} + iCD + iCP\theta_1\left(1 - \frac{1}{n}\right)}}$$

Step 3. Now calculate (for some value of 'n')

$$T_2 = \sqrt{\frac{A}{\frac{D\theta_2 C}{2n} + iCD + iCP\theta_1\left(1 - \frac{1}{n} + \frac{iCD\theta_2 T_1}{n}\right)}}$$

Step 4. The actual value of T will lie between T_1 & T_2.

Select a suitable δT so that $(T_1 - \delta T) > T_2$ and let $T_1 - \delta T = T_1$.

Step 5. Calculate T'_2 by using T'_1. Note that actual value of T will now lie between T_1 & T_2.

Step 6. Keep repeating steps 2 to 5 unless $T_1(^n) - T_2(^n) < 0.5$.

Step 7. Let $T = \dfrac{T_1(^n) + T_2(^n)}{2}$

Step 8. Calculate U for this combination of 'n' and T.

Step 9. Decrease the value of n by 1 and again go through the steps 2 to 8. Stop if U for j^{th} pack is more than $(j-1)^{th}$ pack i.e. stop if $Uj > Uj-1$. This means that EOQ for this size of pack is $(j-1)$.

Step 10. Perform step 1 to 9 for each size of the pack. Then select the pack size for which the cost/unit time is minimum and order the EOQ obtained for it.

Scope for Further Work

The model developed here tries to depict the situation more realistically but has obvious limitations. Models can be developed which consider demand as a function of time, lead time, supply as a function of time, shortages etc. However, the complexity of the model will increase as we go on incorporating these variables. Good approximation methods or approximate solution procedures will be very useful for these models.

Step 4. The actual value of T will lie between T_1 & T_2.

[illegible] T_1 [illegible] $(T_1 + T_2)/2$ [illegible] T_2 and let $T_1 = T$.

Step 5. Calculate T_2 by using [illegible]. Note that actual value of T will now lie between T_1 & T_2.

Step 6. Keep repeating steps 2 to 5 unless $T_1 \simeq T_2$.

$$\text{Step 7. Let } T = \frac{T_1^{(n)} + T_2^{(n)}}{2}$$

Step 8. Calculate Q for this combination of 'n' and T.

Step 9. Decrease the value of n by 1 and again go through the steps 2 to 8. Stop if U for the pack is more than [illegible] pack i.e. stop if $U_n > U_{n+1}$. This means that EOQ for this size of pack is $Q - 1$ [illegible].

Step 10. Perform step 1 to 9 for each size of the pack. Then select the pack size for which the cost/unit time is minimum and order the EOQ obtained for it.

Scope for Further Work

The model developed here tries to depict the situation more realistically but has obvious limitations. Models can be conceived which consider demand as a function of time and other supplies as a function of time, shortages etc. [illegible] the complexity of the model will increase [illegible] using these alternatives [illegible] approximation methods or [illegible] very useful [illegible] these models.

32

Maximisation of Value Engineering Programme

*N. N. Apsingeker**

Introduction

Value analysis or value Engineering, as it is called, is one of the several specialised services recently offered as tools of management. Value Engineering technique differs from other cost reduction techniques, in the sense that it probes into the economic attributes of value. The concept is that by continuous process of planned action, it is possible to improve the performance, increase the value in product and thus reduce costs.

Value Engineering is defined as the relationship between what the function is worth to a buyer and what it costs to him. There are three types of values having relationship with function (a) Use Value – Is the monetary measure of the properties or qualities of an item which contributes to its saleability (b) Esteem Value – Is the monetary measure of the properties or

* Asstt. Indl. Engineer, Hal, Nasik.

qualities of an item which contribute to its saleability, but not to its performance. It does not include use value. (c) Exchange Value—Is the monetary measure of the properties or qualities of an item which enable it to be exchanged for something else. Ordinarily :

$$\text{Use value} + \text{Esteem value} \geqslant \text{Exchange value}$$

Concept of Function

Functions are the natural or characteristic actions performed by an item or properties of an item which enable it to perform the requirement placed on it. To aid in designing an item or in evaluating an existing item, three classes of functions are a 'Basic Function' —is the specific purpose for which the item was designed. (b) Secondry Function—Are the actions which supports basic function and results from a specific design approach (c) Unnecessary Function—are those which are not required either as a basic or a secondary function.

Role of Creative Thinking

Creative thinking helps in providing function in the end use environment at the lowest overall cost considering performance, reliability and maintenance. Assumptions underlining creative analysis are (a) The nature of open ended problem (b) problem solving rules and sphere of influence (c) Creative and analytical processes (d) Individual and group solving.

Techniques for Evaluating Functions

There are many alternatives for evaluating functional approach. 'Analytical approach'—consists of a series of step by step progression of experiment, evaluation and mathematical manipulation till the problem is narrowed to a single justifiable answer. 'Input-Output' is used to examine methods of using the input to cause output in most direct manner, e.g. energy. The 'Synthetic Approach' is used on the hypothesis that creativity can be increased if the psychology of analysis is understood. In 'specialists review approach'—analysis is made in each area as the product passes from design to sale. 'Brainstorming a group technique produces atleast 50 percent more ideas than individuals.

Use of Matrix for Value Decision

A decision matrix makes it possible to compare alternative decisions by analysing the functions, task or objectives of a product by breaking it down into number of requirements. Once the requirements have been determined, the algorithm aligns them with their measure of relative importance. To every expected benefit B_1 B_2... Bn governing choice or decision among available means to accomplish a given end, a real non-negative number W1, W2...Wn is assigned which is initially obtained by dividing number 1 by the number of benefits being considered (1/Bn) then it is varied as the relative importance of each benefit varies from that of other benefits. A positive change in the relative importance of one benefit results in a corresponding negative change in the others. This is imposed by constraints that the sum of the measures of relative importance is equal to unity.

$$\sum_{j=1}^{n} wj = 1$$

Wj is measured along a internal scale extending from 0 (minimum) to 1 (maximum) and unity indicates the given limitations on resources. Each of the available choices is then transferred from minimum (70) required to maximum (90) in percentage points which proved meaningful for all purposes. The expected values of choices can be had by multiplying e. i. j. by Wj.

In the matrix, weights imply relative importance of each benefit. Six benefits or objectives have been considered for evaluation, namely (i) Cost effectiveness (ii) Purity (iii) delivery

(iv) prodn...flexibility (v) Proximity (vi) Financial stability. A range of percentage should be given in such a way that all rating factors depending upon one's requirements should fall with ina lower and higher limits, i. e. best practical and least favourable but acceptable in the range of choice. In the above example, lower and higher limits are 70 to 90 which is the range of choice. For rating purpose, each factor should be reduced to measurable parameters as given below :

	Lower limit tolerance (least we can live with)	Upper limit tolerance (most we can use)
(1) Financial stability	90%	99%
(2) Cost	Rs. 2.5/kg.	Rs. 2.25/kg.
(3) Purity	99.2	99.8
(4) Delivery	Monthly	Weekly
(5) Peak quantity	10000 kg on 10 days notice	50000 kg on 5 days notice

Management Role in VE Programme

Some of the actions by management for effective VE programme are :

(a) Tie upper management level with VE programme.

(b) Eastablish company objectives and overall goals.

(c) Authorise and establish Value Engineering staff organisation.

(d) Authorise and establish adequate staffing.

(e) Develop effective programming planning.

(f) Constantly audit and chase progress.

(g) Provide a merit recognition for outstanding VE programme.

Conclusion

Value Engineering offers a planned co-operative approach and broadened view point in arriving at many of the basic decisions of the industrial enterprise. It is one of the tools which any rational management should seriously consider in utilising the resources under its control. It is a tool which makes work easier, if applied properly. Some of its results, in addition to lower costs, are shortened design times, improved quality and easier production, because all aspects are planned and no loose ends are left out.

33

Evaluation of Physiological Energy Expenditure of Workers in an Indian Forging Industry— A Case Study

Dr. J.M. Mahajan, Mr. Maheshwar Dayal*

Abstract

The optimal working level for 8½ hour working day was evaluated by the method suggested by Dr. Bink. Although it led to satisfactory state of affairs, the workers were still found to be exhausted. Geographical reasons were assigned to resolve this ambiguity because the subject with far less physical fitness had aerobic capacity which was comparable to European workers. Instead of taking aerobic capacity as the physical working capacity for four minutes, the aerobic capacity taken as the P.W.C. for zero minute gave better results and therefore, is recommended to calculate the P.W.C. for Indian workers. This gives P.W.C. equal to 4.5 K cal/min.

* Asst. Prof. Deptt. of Mech. Engg., Indian Institute of Technology, New Delhi-110016.

For different age groups an age factor must be used which may be calculated by a similar detailed study.

Introduction

A certain amount of fatigue is a natural result of all work, but it should not prevent a person from enjoyment of his/her leisure, i.e. physical demand of work should not affect the individual's health and well-being. The optimum level of energy at which individual can work sefely for a 6-8 hours-shift from month to month has normally been defined in terms of percentage of aerobic capacity. Some say a pulse rate of 120, i.e. 30% of aerobic capacity is the safe limit. Christensen found that even on high incentives people at work do not, in general, work at more than 50% of their aerobic capacity.

A sound basis for the limit would be the commencement of anaerobic metabolism, i.e. "excess" lactable derived from the ratio of total body lactate to pyruvate. C.H. Wyndham *et al* have found that the highly trained men can work at 55% of the maximum 0, uptake capacity without anaerobic metabolism occurring in the body. It has been pointed out that the 50% work level should be considered the upper limit with work periods of longer than one hour duration. The 50% work-load must be related to the capacity of the particular muscle involved and not the body as a whole. In most of professional jobs both trunk, arm and leg muscles are engaged and the aerobic work capacity must be appraised similarly. Under certain conditions one can expect a work-load demanding more than 50% of the individual's capacity, but the peak loads must be of short duration.

Physical working capacity (P.W.C.) has been defined as the energy level that can be maintained throughout the working time by an individual with a given level of aerobic capacity. The caloric expenditure averaged over working time depends upon working capacity which depends upon : (i) Capacity for food intake and (ii) Capacity for O_2 uptake.

Capacity for food intake depends upon the body built. Dr. Bink has shown that straight line graph fits well if the horizontal axis measures P.W.C. and vertical axis measures the log of working time. Aerobic work capacity has been considered as the P.W.C. for four minutes—working time. P.W.C. at the theoretical time of 42 hours can be calculated from the food intake.

The Study

The study was made on the workers engaged in heavy muscular work in a forging indusrty near Delhi. The eating habits and the food intake vary so widely that the standard average food intake values cannot be relied upon for the experiment. So the energy available for a theoretical 24 hours working day for all the workers was calculated by averaging the monthly food intane value (determined after thorough consultation with the workers). From this energy available per minute was calculated and plotted against log of working time. P.W.C. for 8½ hours working day in the factory was calculated from the above mentioned graphs according to the relation given by Dr. Bonjer.

$$A=(\log_{10}(5700)-\log_{10}(t)\ a/3.1\ \text{K.cal/min.}$$

where,

A=P.W.C. in k.cal/min.

t =working time in min.

a =aerobic capacity in K.cal/min.

The P.W.C. thus obtained was compared with the actual average physiological energy expenditure (M) of the workers in industry. Actual physiological energy expenditure of a subject was estimated from the pulse rate taken at various times during the day. M/A gives the ratio (b) which may be defined as the degree of utilization of man's capacity.

Results and Discussion

However, the above procedure assumes and utilises the norm of gross energy expenditure equal to approximately 5.2

K. cal/min. frequently used is West European countries. The same may not hold good here. In general comparison, it was found that the subjects consumer for less nutritious food stuff and had not so good body built, but still had comparable aerobic capacity. The high aerobic capacity does not necessarily mean a better physical fitness and stamina of the body. So the measured aerobic capacity increased the P.W.C. when used in the equation suggested by Dr. Bink. If we define Utilization Ratio (u) as the ratio of average total energy consumed during eight hours of working day to the average total energy available during theoretical working time of 24 hours the European norm assumes a Utilization Ratio (u) of 61%, while the values calculated in the study ranged from 72% to 95% with a mean of 81.8%. These values are quite high and must never be used in an eight hours working shift. Because of high Utilization Ratio (u), workers in the industry were fully exhausted; in fact it should not be the case, if the above criteria for calculation of P.W.C. holls true. This may be due to the fact that the workers are continuously accumulating the physiological stress and thus unable to recover fully before they start the next day's work. These conclusions are very obvious in many of the cases where workers were constantly loosing weight. This also explains, why the workers were very sensitive to even light work.

If, however, the aerobic capacity is taken as the P.W.C. for zero time, better results are obtained. For example, for the twenty-years old the average maximum energy available for 24 hours-day was 3458 K.cal., i.e. a gross average of 2.4 K.cal/min. Average aerobic capacity was 18.15 K.cal/min. The Physical Working Capacity for 8½ hours work shift comes to 4.5 K. cal/min. This gives a Utilization Ratio of 63.5% which is very reasonable.

The corresponding equation is :

$$A = \frac{[\log_{10}(4217) - \log_{10}(t)]}{3.625} \times a \text{ K.cal/min}$$

Similar graph is drawn for 40 years old. This gives a Utilisation Ratio of 84%, and the equation becomes.

understood in conventional objective/empirical scientific temper, OR : MS is an undescriptive (title), if, not downright misleading (2). We elaborate, at some length, this diffused area, as these are important to clearly isolate the contributions and limitations of OR, in the context of India.

We may begin with some definitions of O. R. and profit by their brief analysis to clear the context.

"OR is application of scientific methods/techniques/tools to problem involving operation of a system, so as to provide these in control of system with optimum solution to problems."

—Churchman, Ackooff, Arnoff (as quoted in 4)

"OR is applied Decision theory—uses scientific, mathematical, logical means to attempt to cope with problems that confront executive, when he tries to achieve a thorough going rationality in dealing with his decision problems."

—Starr & Miller (as quoted in 4)

"OR is a scientific approach to problem solving for Executive Management. X X constructs Mathematical/Economic/ Statistical descriptive models of decision and control problems to treat situations of complexity/uncertainty X Analysis relation to determine probable future consequences of decision choices and devises appropriate measures of effectiveness to evaluate relative merit of alternative action."

Wagner (2)

"OR is application of scientific (quantitative) method to managerial problems—to extend and refine analytical approach to decision making-"

Defining anything is, of course, a difficult task. Those, who attempt to define a new, growing and necessarily multidisciplinary field like OR, unconsciously try to define it *As If* it is a new discipline by itself, and that accounts for absence of

Multidisciplinary term from foregoing definitions by very well recognised authors, which we consider very vital for proper appreciation and utility of this powerful approach. Optimality and rationality concepts, emphasised in definitions, are unfortunately not absolute concepts, but situational, relativistic system constituent dependent on temporal—spatial system boundary. Bounded rationality is realism. Decision making without emphasis on *Implementation* is in fructuous and O.R. application can not be undertaken in isolations from surrounding managerial environment, tough hopefully objective scientific; hence rational process will have long run impact on entire management process leading to better planning decision, coordination, control, etc. (if not solve very satisfactorily present, specific problem) (2). However, quality of decision making, and methodologically speaking, 'model making' are central aspects of O. R. approach, process and reason centre, on which we must deliberate sufficiently in next section.

Decision Making

Decision making is concerned with choosing between alternative (selecting the best or optimal) given, of course, the objective, criterion of goodness, an alternative-generating process an obviously creative perceptive activity) constraints—both internal and external in terms of all resources, the means to achieve ends. Management is concerned with decision making, hopefully with the aid of OR/MS and in a whole range of activity preceding and following the decision making activity from conception, generation of alternative to implementation, control and replanning. Managers are concerned with present/future states of organisation, policies and operational issues (1), with how things work or should work in the artificial man made organisations/institutions/rules of behaviour (3) etc. Science—the core of OR—following method of enquiry/hypothesis testing empirical evidence free of subjective element, wherever possible, provide a logical basis to choose between alternative.

O. R. in theory and practice has remained primarily concerned with pre-calculating consequence of alternative courses of action, thus indicating the 'best' through its models, without directly being concerned with vital phases, objective/criterion setting, generation of alternatives and implemenation phase which are left to broader process of management, thus remaining as a staff, advisory aid at one point (albeit, important) in the chain from perceptive dreams to reality. 'Management Science' is but a small (though vital) part of Management process.

Complexities in decision situation from economic, technological, environmental and competitive factors, in the corporate sectors are many. Organisations—parts of apparently well knit corporations—pursue inconsistent, contradictory, dynamic goals. Goals are in hierarchical fashion, often without clearity and intercommunications between hierarchy. Between corporations and societal-governmental national/international levels, horizontally and vertically goals get diffused out of focus and contradictions set in a reality yet to be effectively captured in OR conceptual frame work. "OR is not so effective in nonprofit corporation and in government due to lack of clear objectives, and diffused responsibility and authority (2). No wonder, Science, and OR apart, decisions continue to be based on chance, haunch, serendipity, dreams and faith (2).

Model Building

The key concept in OR/MS is mathematical—model building to represent in abstract from the reach reality in problem-solving situation, and then solving the models, to predict and control consequences of alternative actions before committing resources to a course of action. Concept of model making is not new—Engineers and Scientists have made them extensively —physical, structural and mathematical once. However, newness in MS/OR models are in terms of very complex, dynamic situations, in extent, magnitude, consequences, inputs, outputs —a simultaneous consideration of objective(s) and constraints in its search for optimality and often only for a feasible (workable) solution—satisfying if not optimising—involving varieties of variables—physical, organisational, behavioural limitations of all models—in simplifying complexity is well known.

In MS/OR, in this simplification process, admittedly complex reality may be totally lost unless the model makers are conscious and careful. Often, the temptation, advantage and cease of available generalised models may have to be sacrificed to formulate, tailor made, situation specific models relevant to our context. Essence of OR is 'model making' capability, scientific temper, group effort, system view and *Not*, necessarily, theoretical appreciation of underlying mathematical-logical basis of available standard models except for their academic training value. Once this essence is lost sight of, standard models may be imposed on in appropriate problems with well known disastrous consequences. Even without satisfatory specific solution, conceptual value of such Model Bullding exercise can be valuable (3). Search for objective(s), realistic but essential constraints, logical interrelationships and later empirical research to find appropriate quantitative values for models are laborious but real research efforts, often neglected through impatience. Finally, keeping a model updated will require checking up periodically both assumed logical relationship and data base for estimation of parameters—again, often not very seriously undertaken.

OR : Techniques and Application

The most elegant part of OR/MS—in popular mind, synonymous with them—are the new very well known standard models for evaluation, prediction and optimisation (3), such as : Linear & Non-linear programming, Network, Dynamic programming, Goal programming, geometric programming, Stochastic programming, Inventory, Replacement, Queueing, Simulation Decision trees, Forecasting, System Dynamics, Markov analysis (1) (2) (4). Basis for all these models are : Linear Algebra, Finite defferences, Matrices, Vectors, Probability and Statistics, Utility and information theory, discounted cash flow, economics and accounting. Invariably, solution of all models—analytical or simulation dose require use of Computer.

Successful applications of MS/OR, as reported in literature, are numerous and impressive in their range and depth.

The sectors include : Defence all types of business and industry in corporate sector from Aircraft to Mining, Infrastructural sectors such as Transportation, power and other public utilities. Banking and Insurance, Social welfare activities of public Administration, law and police health, education and ecology (3). In all functional areas of planning and Control—in corporate sector—from strategic planning to operational problems in production, Maintenance, Materials, Finance, Marketing and even personnel—OR/MS applications are widely reported. Keeping the numerous well known and reported applications of MS/OR in corporate sector confined to the above summary, particular references to following other, often non-profit, non-corporate sector, is worthwhile to examine relevance of MS/OR in Indian context later. Ecology, conservation, pollution and limits to growth/World Dynamics (5) (27) (31) (32, 32a 32b, 32c) (35) (51); Weather Control (9); Energy systems (36) (37) (38) (46); Public Health and Hospital management (7) (16) (19) (33) (42) (43) (45) (52) and (56); Social Decisions in Utilities (6) (8) (15) and (49); Education, Manpower planning and Human resources accounting (13) (17) (39) (40) (41) (53) (54); Management of water resources (14) (34); Transportation and Distribution (18) (21) (55); Planning and Industrial Development (23) (24) (50); Corporate long range planning (26) (28) (29) (30) (57); Corporate finance (25) (47) (48); Labour Management negotiation (12); Methodological (11) (44) (58) on Simulation, Multiple objectives and hierarchial Models are interesting.

OR in India : Relevance & Potentialities

Within this backdrop of historical development concepts, models, theories and applications, relevance of MS/OR in Indian context may be examined.

In India history of OR is nearly as long as it is in most developing countries. In late fifties, we had associations and formal college level courses and beginning of MS function in some of our industry. Professor Mahalanobis association with Indian planning for 1951 and use of quantitative model is well known. An aggregate thumbnail picture of achievements and growth in O.R. will include : Several University level programmes in OR limited Ph.D. research in O.R. field; Increasing OR content in all collegiate level Management Education; great interest in short term courses, appreciation level in OR for Managers and Public Administration; Management Services Departments, OR cells, Industrial Engineering Departments, Computor Centres, increasingly coming into being for OR/MS type work in large corporate sectors in business/Industry—public and private, in transportation sector—Rail/Airways; power generation and distribution; planning and Control problems in OR/MS application is dominated in forecasting, planning and control problems in operational—production function such as production planning and control, Inventry Management, replacement investment decisions, project Management through PERT/CPM. Finance and marketing functions follow in order of extensiveness of Indian applications. Long range strategic problems in corporate sectors are not very seriously modelled—through static or Industrial Dynamics type models—which is now beginning to attract atleast academic interest.

Except for a few infrastructural sectors like: Transportation and power, MS/OR in India has practically not touched nonprofit, Non-corporate sector. Unorganised Agricultural sector, numerically vast small/cottage industry sector, important social welfare and economic infrastructural activities such as Health, education, Road/Rail transportation, Communication, Energy, Water resources have not come under satisfactory serious OR modelling at national planning, Regional/sectoral or even unit level except for touching fringes of minor operational bottlenecks.

Management Science, thus, along with most other professional activities, is confined to a very myopic and microscopic area, by and large, in national context of priorities and problems.

Our link with and contribution to solving vital and well-known problems of multilaterally developing our society— in the sphere of poverty, health, education, unemployment, disparities of income and opportunities—though exploitation and better utilisation of our natural and human resources—is tenuous far-fetched and invisible. As good staff men even within our narrow confines of few larger corporations often in trivial sectors of economy—we have not bothered to model for finding worthwhileness of objective(s)—short term Vs long term contradictions—hierarchial conflicts with larger and smaller systems—but taking them for granted and sacroscent have dutifully searched for (often) short term profit maximising decisions. Even these recommendations, limited as they are in scope and significance, are not backed up by a true scientific spirit to search for and use relevant data, updating, and very rarely, OR/MS specialist bothers to follow up implementation. Models manipulation, rather than development, is the self defeating concern.

Future scope for OR/MS in India, viewed in the context of the limited achievement, is infinite in its range and variety. In fact, in our state of Development, the scope for any professional activity is tremendous. All our intellectual and physical faculties will have to be strained—with a spirit of dedication and service—in worthwhile priority (rather than personally rewarding trivial) areas—to bring all round development. Planning efforts—in regional/sectoral national level and then in each unit, are to be modelled. New hierarchial model formulations to resolve cascades of conflicting objectives inhibiting efficient and effective implementation are to be intellectually conceived. Dynamism, in terms of multiperiod, is to be built into planned models along with estimation of stochastic parameters, utility scales for subjective value loaded aspects, etc. and for intertemporal and interpersonal distributive problems and for ecological considerations, social accounting and social Cost Benefit models are to be developed for project Investment decisions.

Conclusion

The essential aspects of 'multidisciplinary team' and 'Scientific' and 'system view' in OR must be recaptured to make its contribution worthwhile corresponding to its promised potential. The rise of an 'Individual' OR specialist who can bring wonder all by himself is a dangerous anti-thesis of basic OR/MS philosophy and must be guarded against. Whether an individual or a small cell/department, it must not remain in isolation but must interact—at all states—from conception, through model building to implementation and control.

The spirit of Science in managers and decision makers is the most vital possible reward of OR/MS, and one can look for symptoms of the change in organisation where OR/MS formally have been introduced and indeed in country at large. One must, however, truefully admit that such symptoms are not very strong and therefore OR/MS has much ground to cover in all directions in each organised activity in India from Governmental administration to non-profit welfare activities. We just have to have sense of priority arising out of a service oriented value system to locate where we should start first and concentrate.